THE WHITE PEDESTAL

THE WHITE PEDESTAL

How White Nationalists Use Ancient Greece and Rome to Justify Hate

CURTIS DOZIER

Yale
UNIVERSITY
PRESS
New Haven and London

Published with assistance from the Mary Cady Tew Memorial Fund.

Yale University Press books may be purchased in quantity for educational, business, or promotional use. For information, please e-mail sales.press@yale.edu (U.S. office) or sales@yaleup.co.uk (U.K. office).

Set in Janson type by IDS Infotech, Ltd.
Printed in the United States of America.

Library of Congress Control Number: 2025936139
ISBN 978-0-300-27273-4 (hardcover)

A catalogue record for this book is available from the British Library.

Authorized Representative in the EU: Easy Access System Europe, Mustamäe tee 50, 10621 Tallinn, Estonia, gpsr.requests@easproject.com.

10 9 8 7 6 5 4 3 2 1

In solidarity with those who have already said this but were ignored

Contents

Acknowledgments

MY FIRST THANKS GO to those friends who have shown me, gently, how much my perspective on Greco-Roman antiquity left out, and the harm such omissions might do: Deborah Kamen, Laurialan Reitzammer, Angelo Mercado, Rachel Friedman, Tara Mulder, Elizabeth Young, Elise Archias, Corinne Crawford (*in memoriam*), and Taneisha Means. The white nationalists profiled in this book fear relationships such as these because friendship across difference has such power to open minds and change hearts.

Similar thanks go to the many colleagues who challenged me, in person and in print, to strive to make this project an intervention against white supremacy and not merely an elaboration of it: Shelley Haley, Jackie Murray, Rebecca Futo Kennedy, David Lupher, Dani Bostick, Judy Hallett, Sarah Bond, Dan-el Padilla Peralta, Joel Christensen, Donna Zuckerberg, Emily Greenwood, Cecilio Cooper, Nora Galland, Cord Whitaker, Jonathan Hsy, and all the other participants in the Race B4 Race First Book workshop that Cord and Jonathan directed.

It is a commonplace of acknowledgments sections to accept responsibility for all remaining errors, and I do, not only for those of fact but also, as I continue on my journey, for those of politics. On that journey I am grateful too for the support of Denise McCoskey, Katherine Harloe, Patrice Rankine, Young Kim, and Margaret Williamson, mentors who believed not only in this project but that I could be the one to do it. The encouragement of colleagues including Katharine White, Natasha MacBean, Sergio Gutiérrez Negrón, and Naomi Campa has been similarly invaluable, as has been my daughter's faith in me, all the more nourishing for its innocence of the subject of this book.

Material support is every bit as important as the intellectual. An award from Harvard's Loeb Classical Library Foundation allowed me to dedicate myself full-time to writing this book, as did research leaves from Vassar College.

In past generations scholars would sometimes thank their wives for typing their books, leaving out how those women (I am sure) improved the manuscripts while doing so. They deserved to have their contributions recognized more explicitly: my developmental editor, Sara Streett, assisted with every aspect of writing except the typing, editing and making suggestions both stylistic and substantive on innumerable drafts over many years and saving me from countless errors and false steps; Sabrina Haenze, Brian Murphy, Sam Glaser-Nolan, and especially Robin DuBlanc and Roberta Klarreich offered similarly helpful advice in the final stages.

Every scholar should be as fortunate as I have been to have the support of Vassar College's library staff, especially Deb Bucher, Lydia Smith, and Emily McNeil; of the student research assistants who have been my partners since the launch of *Pharos* in 2017: Anne Boyd, Hannah Broholm-Vail, Daisy Catling-Allen, Andrew Szente, Ji Baek, Tao Beloney, Carina Leung, Ann John, Maeve Smith, Helen Ambrose, Iris Leach Dowe, and Sabina Hawkes; and of my editor at Yale University Press, Heather Gold, who from the beginning understood and believed deeply in this project.

Finally, I thank my wife, Emily. When I took her to see Bernini's sculpture *Apollo and Daphne*, excited to introduce her to a famous work of art that had inspired my career, she immediately recognized what it portrayed: "That's a rape." I met that observation with defensiveness then, but it set this project in motion—by forcing me to look with such clear eyes at what I had idealized—long before it took on its present form. Years later, in researching this book, I found an essay in a white nationalist publication that took for granted that observers would identify with Apollo and his desire. If not for the intervention of Emily and many others named above, that essay could have described me.

The manuscript of this book was finalized shortly after the election of Donald Trump to a second term as president of the United States, when it was too early to tell whether, or how, his administration's priorities might resonate with the ideologies I describe. But even though many contemporary events appear in these pages, this is not a study of a particular time or even of a particular group of people. The entanglement of Greco-Roman antiquity with white supremacist politics has a long, long history. Very likely it has a long, long future as well.

I wrote this book to try to contribute, in my own small way, to the emergence of a better discipline of classical studies and the creation of a better world, however long that might take. To Emily, I wish a better life for us as well.

A Note on White Nationalist Sources

White nationalist intellectuals seek academic legitimacy by imitating the conventions of scholarly discourse in their publications. To cite these publications in the same manner that I would cite other scholarship would confer such legitimacy, as well as visibility. Therefore I do not cite publications from white nationalist websites in my notes. Interested researchers will be able to locate them from my descriptions.

THE WHITE PEDESTAL

Introduction
Confronting the Past

WHAT DO YOU PICTURE when you think about ancient Greece or ancient Rome? White marble columns, gleaming under a deep blue Mediterranean sky? A Roman military legion, battle standards flapping in the breeze? Or do you see something more like Raphael's painting *The School of Athens*, in which men in robes—many of them bearded, several of them bald—gather to discuss philosophy? Or maybe you see Greece and Rome as they are portrayed in film: Monty Python's *Life of Brian* (1979), Disney's animated *Hercules* (1997), or Brad Pitt as Achilles in Wolfgang Petersen's *Troy* (2004). Video games like *Assassin's Creed: Odyssey* or *Rome: Total War* show us the ancient world too. Millions of people have read the *Percy Jackson and the Olympians* series. In the *Iliad*, Homer says that there were so many warriors in the Trojan War that he could never name them all.[1] He would fare no better in attempting to list all the representations of Greece and Rome in books, television, film, and other media. There are just too many.

Whatever you are imagining, ask yourself how you feel about ancient Greece and Rome. Fascination? Excitement? A sense of grandeur and beauty? Do you have a sense that ancient Greece and Rome are important, perhaps even foundational, to understanding the modern world? That they have exerted a special and beneficial influence on modern literature, politics, law, religion, even science? If you do, you are not alone. In 2024 the market research firm YouGov published survey data showing that more than half of Americans viewed ancient Athens favorably, and that about half of Americans who said they knew something about the Roman Empire believed it had a positive impact on the world.[2]

Large numbers of Americans feel this way because the idea that the ancient Greco-Roman world is important, admirable, and foundational is omnipresent in American culture. For one thing, public intellectuals are always telling us that this is the case. Nicholas Kristof illustrates the "lesson[s] of history" in the *New York Times* by quoting the ancient Greek playwright Aeschylus. Cornel West has called the literature and philosophy of ancient Greece and Rome the "crème de la crème of our civilization."[3] For another, museums devote entire rooms to classical art, even though it was produced during a relatively short period of time in a relatively small region of Europe, alongside other rooms that attempt to present the complete artistic history of entire continents in a similar-sized space. The most important buildings in our nation's capital, on many university campuses, and in countless cities and towns, feature architecture that evokes the Greco-Roman world. We use Roman numerals to count Super Bowls in order to indicate the cultural importance of this annual game. Once you begin to notice how pervasive this admiring attitude toward Greco-Roman antiquity is, it is hard not to keep seeing it.

What may be less visible is that this admiration is especially widespread among American white supremacists. Online, social media accounts hiding fascist sympathies behind the promotion of what they term "traditional" values frequently feature Greek sculptures as profile pictures. A channel on the social media platform Telegram devoted to encouraging its eleven thousand subscribers to harass Jewish people used a bust of the Roman orator Cicero as its avatar. In the discussion forums on Stormfront.org, the oldest neo-Nazi website in the world, contributors frequently invoke the civilizations of Greece and Rome as proof of the superiority of white people. Offline, too, this obsession with the ancient world informs real-world activism. The group known as the Proud Boys, whose leaders have been convicted of multiple felonies in connection with the January 6, 2021, attack on the U.S. Capitol, uses the laurel wreath—an ancient Greek symbol of victory—as its logo. When members of the Proud Boys engaged in what a judge later described as "hateful and overtly racist conduct" outside a predominantly African American church in Washington, DC, they were joined by a man who had earned himself the nickname "Based Spartan" because he wore a Spartan-style helmet when he attended white supremacist rallies and beat up counterprotestors.[4] For those of us accustomed to associate Greco-Roman antiquity with sophisticated philosophy and artistic beauty, violent and hateful actors taking inspiration from the ancient world strikes a deeply incongruous note that might be laughable—if the consequences of that admiration were not so disturbing.

It is tempting to dismiss such appropriations of Greco-Roman antiquity by hate groups as nothing more than "the products of twisted minds," as one journalist put it.[5] Brawlers in polo shirts decorated with laurel wreaths or wearing a replica Spartan helmet, alienated loners in neo-Nazi Web forums or on social media . . . what, it seems reasonable to ask, could such people really know about history? The high-minded philosophy and artistic achievement for which ancient Greece and Rome are celebrated seem incompatible with anything so repulsive as racism. Ancient Rome stands as an example of a cosmopolitan, multicultural empire. Ancient Greece is known as a society in which narrow and repressive attitudes toward sexuality had not yet taken hold. This hardly seems like a world that could provide suitable models for the hateful politics of white supremacists.

This is a book about just how suitable models from Greco-Roman antiquity are, in fact, for those who wish to promote abhorrently racist ideas. Greco-Roman antiquity's reputation as a high point in European history has eclipsed the fact that some of the most widely admired figures in ancient literature and philosophy endorsed ideas that modern white supremacists share, and that the social and political realities of the ancient world provide models for political systems that contemporary white supremacists would like to establish in our communities. Hate groups' appropriations of ancient history throw these aspects of ancient culture into stark relief. They do the same for the way that history has been studied and described by later generations, revealing that famous and influential historians and intellectuals—people few of us are accustomed to think of as white supremacists—have used the ancient world to normalize racism, antisemitism, and xenophobia. And most important, this material compels us to recognize that the uncritical admiration so many of us are taught to feel toward ancient Greece and Rome—by popular films and television shows, yes, but also in some cases by our teachers—provides fuel not only for the racist activism that is described above and throughout these pages, but also for the maintenance of white supremacy in our society as a whole.[6]

Some precision in terminology is necessary, since my discussion treats phenomena ranging from overtly racist activism to assumptions about human difference that many Americans harbor without realizing it. Many examples of racist admiration for Greco-Roman antiquity that I will discuss are associated with individuals who either used the term "Alt-Right" to describe themselves or had that term applied to them by journalists. However, in what follows, I avoid the term, which is now recognized as a euphemism that obscures how those who used it had merely repackaged older racist and antisemitic ideas in forms that promoted white supremacy to a potential global audience of millions of people by capitalizing upon the growth of unmoderated online communities within which reactionary ideologies flourished.[7] Instead I have adopted the term "white nationalist" to describe both the movement and the ideas I discuss, recognizing that all terminological choices require trade-offs.

"White nationalist," like "Alt-Right," was originally adopted by members of the movement in a play for respectability. For this reason, the historians of racism Kathleen Belew and Ramón Gutiérrez recommend against its use, preferring "White Power."[8] But for the particular subset of white supremacists that I consider here, namely, the authors of historical essays appearing in publications notorious for their promotion of white supremacist thought, I believe "white nationalist" is best because it conveys that their objectives are not only racial but political: not simply the assertion of white superiority but the development and implementation of customs, social practices, policies, and laws necessary to create a white supremacist society. The most utopian of these thinkers even envision the creation of a racially pure nation: the white ethnostate. In my view, "white nationalism" best captures the full extent of this movement's aims.

But racism in America festers far beyond the white nationalist organizations I profile here. I understand "white supremacy" to be an umbrella term that describes the pervasiveness in contemporary American thought of ideologies that not only posit the superiority of white people but also promote and maintain political and social hierarchies in which white people wield more power and enjoy greater access to wealth, healthcare, food, employment, safety, housing, education, information, and comfort than others. Those supporting white supremacy may do so online or in the "real world," violently or behind a genteel veneer, and explicitly and openly or implicitly and unknowingly, as members of racist organizations or as people who simply ignore the inequality that such systems produce. The individuals, organizations, and publications that are the focus of my study fall squarely into the former category, but a careful study of their methods, and in particular of their engagement with Greco-Roman antiquity, reveals much more about the insidious pervasiveness of racist ideologies in the United States than the size of these organizations, or the apparent narrowness of the subject, might at first glance suggest.

To be fair, the examples of white nationalist fascination with Greco-Roman antiquity that I have cited thus far reflect only superficial engagement with it. The man known as Based Spartan probably doesn't know much more about the history of Sparta than what he learned by watching the 2006 film *300*, which recounts the battle of Thermopylae in the style of a comic book. The images of classical sculpture used as avatars on social media can be found by a simple Google image search. What, it seems reasonable to ask, do these claims of racial continuity have to do with the actual history of the Greco-Roman world?

For many years, conventional scholarly wisdom has held that the answer to this question is "Not much." The ancient Greeks and Romans did not primarily define themselves, or other people, by the color of their skin. Sources show that they noticed differences in appearance between people but did not assign the same meanings to these differences that modern pseudoscientific concepts of race do.

Whereas modern racial theories associate whiteness with civilized superiority, in antiquity white skin was often associated with weakness and effeminacy or, because the Greeks and Romans living in what we now call southern Europe regarded people from farther north as uncivilized, with ferocity and barbarism. And whereas modern racism promotes an association between Blackness and ugliness, in antiquity black skin was often associated with beauty, as ancient descriptions of the Ethiopians attest. In Homer's *Odyssey*, when Athena restores the disguised and bedraggled Odysseus to a form that will be most recognizable to his son, she gives his skin a color that is described with the same Greek word used elsewhere to describe night, darkness, soil, and ink.[9] The stark differences between ancient and modern attitudes toward skin color reveal that all such judgments about skin color are arbitrary, changing over time as a society's assumptions about human difference change.

White nationalist interpretations of history ignore this because it undermines their insistence that racial identities reflect natural biological realities. An ancient Greek sculpture as a profile picture for a white nationalist social media account makes an implicit claim that modern white people are the racial descendants of the ancient Greeks and that the alleged superiority of the ancient Greeks as sculptors (in this case) proves the superiority of modern white people. But the very category of whiteness and the meanings assigned to white skin were invented in the seventeenth century in order to justify the enslavement of black Africans by designating them as fundamentally different from, and inferior to, the people enslaving them.[10] Nearly all white nationalist interpretations of ancient history, by contrast, depend on making the invented category of whiteness seem natural and eternal. One method for claiming this is to retroject anachronistic racist ideas about whiteness onto the ancient Greeks and Romans, none of whom would even have understood the significance modern racial theories grant to skin color, let alone shared those assumptions about it.

But that doesn't mean we should simply ignore the white nationalist application of modern racial theories to Greco-Roman antiquity. The ancient world was anything but a paradise of tolerance and acceptance of difference. Ancient Greek and Roman thinkers articulated many theories of human difference that ranked groups of people as inferior, using different criteria from those employed by modern racism but applying them to the same ends: the marginalization of those deemed different and the justification of violence against them.[11]

For example, assumptions about the inferiority of women justified granting them fewer political and civic rights than men; women who defied these restrictions could be prosecuted and penalized. Citizenship, especially in classical Greece, was generally determined by birth, with little or no opportunity for the naturalization of those born elsewhere. Athens even imposed special taxes on foreign-born residents and made them liable to special penalties if they attempted to participate in the civic life of the city-state. Greek hostility toward the "barbarian" marks the beginning of twenty-five hundred years of European dismissiveness and suspicion of Asia. And ancient Greece and Rome were slave societies, with no abolitionist thought to speak of. Even though ancient practice differed from American slavery in important ways—any prisoner of war could be reduced to slavery, with the result that enslaved people came from all over the Mediterranean world and did not share any physical characteristics, whereas in the United States slavery was predicated on and justified by anti-Blackness—ancient enslavers adopted beliefs about the alleged laziness, rebelliousness, and sexual promiscuity of enslaved people quite similar to those that American slaveholders adopted to justify their dehumanization and exploitation.[12] Whether or not a person who wears a Spartan helmet to a rally or uses a Greek sculpture as their profile picture knows this history, the ancient world provides plenty of fodder for those who want to claim that modern racism is justified because celebrated ancient societies recognized the fundamental superiority and inferiority of different types of people.

More than a few classical scholars have dismissed the significance of these aspects of Greco-Roman society, arguing that Greece and Rome should not be judged harshly for committing what one describes as "the sins of humanity, discoverable in all times and places." Those who make this argument are likely unaware that it is the same argument found in the preening celebrations of white history and culture in white nationalist publications. The editor in chief of one of these, for example, has written that "if slavery is somebody's 'original sin,' it's sure not ours," citing the example of Arab slave-trading in Africa dating back to late antiquity. Certainly the history of world slavery is one of staggering brutality and violence that transcends any one place or time period. But the defensive stance described above ignores that the violence and the oppression practiced in the ancient world have exerted an incalculably greater influence than those of other "times and places." No one in eighteenth- or nineteenth-century America cited Arab slavery to justify the enslavement of Africans. They invoked Greco-Roman antiquity as proof that slavery was compatible with the aspirations of any sophisticated, enlightened, and powerful civilization, whether classical Athens, the Roman Empire, or America itself.[13] In this they made the same assumption about their audiences' attitudes toward Greco-Roman antiquity as modern white supremacists do—that such analogies are persuasive.

It is no coincidence that the same historians who dismiss ancient Greco-Roman slavery as a product of its time tend to be most invested in the idea that Greco-Roman antiquity provides the foundation for the set of admirable and beneficial values that have conventionally been grouped under the heading of "Western civilization."[14] As historians such as Naoíse Mac Sweeney and Josephine Quinn have so amply demonstrated, this narrative of history leaves out much more than it explains. It minimizes both the contributions of diverse cultures to those aspects of modernity that we find most worthy of celebration and the violence by which the regions conventionally (and arbitrarily) designated as "the West" ensured that they enjoyed the fruits of modernity more fully than people living outside those regions.[15] The violence of slavery is just one aspect of that history that the prestige of Greco-Roman antiquity has been used to justify. If we are going to claim that the ancient world is foundational for aspects of modernity that we wish to celebrate, we must acknowledge its foundational influence as a source of legitimacy for violence, colonialism, oppression, and exploitation, too. We must do this not in order to feel guilty, as some critics claim, but in order to fuel the moral outrage that should inspire us to create a better world than the one the influence of the ancient world helped build.

For this reason, alongside this book's exploration of the underrecognized presence of racist ideas in ancient thought, I present historical examples of political figures and professional historians using the ancient world in much the same way that contemporary white supremacists do: to justify violence and oppression. In this I draw on the work of many scholars who have detailed this intellectual history, finding Greco-Roman antiquity implicated not only in the defenses of slavery noted above but also in the racial nationalism that attended the creation of modern nation-states and European imperialism in the eighteenth and nineteenth centuries. My more selective history focuses on the points of similarity between the arguments made in these historical sources and those made by contemporary white supremacists.

The most well known of these critical studies of the historical entanglement of scholarship on Greco-Roman antiquity and white supremacy is the first volume of Martin Bernal's *Black Athena* (1987). Bernal argued that European historians from the seventeenth century onward promoted the same baseless claim of continuous racial identity between ancient Greece and modern Europeans that the contemporary white nationalists profiled in this book make. The public controversy and academic backlash that Bernal's work provoked continues to obscure the fact that Black intellectuals and historians such as Charles W. Chesnutt, Anna Julia Cooper, and W.E.B. Du Bois had been challenging the white supremacy inherent in these dominant idealized views of Greco-Roman antiquity since at least the nineteenth century.[16] It also prevented classical scholars from grappling with the fact that although those who invoke the ancient world in support of racism may be misrepresenting history, theirs is a misrepresentation that has also been promoted by prominent and influential individuals working in the political mainstream and wielding considerable influence both on public policy and on popular perceptions of history. To label contemporary white nationalists "extremists," as many observers do, ignores how popular and influential their understanding of history has been.

Since my primary objective is to expose the similarities between the attitudes toward Greco-Roman antiquity held by modern white supremacists and mainstream intellectuals, each chapter is organized around an idea that informs violent white nationalist activism in the contemporary world. My first chapter introduces the major white nationalist intellectuals whose treatment of ancient evidence best illustrates this similarity, taking the antisemitic and xenophobic conspiracy theory of the "Great Replacement" as an illustrative case of the degree to which contemporary white nationalist thought finds support in both ancient evidence and influential mainstream interpretations of it. I then turn to the less obvious but equally pernicious—and, I argue, more widely accepted—ideas upon which the white nationalist worldview is based, making this book as much an exposé of how history can be made to support hateful political ideologies as an introduction to white nationalist thought itself. These component ideas and their associated assumptions are:

> White men have a duty to defend whiteness against the forces that threaten it. Masculine heroism will be essential to this defense, and violence may be justified and necessary.
>
> Such heroism is necessary because the contemporary world has degenerated from a past golden age. Only white nationalist politics can repair and regenerate the contemporary world.
>
> Race is a biological reality. Since whiteness constitutes a real and meaningful identity, it is worth fighting for.
>
> The white race is superior to all others. This is the most familiar aspect of white supremacist thought (it's right there in the name), but it has meaning only in relation to the others. Decline is a serious problem only if it threatens something of special value. The white race is worth fighting for not merely because it is real but because it possesses that special value.
>
> Hierarchy is natural and desirable. The superiority of white people means that white people should rule over others, and inferior people should accept this.
>
> Difference leads to violence and conflict. Inferior people are unable to coexist peacefully with white people, either because they resent white superiority or because violence is inherent to their natures. This last belief brings my discussion full circle to insistence on the supposed decline of the contemporary world, which nationalists attribute in large

> part to faith in egalitarian ideals and multiculturalism. Hence the fantasy of the ethnostate: a racially pure nation in which white people can live in harmony with each other, insulated from the violence of all others.

Beginning with white nationalist articulations of these ideas, each of the following chapters surveys the aspects of Greco-Roman antiquity that white nationalist intellectuals turn to as respectable models for these ideas, documents the ways that influential historians and politicians have promoted similar understandings of those sources, and invites reflection on the persistence of those ideas in contemporary American thought. Any surprise that white nationalists take an interest in Greco-Roman antiquity may give way to surprise at just how frequently ancient sources articulate ideas congruent with white nationalist thought. And an encounter with the long history of respected intellectuals promoting identical or similar understandings of ancient evidence should, in turn, prompt a recognition that the investment of contemporary white nationalist intellectuals in Greco-Roman antiquity is not so much surprising as it is inevitable, given the pervasiveness of the ideas that structure this book both in the scholarship of past ages and in the dominant, but often unspoken, attitudes of the present.

There is a danger, in a book like this, that such attention could minimize the abhorrence of those ideas by "taking them seriously," by implying that they are worthy of detailed consideration or that the inspiration white nationalists take from ancient history is nothing more than an interesting dimension of extremist thought. Let me leave no doubt. I condemn the ideas surveyed in this book, and I mourn the untold human suffering and violence that these ideas have sanctioned, and continue to sanction. The patent injustice of this history demands, however, more than condemnation and grief from those who have benefited from it. It demands reflection upon how and why this history of violence unfolded as it did. This study of racist ideas seeks to explain how these ideas are perpetuated, how they are given respectability, and how they retain it. The prestige of Greco-Roman antiquity does not, on its own, explain this history. But it has played a role in that history, a role that dominant perspectives on the significance of the ancient world either ignore or actively suppress.

Confronting the ugly realities of the ancient world through the work of white nationalist intellectuals also requires confronting some ugly realities about the contemporary world. The ideas that structure this book enjoy currency far beyond the white nationalist communities in which they are openly stated and embraced. One has only to look at the inequities that racism continues to produce in twenty-first-century America to realize that the congruences between white nationalist and mainstream thought are not limited to the interpretation of Greco-Roman antiquity.[17] We are surrounded by institutions and systems shaped by white nationalist ideas as surely as we are surrounded by references to, and representations of, the Greco-Roman world. Perhaps the study of white nationalist engagement with the latter can help us recognize the pervasiveness of the former.

So if the investigation this book offers seems grim, joyless, and exhausting, and if you find yourself yearning for one of the countless books about how exciting, impressive, or inspiring the ancient world is, bear in mind that that's what the white nationalist movement expects you to do. In fact, it's what they need you to do, because they need the Greco-Roman world to retain the prestige they seek to harness in support of their hateful politics.

Inevitably our identities shape our view of history, the world, and ourselves. From this point of view, I am not a promising candidate as an investigator of the pervasiveness of white nationalist ideas in classical studies and American society at large. As a white, straight, Christian man I am not so much the target of racism as the target audience of white nationalist rhetoric. Those who have experienced racism, as I never have, may find some aspects of my analysis frustratingly obvious, and the rehearsal of the details of all-too-familiar white supremacist ideologies traumatic.[18] They do not need to have the racist ideas that underpin the violence they have experienced explained to them. This book represents my own journey from ignorance to a still-evolving understanding of the role that race and racism have played in the formation of my identities, both as a classical scholar and as a white American.

Much has been written about "white privilege" in the last decade, but the most basic form of that privilege is the freedom to live without thinking about race. This extends to the privilege of not thinking about the racial politics of the study of Greco-Roman antiquity. I never did until I started conducting research for this book. Just as I have always felt at home in the United States, confident that the ideals of American democracy apply to me and, until I began researching this topic, ignorant of the myriad ways the benefits of those ideals are inequitably distributed, I have always felt at home in the study of the Greco-Roman world because I had no reason to question (and even benefited from) the subject's prestige. As this book shows, this prestige has lent legitimacy to all manner of violence and oppression. Unaffected by that legacy, I could derive a feeling of self-worth from my expertise in the study of a culture widely considered "the most significant starting point of Western Civilization," as the influential Yale University historian and classical scholar Donald Kagan puts it in a lecture.[19]

It took the study of white supremacist appropriations of history, and the disgust I felt when encountering them, to shake me out of my complacency. I began researching this material in 2017 when, inspired by colleagues in classical studies who began raising awareness in public venues about the ways that misogynists, xenophobes, and white supremacists were invoking Greco-Roman antiquity, I launched a website, *Pharos: Doing Justice to the Classics*, to document and respond to appropriations of Greco-Roman antiquity by hate groups online. When I announced the project, I promised to "detail the inaccuracies, omissions, and distortions" I found. I believed (then) that my job as an expert was to show that the historical reality of antiquity had to be distorted in order to support racism. With hindsight, however, I have come to understand that this impulse served more to protect myself from the charge of racism than to promote racial justice. Such defensive scholarship constitutes what Mathura Umachandran and Marchella Ward, following postcolonial theory, have identified as a "settler move to innocence," by which the beneficiaries of white supremacy attempt to distance themselves from it.[20]

The more research I conducted, however, the harder it became to distinguish white nationalist perspectives on antiquity from my own. When I came across a website claiming that the Roman emperor Augustus subscribed to the Great Replacement conspiracy theory because he once said that "it is neither pleasing to heaven nor creditable that our race should cease . . . and the city be given up to foreigners," I assumed that white nationalists had put these words into his mouth. They turned out to come from a speech that the historian Cassius Dio claims Augustus delivered in support of his legislation promoting marriage and childbirth in Rome.[21] When I learned about an antisemitic book from 1910 that claimed Jewish people were a "Negro" sub-race, I initially mocked how far racists would go to systematize their hatreds. My scoffing turned to chagrin when I learned that its author, Arthur Talmage Abernethy, was a professor of Latin. And as I read an essay in a white nationalist magazine describing how studying ancient Greek society could reveal the timeless and unique qualities of white people, my skin crawled when I found the essayist making an argument I had heard in a course I had taken: that the Homeric epics deserve special study because they possess a greater emotional range and narrative sophistication than what the essayist described as the "thin tales of Egypt and Babylonia." I do not know what my professor in that course—an award-winning scholar—had intended me to learn from this comparison, but I know that I reached a conclusion similar to the one the magazine was pushing. Again and again, what I had at first found outrageous and offensive turned out to be familiar from my own education. As I read that article, I reflected that I had never even taken the time to read *The Epic of Gilgamesh* to see if I agreed with my teacher's dismissive claim about it.

It was uncomfortable for me to come to the realization that the version of history that I studied and admired concealed a racist and violent history. Such a realization, however, should prompt not shame but clarity about what attitudes—whether toward antiquity or toward our fellow human beings—we wish to cultivate in the future. When I refer to individuals whose scholarship reproduces conceptions of the ancient world that resemble those of white nationalists, I do so not to "call them out" as racists. I have believed, and taught, many of those perspectives myself. I do so, rather, to illustrate how common it is to learn and reproduce the modes of thinking that white nationalists depend on to make their arguments persuasive. Indeed, as Andrew Garrett's study of the work and legacy of anthropologist Alfred Kroeber shows, too much focus on individuals can blind us to the larger systems of thought and practice that nourish and maintain white supremacy.[22] Few of us who live in a racist society are innocent, but all of us can be agents of change.

Ibram Kendi has written that "the heartbeat of racism is denial."[23] This book is my attempt to counter the denial of any relationship between white supremacy and the study of Greco-Roman antiquity. It was the patent racism of white nationalist treatments of Greco-Roman antiquity, combined with the learning and sophistication evident within them, that forced me to recognize the extent to which I had absorbed and maintained racist understandings not just of the ancient world but of my own. Each chapter of this book is an invitation to experience a similar process, beginning with disgust or mockery, leading to surprise at both the extent and depth of the history that white nationalists can draw on, and finally to a recognition of the familiarity of the ideas that white nationalists use history to support. There is no shame in recognizing these ideas within ourselves. It is what we do next that matters.

CHAPTER ONE

The Who and Why of White Nationalist History

When Fox News canceled *Tucker Carlson Tonight* in 2023, the network lost an extremely popular host. Carlson's show had been at or near the top of cable news ratings for years. A 2021 headline in *Time* declared him "the most powerful conservative in America." The press release canceling the show gave no explanation for Carlson's firing, but what might appear to be the most obvious reason—his increasingly inflammatory political opinions—does not seem to have troubled network executives too much. For example, they apparently did not mind that advertisers had boycotted Carlson's show several times throughout its seven-year run. To judge from his ratings, which continued to improve even amid these boycotts, audiences loved the same political opinions from which advertisers sought to distance themselves, and for many years, at least, that was enough for the network. Until it wasn't.[1]

For the last several years of his tenure at Fox, one of Carlson's signature preoccupations was a conspiracy theory known as the "Great Replacement." This conspiracy theory holds that world governments, media organizations, and in some cases Jewish interests are promoting immigration, intermarriage, birth control, and abortion as a means of bringing about the extinction of white people. Before Carlson began promoting this conspiracy theory, it was unknown outside the circles of avowed white nationalists and neo-Nazis. By the time he left Fox, prominent politicians had embraced this theory, and surveys in the United States found that nearly a third of Americans, and between half and two-thirds of Republicans, accepted it in some form.[2]

Like other conspiracy theories, this one did not arise out of thin air: demographic data do indeed show that the percentage of people whom demographers designate as "white" is declining in the United States and many countries in Europe, but these changes are caused by changes in how census takers and respondents define the term "white," not because of anything so sinister as a coordinated campaign of "replacement," let alone "genocide." Unlike many other conspiracy theories, however, this one has exacted a brutal toll: mass murderers who have targeted Muslims, Latinos, and Black people in Christchurch, New Zealand; El Paso, Texas; and Buffalo, New York, all said in their manifestos that this conspiracy theory inspired their attacks.[3]

The wide popularity of the idea of the "Great Replacement," and the racist violence it has inspired, conceals that the phrase originates from a source quite remote from that of cable news provocateurs and racist terrorists. It comes from the title of a book by a French intellectual, Renaud Camus, who was educated at the Sorbonne, one of the oldest and most distinguished universities in the world, and who has won literary awards for his essays and novels, including one from the Académie française, France's premier authority on language and literature. Camus was even affiliated with radical politics: before the publication of *Le Grand Remplacement,* as his book is titled in French, he was best known for his involvement in the French gay literary scene of the 1980s and '90s. Camus has insisted in interviews that he does not consider his "general conception of the world . . . 'racist,'" and he certainly defies the stereotype most Americans have of someone who holds such beliefs: we expect them to be poor, uneducated, unruly, and probably living somewhere rural. But one reason this stereotype persists is because it reassures those of us who do not conform to it that we have nothing to do with racism. Men like Camus—educated, refined, intelligent—challenge this comforting belief. And their existence invites us to look beyond the most visible exponents of white supremacy—street brawlers, mass murderers, and rioters—into the minds that develop and refine the ideas that inspire them.[4]

What we find when we delve into this world, which political scientists describe as "the intellectual radical right," is in some ways predictable but in others surprising. As one might expect, nearly all of the members of this community are men who identify as white, although there are a few women, Jewish people, and even people of color. Their association with white nationalism should not be taken to indicate the diversity of the movement but the insidiousness of its ideas: one survival strategy for people marginalized by white supremacy is to seek apparent safety in the middle of its hierarchies rather than risk relegation to the lowest social ranks. But beyond these demographic elements, these "highbrow white nationalists," as they have also been called, resemble Camus much more than they do the men who put on Spartan helmets and attacked the U.S. Capitol. Many of them possess PhDs and other advanced degrees. They are fluent in several languages. Some of them have held positions at well-known colleges and universities. And they write—not rambling, paranoid manifestos like those of the terrorists who grab headlines, but books and essays that bear all the hallmarks of serious journalism and academic work: argument-driven paragraphs, footnotes citing sources, and bibliographies. Instead of racial slurs, their style features scholarly-sounding euphemisms for racist ideas, such as "human biodiversity," "cultural Marxism," or "traditionalism." And they have quite a lot to say about Greco-Roman antiquity.[5]

In fact, material from the ancient world played a role in establishing the respectability of the Great Replacement conspiracy theory. *Le Grand Remplacement* begins with a discussion of the Platonic dialogue *Cratylus*, in which the character Hermogenes attempts to refute Cratylus's argument that words have "natural" meanings. He argues instead that the relationship of word to meaning is arbitrary. To cite one example from the dialogue, it is only by custom that the word *horse* refers to the four-legged animal that people ride. Camus summarizes this argument and then wonders which character's reasoning applies to "Frenchness." If Hermogenes' does, he says, then a government can simply make a person French by conferring citizenship upon them. Camus suggests that Cratylus's position better reflects the reality of national identity, which is not, he argues, an arbitrary designation but must be based on "ancestry, long experience, shared history, blood, race, love, culture, [and] civilization." The dialogue itself does not conclusively endorse one position or the other, but Camus makes Cratylus's position the basis of his claim that declining birth rates and (especially) Muslim immigration pose an existential threat to "Frenchness."

Camus's use of Plato epitomizes the appeal of Greco-Roman antiquity to white nationalist intellectuals. Plato is one of the most respected thinkers in human history. The philosopher Alfred North Whitehead, for example, famously wrote that "the safest general characterization of the European philosophical tradition is that it consists in a series of footnotes to Plato."[6] By beginning his analysis with Plato, Camus suggests (first) that he should be trusted because he possesses this familiarity with so distinguished a philosopher, and (second) that Plato agrees with him. To question Camus, it is implied, would be to question Plato. Furthermore, white nationalist intellectuals know that Plato's work contains many ideas congruent to theirs, such as making eugenic programs an integral part of the ideal state described in *The Republic*. And they know that most people believe that ideas expressed by Plato are worth taking seriously. Plato's sterling reputation, combined with his endorsement of violence and hierarchy, makes his work an ideal tool for the promotion of white nationalist ideas.

None of the manifestos that cite the Great Replacement mention Plato. They don't even mention Renaud Camus. By the time their authors learned about the conspiracy theory, it had been translated, repackaged, and simplified through a process of repetition that would be impossible to trace. But someone had to take the idea seriously enough to begin that process of repackaging it. We can never know what that first unknown translator saw in Camus's subtly written philosophical tract that made them promote it to the world, beginning a process that would ultimately lead to its consumption by people who would translate it into real-world violence. But linking Plato's name with the theory suggests that it possesses intellectual seriousness and depth.

A History of White Nationalist Classics

If the white nationalist intellectuals whose thought I investigate bear little resemblance to the picture Americans hold in their heads of racist activists, it is because white supremacist activism has evolved over the past half century. Following the defeat of fascist regimes in the Second World War, especially the revelation of the scale and bureaucratic sophistication of the Holocaust, it became socially unacceptable to show open sympathy toward political ideas associated with fascism, such as eugenics, ethnic cleansing, antisemitism, and authoritarianism. New laws, particularly in Europe, disrupted fascist organizing. Political parties associated with fascism were banned. The display of fascist symbols, particularly the swastika, was and continues to be prohibited or restricted in many countries. European fascism, marginalized and discredited by these changes in law and public opinion, entered a period of reorganization and reconfiguration.[7]

One of the reconfigurations of fascism that emerged in the 1960s and 1970s was a movement that described itself as the "European New Right." This took shape first in France among the group of thinkers that coalesced around Dominique Venner, a veteran of the Algerian war in France who served a prison sentence for his membership in a terrorist organization that attempted to prevent Algerian independence, and the philosopher Alain de Benoist. Venner is notable for his frequent references to Greco-Roman antiquity and his public prominence—he called the Homeric epics the "founding poems of the European soul" and won a prestigious prize for historical scholarship from the Académie française—but it was de Benoist who pioneered the development of new intellectual and philosophical arguments in favor of white separatism while disavowing the violence and overt racism that characterized earlier movements.[8]

The *Nouvelle Droite* (New Right), as de Benoist's movement became known, aimed to work within existing political systems to achieve its goals. Gone were the most familiar trappings of fascism: the swastikas, paramilitary exercises, and political parties worshipping charismatic strongmen. De Benoist, a Sorbonne-educated journalist who is said to own the largest private library in France, abandoned these symbols and concepts, perhaps because he understood that they would not be persuasive to the public of contemporary Europe. He replaced them with political tools more suited to his talents and temperament: ideas.

Central to de Benoist's new campaign of ideas was the concept of "metapolitics." This holds that before a movement can achieve political success in the form of winning elections, passing laws, and enacting and enforcing policies, it must make its ideas acceptable and respectable among those whom it expects to support its candidates and politics. To this end, de Benoist and his colleagues formed a think tank to promote their ideas, the Research and Study Group for European Civilization. The French version of this name (*Groupement de recherche et d'études pour la civilisation européenne*) produced an acronym that placed the classical world at the center of its play for intellectual and political respectability: GRECE. In part, this turn to Greco-Roman antiquity is a clue to the fundamental continuity between the European New Right and earlier fascist movements. Greco-Roman antiquity was a favorite point of reference for the analogies Mussolini drew between his military ambitions and those of the Roman Empire, for example, or for Nazi theories concerning the superiority of white Europeans and the ancient valor of the German people. But de Benoist's choice of acronym may also be understood to reflect a belief that the prestige of Greco-Roman antiquity could be harnessed to make fascist ideas respectable among a general public that recoiled at open fascism but retained respect and admiration for an ancient world in which, as de Benoist would have known, he could find many articulations of ideas resembling his own. Camus's citation of Plato in *Le Grand Remplacement* was thus textbook metapolitics. And the subsequent influence of Camus's theory is not the only sign that the metapolitical project of the European New Right has begun to bear fruit. The spread of similar New Right groups in other European nations, such as the *Neue Recht* in Germany, makes clear that political bans did little to eradicate the appeal of fascist ideas. And five decades after GRECE was founded, far-right political parties have begun to win seats in European parliaments and legislatures.[9]

The theory of metapolitics advocated by de Benoist and his circle found few adherents in the United States following the Second

World War, where fascist sympathizers faced fewer cultural and legal obstacles. Segregation, for example, continued to be enforced by law and custom even amid public horror at the racial policies of the Nazi regime. Constitutional protections for freedom of speech and freedom of association allowed for open continuation of fascist activism: George Lincoln Rockwell, for example, founded the American Nazi Party in 1959 and openly promoted segregation, Holocaust denial, and anti-Black racism until his assassination by one of his followers in 1967, just after he had decided to stop using the most provocative symbols and regalia of German Nazism.[10]

Rockwell himself did not make much use of Greco-Roman antiquity in his propaganda, although later neo-Nazi leaders have attempted to claim (falsely) that the "Hitler salute" so integral to their rallies is an ancient Roman gesture. In 2018 the "commander" of one notorious organization promoted this identification to a journalist; so too did defenders of Elon Musk, following his use of a gesture at Donald Trump's 2025 inauguration that many observers considered similar to that of the National Socialists. But the historical links between Greco-Roman antiquity and organized white supremacy are deeper than this. One of the most influential thought leaders in postwar American white nationalism was, in fact, a professor of classics. This was Revilo Oliver, who maintained a friendly correspondence with many of the most prominent classical scholars of his day, even after one of his essays attracted national attention for attributing President Kennedy's assassination to a Jewish conspiracy.[11] Like de Benoist and other intellectuals of the European New Right, Oliver showed his wide learning in his many publications, including by making reference to Greco-Roman antiquity, as might be expected of a professional scholar. Unlike de Benoist, however, Oliver continued to lard his writings with overtly racist and antisemitic proclamations that earned the admiration of people who had already joined the movement but contributed little to making their views broadly respectable.

The same may be said of another highly educated American white nationalist who exerted considerable influence in the latter half of the twentieth century. William Luther Pierce held a PhD in physics and taught at Oregon State University before leaving the academy to work for Rockwell shortly before Rockwell's assassination. Pierce is best known as the author of *The Turner Diaries*, an apocalyptic novel that inspired the terrorist who blew up the Murrah Federal Building in Oklahoma City in 1995, killing 168 people and injuring hundreds more. This act of violent terrorism did little to win converts to white nationalism, undermining the metapolitical work Pierce had also undertaken, which included a series of articles claiming to trace the history of the white race and featuring sections on "Hellenes and Dorians," "Nordic Latins," and "Nordic Romans." It would not be until the new millennium that white nationalists in the United States, sensing that the liberalization of the Republican Party's immigration policies under President George W. Bush had alienated conservative white people and, later, capitalizing on white racial resentment over the election of Barack Obama to the presidency in 2008, would begin translating the principles of European-style metapolitics into an American context.[12]

A typical example of the practitioners of that mode of white nationalist thought is Kevin MacDonald, an emeritus professor of psychology at California State University, Long Beach, who has published extensively in academic journals in the field of evolutionary psychology. In the 1990s, he also published a three-volume series of books at a mainstream press (Praeger) that earned him the title of "the neo-Nazi movement's favorite academic" from the Southern Poverty Law Center.[13] In these books, MacDonald attempts to give scientific legitimacy to antisemitic conspiracy theories and canards. In one section, he suggests that if white Europeans had maintained the harsh xenophobia and eugenic priorities of classical Sparta, they would not have succumbed so easily to what he regards as hostile Jewish influence. The publication of this series established MacDonald's reputation in white nationalist circles. Today he is the editor in chief of the *Occidental Observer*, a website dedicated to "White Identity, Interests, and Culture," and the *Occidental Quarterly*, a publication that imitates the format and style of a peer-reviewed journal. MacDonald epitomizes the profile of the white nationalist intellectual that interests me: highly educated, he had a successful career before applying that education and position of influence to the promotion of white nationalist ideas.

MacDonald constitutes just one example of the numerous white nationalist thought leaders who deploy Greco-Roman antiquity in their publications. Greg Johnson holds a PhD in philosophy and serves as editor of the website Counter-Currents, where he has published a ten-part essay, "What Socrates Knew," alongside translations of European New Right thinkers, including an essay by de Benoist's colleague Dominique Venner entitled "Homer: The European Bible." The government of Norway considered Johnson enough of a threat to public safety that they arrested and deported him in 2019. Jared Taylor, who grew up in Japan as the son of Christian missionaries and holds degrees from Yale and Sciences Po in Paris, has published *American Renaissance* since 1994, first as a print magazine and later as an online journal; its logo features a classical column. Arktos is a Swedish publishing company known for translating the books of the European New Right into English. One editor in chief was Jason Reza Jorjani, who was fired from his lectureship at the New Jersey Institute of Technology when an undercover journalist recorded him predicting that in the near future Adolf Hitler would be regarded as a "great European leader" comparable to Alexander the Great. Jorjani was succeeded at Arktos by John Bruce Leonard, whose biography at Arktos's website stated that he had "studied . . . in a university curriculum based exclusively on the great books of the Western Tradition."[14] These men, and the other intellectuals whose work they publish, are engaged in the metapolitical project of making white nationalism respectable, and all of them turn to the Greco-Roman world to do so.

None of these men are household names, but we should not underestimate the influence they wield and the resources they possess. The development of metapolitical theory and the reach of the internet have produced a new era of white nationalist activism. Never before have hate groups been able to reach untold millions with such rhetorical tools. A member of Donald Trump's 2016 presidential campaign staff promoted articles from *American Renaissance* to news outlets covering the campaign. Many of the publications discussed in this book receive funding from nonprofit foundations established by wealthy individuals to support white supremacist activism, such as the Pioneer Fund, founded by the heir of a textile fortune in 1937, or the Charles Martel Society, founded in 2001 by a nephew of the founder of the conservative publishing house Regnery. Such foundations receive individual contributions as well: the VDARE Foundation, which supported the publication of the anti-immigration website of the same name, received more than $4 million in tax-deductible contributions in 2019.[15] These positions of influence are fragile: as I was finishing this book, VDARE's publisher announced that he was shuttering the twenty-five-year-old website, having run out of money to pay for legal fees relating to an investigation of the organization's nonprofit status by the New York State attorney general's office. But if the long history of white nationalist activism in the United States is any indication, it seems likely that new organizations and publications will spring up to take its place.

These facts alone justify scrutiny of these white nationalist activists, so that their deadly ideologies might wither in the light of notoriety and condemnation. But I have primarily marked out this particular subset for detailed study because, unlike the Proud Boys, the Oath Keepers, Based Spartan, and social media trolls who use classical sculptures as profile pictures, these thinkers engage with Greco-Roman antiquity in ways that are anything but superficial. The assumption that racists must be uneducated may lead us to expect to find distortion, misuse, and abuse of history in their writings. But what we actually find is much more disturbing. We find that they know much more about history than we give them credit for. They know, for example, that they do not need to distort or misrepresent the writings of many ancient philosophers and historians in order to find ideas in them quite similar to those that inform white nationalist politics. In this respect, white nationalist intellectuals often see the ancient world with clearer eyes than those who assume such interpretations depend on distortion or lies.

A comparison between the misogynist communities analyzed by Donna Zuckerberg in her 2018 book *Not All Dead White Men: Classics and Misogyny in the Digital Age* and the white nationalists with whom I am concerned here illustrates the sophistication of white nationalist engagements with Greco-Roman antiquity. The "pickup artists," "involuntary celibates," and "men's rights" activists that Zuckerberg profiles share with white nationalists an understanding of the rhetorical usefulness of the prestige of ancient thinkers. One of Zuckerberg's primary examples is ancient Stoicism, particularly the form that Roman philosophers articulated.

Roman Stoicism's conceptions of virtue, wisdom, and the good life are, by and large, deeply and explicitly gendered in masculine terms. This system of thought, which makes women base and irrational by nature, serves very well the interests of modern men who seek to justify the relegation of women to second-class status and to control their sexuality and freedom.[16] Classical scholars and philosophers who have welcomed the rising popularity of Stoicism among modern audiences would do well to note this point of intersection with misogynist politics.

White nationalist intellectuals may agree with male supremacists about the proper role of women in society, but they do not share their enthusiasm for Roman Stoicism. An essay in what was for a time the premier venue for intellectuals who identified themselves as "Alt-Right," Richard Spencer's online journal *Radix*, illustrates this. This essay condemned Stoicism as an individualistic philosophy that fosters "rootlessness" and alienation in service of what the essayist argues is a Jewish goal of eroding feelings of connection and solidarity among white people. Whereas misogynists have simply identified ideas that the Stoics share with them, the essayist for *Radix* has grounded his critique in an understanding of the historical context of Roman Stoicism. This philosophy flourished in the time of the Roman Empire's maximum extent, and its emphasis on the cosmic powerlessness of the individual is transparently a response to the disruption of traditional social structures that the increasing cosmopolitanism of the capital cities of the empire accelerated. White nationalists condemn all multicultural societies as degenerate and chaotic—the classical scholar Revilo Oliver attributed Stoicism's development in Rome to "racial agglomeration"—and for them, Stoicism's contemporary popularity reflects the modern world's succumbing to a similar trend. We may reject the very premise that cosmopolitanism presages decline, and we may condemn the antisemitic spin that the *Radix* essayist puts on his diagnosis of that alleged decline. But we must recognize that he nevertheless possesses a deeper understanding of the historical origins of Stoicism than many of the self-help gurus—whether openly misogynist or not—who promote this philosophy to modern audiences.

White nationalist intellectuals know, too, a great deal about how Greco-Roman antiquity has been interpreted over the centuries. Study of the classics has traditionally been the province of political and social elites, and its interpretation has accordingly reflected the biases and prejudices of those elites.[17] So it is easy for white nationalist intellectuals to find examples of respected historians whose understanding of the ancient world promotes racism, antisemitism, xenophobia, and homophobia, and to cite them as proof that white nationalist ideas have been taken seriously by respectable thinkers in the past and should be taken seriously in the present. Nearly all of these older interpretations have been challenged by modern specialists, but it takes many years for specialist research to alter public perceptions of the ancient world. Popular representations are more likely to draw on the traditions that white nationalists turn to than on cutting-edge scholarship. And, as we shall see, even within the scholarly community, older assumptions about the ancient world persist, particularly in work that seeks to speak to the broader public and not only to academic specialists.

In the analysis that follows, I will correct some distortions of history found in white nationalist analyses of it, especially when they are imposing false modern ideas about the biological reality of race on the ancient world, and I will point out how contemporary research has invalidated some of the assumptions underlying their claims. But this is not a book about how white nationalists have twisted historical fact to fit their racist agenda. This is a book about the presence of white nationalist ideas in the Greco-Roman world, and the influence of such ideas on the way that history has been preserved, remembered, and interpreted. Because these two dimensions of the relationship of Greco-Roman antiquity to white nationalist ideas reinforce each other in white nationalist thought, and so are intertwined throughout my analysis, it is worthwhile to distinguish them conceptually from the outset.

Popular idealized conceptions of ancient Greece and Rome have rendered the presence of hateful ideas in ancient thought less visible, either by ignoring the texts that contain them or by minimizing their presence in familiar texts. White nationalist intellectuals know of the existence of these texts and promote them as evidence that distinguished ancient thinkers shared their hateful views. This is an act of distortion only insofar as these intellectuals avoid citing ancient texts that contradict or complicate the passages they do cite.

Such curation of ancient evidence is merely the inverse of the same, more mainstream, act of curation that avoids citing passages that complicate the idea that ancient thinkers promoted high-minded ideals and sophisticated philosophy. Ancient texts do articulate racist ideas. Too few people outside white nationalist circles know this.

My treatment of the ways that material from Greco-Roman antiquity has been used by later historians and politicians to promote violence and oppression is informed by the fact that all aspects of the ancient world—the texts Greek and Roman authors wrote, the monuments their civilization erected, its sculptures—have been made to mean different things in different periods of history.[18] Many white nationalist interpretations of ancient material, although they would have been incomprehensible to the people who actually lived in ancient Greece or Rome, were first articulated by influential historians and intellectuals. And if, because of the influence of those who articulated them, these interpretations have established harmful public attitudes about human difference, shaped laws regarding those differences, and justified violence against those people who have been marked as different, it is not enough to assert that the ancient meaning of the text was different than what it has been made to mean. An interpretation may be "wrong" and yet still be significant and influential. To label such cases a "distortion" or "abuse" of history may shield ancient material from association with racist ideas, but it cannot undo the violence such interpretations have legitimized. And it does nothing to unseat those racist ideas that, having gained currency through their association with the ancient world, persist even after professional scholars have abandoned the interpretations that helped establish them. White nationalist intellectuals take these histories of interpretation seriously precisely because of their distinguished pedigrees. If we care about understanding how racist ideas become popular and maintain their hold on our minds, we must do the same.

Antisemitism, Ancient and Modern

The example of antisemitism illustrates well how white nationalist intellectuals do not need to distort or misrepresent Greco-Roman antiquity to find support for their ideas in it. It will be impossible here to catalogue all the racist canards and conspiracy theories about Jewish people that circulate in white nationalist thought, but a central claim is that Jewish people seek to weaken "white societies" for their own benefit. A series of beliefs about Jewish people has been propagated to make this claim seem plausible, such as that all Jewish people hold non-Jews in contempt, or that Jewish people are particularly skilled at infiltrating and taking control of influential institutions (the most well-known conspiracy theories focus particularly on entertainment media and banking). In a society accustomed to think of racism as relating only, or primarily, to skin color, it is necessary at the outset to identify that these beliefs about Jewish people depend on the same type of logic that racist prejudices toward Black people or immigrants do. They all require accepting that a group of people all share the same qualities, attitudes, and characteristics.

Even many professional historians are not aware of just how explicitly Greco-Roman authors express beliefs like these about Jewish people. One of the earliest references to Jewish people outside of Hebrew sources comes from the Greek historian Hecataeus of Abdera, who wrote in the fourth century BCE. His work does not survive, but a later summary of it attributes to him the claim that the Jewish way of life was "misanthropic" and "hostile to foreigners." Four hundred years later the Roman historian Tacitus, too, asserted that Jewish people evince "hostile hatred toward all others." Alongside this assumption, we find claims about Jewish influence that would not be out of place in the most vicious conspiracy theories. The first-century geographer Strabo wrote that "this people [the Jews] has already made its way into every city, and it is not easy to find any place in the habitable world which has not received this nation and in which it has not made its power felt." A generation later, the Roman philosopher Seneca declared that "the customs of this accursed race have gained such influence that they are now received throughout all the world." In a speech delivered in 59 BCE, the Roman orator Cicero assumes that his audience subscribes to this view as well, stating that he will "speak in a low voice" so as not to provoke Jewish people in the audience, adding, "You know how numerous that crowd is, how great is its unanimity, and of what weight it is in the popular assemblies."[19]

All of these passages are cited in white nationalist publications; the passage from Cicero may explain why the antisemitic Telegram channel mentioned above used his image as its avatar. Some publications, it is true, circulate a version of Cicero's speech with modern additions that heighten its antisemitism ("the Jews belong to a dark and repulsive force"). It was this invented version that was cited in the manifesto of the man who in 2009 murdered Stephen Tyrone Johns, a security guard at the U.S. Holocaust Museum.[20] But in general, white nationalist intellectuals understand that they do not need to modify or distort the hostility toward Jewish people found in ancient sources, ranging from famous authors like Tacitus to little-known fragments from otherwise well-known figures (the line from Seneca comes from "On Superstition," which survives only in quotations in Augustine's work) to ancient thinkers known only to specialists, like Hecataeus of Abdera. White nationalists are able to muster such an impressive range of sources because they know how to do their research. They cite these passages from respected works of scholarship, such as the distinguished Israeli historian Menahem Stern's two-volume reference work *Greek and Latin Authors on Jews and Judaism* (1974).

These publications make clear why they cite ancient sources. An essay in the *Occidental Quarterly*, for example, by the translator of a new edition of Hitler's *Mein Kampf*, quotes many of these passages to illustrate, he says, that those who hate Jewish people share this hatred with "prominent and brilliant individuals, by all other accounts men of genius." Such hatred, the argument goes, is therefore justified. The logical fallacy behind this argument seems laughable (X is true because smart person Y said so) until one remembers just how influential this argument has been. Certainly, Nazi historians combed ancient sources to corroborate their antisemitic views, but they were drawing on well-established historical methods in doing so. Arthur Hertzberg has documented how major figures in the European Enlightenment, especially Voltaire, justified antisemitism with "charges [that], without exception, descended from . . . classic[al] sources." The ancient historian Theodor Mommsen, who won the first Nobel Prize for Literature, argued that Jewish people are themselves to blame for hatred against them, and claimed in his *History of Rome* that "Judaism was an effective leaven of cosmopolitanism and of national decomposition." So it is not just ancient thinkers whom white nationalists can claim as predecessors. They can, and do, point also to the historical arguments of luminaries like Voltaire and Mommsen as proof of the distinguished intellectual pedigree of their beliefs. This is why I avoid terms such as "far right" and "extremist" in my analysis: many of the white nationalist claims I discuss have histories that are anything but extremist. Many of them continue to enjoy acceptance today, as Deborah Lipstadt, an authority on Holocaust denial who has served on the memorial council of the U.S. Holocaust Museum, has documented most recently.[21] Few people may read Strabo or Cicero, but the attitudes that their authority helped establish persist.

Especially for scholars, it is tempting to counterbalance expressions of hostility toward Jews by pointing out that more positive portrayals can be found in ancient sources. The philosopher Aristobulus of Alexandria (second century BCE) records a story that a Jewish wise man impressed Aristotle and made significant contributions to the philosophical conversations of learned Greeks. Numinius of Apamea (second century CE) wrote that Plato got all his best philosophical ideas from Indian Brahmans, Egyptians, and Jews. "What is Plato but Moses writing in Greek?" he asked. There was even a story that the Spartans and the Jews shared a common ancestor.[22] No modern historian accepts this story as fact, but (needless to say) white nationalists who fetishize the Spartans as paragons of white masculine heroism never mention it. Such passages highlight how white nationalists curate a narrow conception of Greco-Roman antiquity that suits their political objectives. It's a valid critique, except for the fact that this narrow, curated view of antiquity is the one propagated by most popular treatments of ancient history and even most educational curricula. If you have any familiarity with Greco-Roman literature, you've heard of Tacitus, Cicero, and Seneca. Hardly anyone knows about Aristobulus of Alexandria or Numinius of Apamea, not even professional scholars.

A different scholarly approach to such claims is to argue that there is a meaningful difference between ancient hostility toward Jewish people and the racial antisemitism of the contemporary world. Scholarship that articulates this distinction demonstrates conclusively that hatred of Jewish people has taken different forms and functioned in different ways throughout history, thereby undermining white nationalist claims that antisemitism is "natural" or inevitable. But such scholarship's treatment of ancient material tends to argue that Greek and Roman attitudes cannot be considered antisemitism because they do not depend on the same pseudoscientific claims that inform modern antisemitism. In my view, this distinction is difficult to maintain: the Roman satirist Juvenal, for example, assumes that Jewish children will always reproduce their fathers' "contempt for Roman laws." This looks to me very much like the biological reasoning of nineteenth-century race pseudoscience. Like the parallel claim that Greco-Roman antiquity had no concept of race, claims that the ancient world did not practice antisemitism run the risk of minimizing or erasing the hatred and violence inherent in ancient sources, ignoring the impact that such passages—however they were understood in antiquity—have had on antisemitic beliefs and violence in the present. The terrorist who murdered eleven people and injured six others in 2018 at the Tree of Life Synagogue in Pittsburgh accused Jewish organizations that support refugees of "bring[ing] invaders that kill our people."[23] This is an accusation not so different from Mommsen's claim that Judaism contributed to "national decomposition" in Rome. It is possible to affirm that antisemitism has a long, even ancient history while attending to the myriad variations and mutations over many years that prove it is neither natural nor inevitable.

White nationalist antisemitism thus typifies the noxious blend of racist fantasy and historical fact that contributes to the ongoing persistence of this vile hatred. On the one hand, it transparently depends on debunked pseudoscientific theories that collapse the very real diversity of Jewish people worldwide into a monolithic mass of racial aliens who all allegedly share attitudes and motivations hostile to white people. This is a racist lie, pure and simple. On the other hand, white nationalist intellectuals can claim, without distortion, that respected ancient thinkers expressed hostility toward Jewish people that resembles white nationalist attitudes, and furthermore that Enlightenment intellectuals believed that this testimony proved that such hostility is justified in modern times. The historical material serves to fortify the racist lie at the heart of antisemitism.

Naming this rhetorical strategy clarifies the role of the historian in confronting white nationalist history. An approach that seeks to cleanse the past from complicity serves only the interests of the deceased—and of those of us who stake our professional reputations on the prestige of that history. By contrast, an approach that recognizes that the weakness of the way white nationalist intellectuals cite histories lies not in their use of history itself, but in the racist fantasies they use that history to legitimize, can focus its energy on exposing the latter: scholarship in service not of the reputation of the past, but of the moral demands of the present.

CHAPTER TWO

The Last Stand against Modernity

On January 6, 2021, a mob of rioters attacked the U.S. Capitol building as members of Congress were gathering to make a formal count of electoral votes from the recent presidential election. The rioters' objective seems to have been to prevent Joe Biden, the winner of the election against then-president Donald Trump, from taking office: a few hours earlier, Trump had told his supporters, many of whom participated in the riot, that "this election was stolen from you, from me and from the country." But the symbols of white supremacy on display at the rally—a noose hung outside the building, a Confederate flag flown inside it—reveal that it was more than support for a particular candidate that motivated the rioters. "This is our house," declared one of the rioters upon entering the Capitol. As historian Lyra Monteiro noted, "By 'our,' they mean white people's."[1]

Alongside these racist symbols were several drawn from Greco-Roman antiquity, primarily related to classical Sparta. At least two rioters wore Spartan-style military helmets, and another flew a flag bearing the Greek slogan *Molon Labe*, the words the Spartan general Leonidas supposedly spoke to an envoy from the Persian Empire who invited the Spartans to hand over their weapons in order to receive better treatment following the Persian invasion of Greece. The English translation of these words appeared on numerous other flags at the riot: "Come and Take Them." Less visible at the riot were the ways that the groups participating in it also looked to the Spartans for inspiration. The Proud Boys, whose logo features a classical laurel wreath, had praised Sparta as "the ultimate example of a warrior society" on their (now defunct) website. The Oath Keepers had announced in a 2018 interview on the conspiracy theory website Infowars that they were forming paramilitary "Spartan Training Groups." Leaders and members from both groups have been convicted of multiple felonies in connection with the January 6 riot.[2]

With these symbols the rioters claimed to be taking a similarly heroic stand in defense of their nation. Trump's rhetoric was tailored to this self-image. He gave the name "Save America" to the rally at which he told them, "If you don't fight like hell, you won't have a country anymore." According to the analogy created by those who donned Spartan-style helmets, Leonidas and his troops "fought like hell" to prevent the Persian king Xerxes from imposing monarchy on Greece. Those in the mob who believed—wrongly—that the election had been undemocratic could see the riot as a heroic stand against tyranny. It was all a baseless conspiracy. There is no evidence that the election was anything but fair and democratic.[3] But it is a lot easier to engage in violence on behalf of lies when you see yourself as a modern-day version of a noble and heroic warrior.

White nationalist intellectuals disavow violence and distance themselves from events like the Capitol attack. They claim to be preoccupied, instead, with laying the intellectual and cultural foundations for political change within existing political institutions, by, for example, persuading sufficient numbers of white people to support overtly white supremacist policies. But persuading white people to do this requires convincing them to accept a whole range of racist conspiracy theories, including the belief that governments worldwide, under the influence of Jewish people, are actively seeking the dilution and extermination of the white race. Surveys conducted by the political scientist Robert Pape found that belief in the Great Replacement conspiracy theory was, in fact, the "key driver" of participation in the insurrectionist movement, including the January 6 attack.[4]

It is one thing to believe this white supremacist lie; it is another thing to engage in violence because you believe it. Yet the recent history of racist violence in America, from the paramilitary and skinhead groups of the 1980s and 1990s that waged a "racial holy war" against Black and Jewish people to the more than 170 violent attacks that have taken place since the Oklahoma City bombing in 1995, shows that plenty of people make the leap from white supremacist thought to real-world terrorism.[5] Analogies between white nationalist activism and Spartan warriors and other ancient models of heroism foster such violence. They legitimize the white nationalist belief that such violence is justified and indeed necessary for the preservation of the white race. They allow, in short, violent terrorists to view themselves as noble defenders of their civilization.

Sparta: "The Unity and Vigor We Have Left Behind"

The Spartans are so popular among white nationalists because they epitomize stereotypically masculine attributes in opposition to foreign invasion, thanks to their role in opposing the Persian Empire's invasion of Greece. White nationalists are not the only ones fixated on this aspect of Spartan history, however. Popular representations of the Spartans focus on it as well. It is tempting to think that the rioters who put on Spartan helmets and tried to overthrow the government on January 6, 2021, did not know anything more about Sparta than what they saw in Zack Snyder's blockbuster 2006 film *300*, which glorifies the heroism of the Spartans at the battle of Thermopylae, especially that of their leader Leonidas. To be sure, the film ticks all the boxes required for a white nationalist portrayal of heroism. The conspicuous near nudity of the Spartans emphasizes their white skin, inviting white viewers to imagine a racial link between themselves and these ancient people who did not, in fact, define themselves by their skin color. Combine this with the portrayal of the invading Persians as decadent and monstrous in contrast to the muscular masculinity of the Spartans, and it is little wonder that *American Renaissance*'s review of the film, entitled

"Why Men Fight," said it "could be the best film ever made about ancient Greece."[6]

White nationalist intellectuals, however, have been cultivating the same symbolic understanding of classical Sparta for generations. The most notorious white supremacist invocation of Spartan heroism is that of the Nazis: Hitler wrote in *Mein Kampf* that the Greeks provide inspiration for "a culture that is fighting for its existence," and when the Nazi propagandist Joseph Goebbels visited the site of classical Sparta he declared, "I truly feel I am in a German city."[7] But Nazi Laconophilia is only one node in a far-reaching history of white supremacist idealizations of Spartan heroism.

David Lane is remembered among white nationalists for popularizing the slogan known as "the fourteen words": "We must secure the existence of our people and a future for white children." But the public remembers him for his involvement in the 1984 murder of the Jewish talk show host Allan Berg. While serving his 190-year prison sentence for that crime, Lane founded a press that published an essay entitled "Leonidas the Spartan." This essay deviates from Lane's usual focus on historical analogues drawn from Germanic mythology, but it makes explicit the racial dynamics that would later characterize the portrayal of the Spartans and Persians in *300*, calling Thermopylae "a model of heroism for white people everywhere." So too did an essay published by William Luther Pierce, the author of the apocalyptic novel that inspired the Oklahoma City bombing, entitled "Leonidas and the Spartan Ethos." This essay, written by an editor of the Holocaust-denying *Journal of Historical Review*, predicted that the "memory of Thermopylae's defenders will live as long as the White race." More recently, Costin Alamariu, who holds a PhD in political science from Yale and whose publications under the pen name "Bronze Age Pervert" have been praised for their perceptiveness by a member of Donald Trump's National Security Council, describes the Spartans in his book *Bronze Age Mindset* as "the most brilliant men . . . [who] easily imposed the intensity of their magic charisma on foreigners."[8] At *American Renaissance*'s 2021 conference, Jared Taylor concluded his speech on the supposed threat of "extermination" that white people face by exhorting attendees to "choose to be like the countless white heroes who have laid down their lives in glorious causes."

His first example was "the Greeks who fought the Persians at Thermopylae."

This interpretive tradition emphasizes a certain form of masculinity that the Spartans supposedly represent. "Leonidas and the Spartan Ethos" employs a Greek word that Homer used primarily, though not exclusively, for the heroism shown by warriors in the Trojan War, arguing that "it was on the battlefield that the Spartan *arete*, or manly excellence, found its chief expression." Bronze Age Pervert presents the Spartans as "men who really didn't have any hangups, who weren't repressed at all." Of crucial importance to this line of thinking is the assumption that any devaluation of this type of masculinity poses an existential threat to a civilization. This, an essayist for the *Occidental Observer* insists, is the fundamental insight that the ancient Greek historian Herodotus reveals through his narrative of the Persian invasion of Greece (a narrative that, this essayist notes, provided many of the most memorable lines in the film *300*). The final scene of the final book in Herodotus's *Histories* is a flashback involving the Persian king Cyrus, the grandfather of Xerxes. In that scene Cyrus rejects a proposal to move the empire's capital to Media, which Cyrus had just conquered, because "soft lands tend to breed soft men."[9] Herodotus's placement of this flashback at the end of his narrative has puzzled professional historians but it makes perfect sense to white nationalist intellectuals as a conclusion to a historical narrative that they claim illustrates how "values and habits of weakness can lead to the fall of one's people."

White nationalists hold up the standard of masculinity supposedly set by the Spartans as the antidote to this dire fate. *American Renaissance* praised *300* for its portrayal of "the unity and vigor we have left behind." Such unity and vigor, this argument goes, were integral to defending Greece against foreign invasions, and should be cultivated again in the face of modern "invasions" that white nationalists believe currently threaten "the West" in the form of immigration. The second issue of the *Occidental Quarterly*, published in 2002, featured an essay that "pa[id] tribute to those who, throughout the history of the West, courageously repulsed alien invading forces." The first example given by the author, who has also published a scholarly book on medieval Christianity and later founded an anti-immigration organization in Westchester County,

New York, was Thermopylae, which he called "the first great battle for the survival of the West." In 2013, the American neo-Nazi Andrew Anglin filed a report on his Daily Stormer website from a rally organized by Greece's Golden Dawn political party at the site of Thermopylae. Anglin contrasted the Spartans, who understood, he argued, "that in giving their lives, they were assuring the survival of their progeny," with "vile White men who today are selling us out to the Jews and their savage hordes." At the peak of their appeal, Golden Dawn held twenty-one seats in the Greek parliament. After the party was banned from elections, some of its former members formed a new party that won seven seats in Greece's 2023 elections. This party, which was later banned from subsequent elections, was known as the Spartans.[10]

Ultimately, all of these commemorations of the battle of Thermopylae serve to ennoble and justify violence, particularly against those whom white nationalists identify as "invaders" or as otherwise complicit in the racial weakening of white-dominated societies. It is impossible to demonstrate a conclusive link between such celebrations of violence and the enactment of real-world violence. But it seems more than coincidental that several members of Golden Dawn, a political party that has commemorated the battle of Thermopylae every year since at least 2008, are now serving prison terms for murder or attempted murder. Among their victims was the anti-fascist rapper Pavlos Fyssas, killed only a few weeks after the commemoration that Anglin attended. White nationalist discussions of the film *300* hardly mention its celebration of violence, a primary topic of reviews in the mainstream press. But this aspect of the film does not seem to have troubled audience members at the film's premiere at the Berlin International Film Festival, who gave it a standing ovation.[11] Nor does it seem to have troubled audiences elsewhere. *300* grossed more than half a billion dollars worldwide.

The Mainstream Mirage

When understood as a model of masculine resistance to the threat of foreign invasion, Sparta makes an ideal model for white nationalism. But there is a further aspect of Spartan heroism that makes it even more attractive to white nationalist thinkers: this conception of Sparta corresponds closely to the dominant conception of masculinity that contemporary media, film, and television—not just *300*—idealize and celebrate. Contemporary portrayals of masculinity often link strength and honor with physical aggression and violence.[12] In such a media environment, it is unsurprising that Sparta is respected far beyond the white nationalist community. But such conflation of violence and honor presents a rhetorical opportunity to white nationalists, who claim Sparta as a model that casts violent masculinity and xenophobia as principled and noble.

For example, extremism researcher Cynthia Miller-Idriss has documented private boxing gyms in France and in Quebec that recruit young men into white nationalist politics: one of them is called "L'agoge" after the Spartan educational system described by Xenophon, and the other is called "La phalange," which evokes not only the ancient Greek military formation known as the phalanx but the name of Spanish dictator Francisco Franco's political party, Falange. As Miller-Idriss shows, such organizations cultivate feelings of "solidarity, heroism, and brotherhood" among those they hope will become activists—foot soldiers, even—on behalf of white nationalism, while downplaying the "violence, risk, and danger" such activism entails.[13] Come for the self-respect, stay for the racist politics.

This is not a matter of white nationalists attaching racist and violent themes to a popular and politically neutral symbol: the film *300* is only the most prominent example of how frequently popular representations of Sparta incorporate such ideas. Emma Bridges has traced how novelistic treatments of the Persian Wars, as far back as the nineteenth century, contrast the barbarism, despotism, and treachery of the Persians with the patriotism, heroism, and excellence of the Greeks. The most influential of these was Stephen Pressfield's *Gates of Fire* which, according to the classical scholar Lynn Fotheringham, featured the same "western triumphalism and orientalist caricature" as the film *300*. This historical novel may not have reached the millions that *300* did but it has appeared on the "Professional Reading Lists" issued by the U.S. Marine Corps' Commandants and the U.S. Army Chief of Staff. And the series of grueling athletic competitions marketed as the "Spartan Race" invites participants to see themselves in this same mold; according to the sports historian Gavin Weedon, the rhetoric of the founder of the company that puts on these races echoes the "concerns about the supposedly emasculating effects of civilization, especially for Anglo-Saxon boys," that characterized the eugenics movement of the early twentieth century.[14]

Nor is this conception of Sparta as a noble, hypermasculine warrior society a matter of the imposition of modern preoccupations on an ancient canvas. Already in antiquity Sparta was renowned for these qualities. Herodotus's description of the battle of Thermopylae is replete with vignettes that celebrate the defiant heroism of the Spartans. Many of these appear unaltered in *300*, such as the reply of the Spartans when they are told that the Persian army is so large that its archers' arrows block out the sun: "Then we will fight in the shade." Herodotus reports, too, that the heroism of Leonidas and his men inspired those living around Thermopylae to erect a monument commemorating them. Every modern retelling of the battle includes the inscription they commissioned for this monument from the famous poet Simonides: "Go tell the Spartans, passerby, that here, by Spartan law, we lie." White nationalist essays on Spartan heroism quote liberally from the descriptions of Spartan customs found in Xenophon and Plutarch that celebrate the discipline and physical fitness of Spartans. These include the legendary Spartan lawgiver Lycurgus's laws against luxury, the physical and moral strength that the harsh educational system instilled, how men lived in barracks with their fellow soldiers rather than with their families. Some details from these sources positively affirm white nationalist beliefs, such as Lycurgus's prohibition against Spartan citizens living abroad, how the elders examined newborn infants and killed any that were deformed, and how the Spartans maintained control of the people they enslaved by making the indiscriminate murder of a few a rite of passage for young citizen men.[15]

None of these sources are unbiased. Xenophon's description of Sparta is shaped by his partisan desire to make an unfavorable comparison between the Sparta of his time and that of the past. His work made a major contribution to the establishment of the fantasy of Spartan masculinity and military supremacy that informs popular and white nationalist representations of Sparta to this day. Plutarch's description, written many centuries after the battle of Thermopylae, preserves and amplifies this fantasy. Stephen Hodkinson has argued that if one takes into account the biases of these literary sources and considers carefully the archaeological evidence of classical Sparta, one concludes that it was, in fact, not much different from other Greek city-states, even in terms of military strength.[16]

But this historical fantasy of Sparta was regarded as historical fact for thousands of years before it began to be seriously questioned. For example, the "philosophes" who laid the intellectual foundations of the French Revolution in the eighteenth century made Sparta a model for how morality and virtue could coexist with individual freedoms. It's an argument that depends on accepting Plutarch's description of Lycurgus's laws as historical fact (as well as ignoring Sparta's slave economy). In the United States, the Texans who died at the battle of the Alamo in 1836 were immediately compared to the Spartans at Thermopylae in political speeches, editorials, legislative resolutions, and, finally, the words that appear on the Alamo memorial at the Texas State Capitol: "Thermopylae had her messenger of defeat, the Alamo had none." The "messenger" of Thermopylae refers to the ancient epigram instructing a "stranger" to deliver the news of the Spartans' heroism. As noted above, this epigram is central to the myth that makes the Spartan self-sacrifice noble rather than, say, ill considered and reckless. By reproducing this myth, the Alamo comparison contributes to what has been called a "Heroic Anglo Narrative" of the Alamo that has been used to demonize Mexican Americans living in Texas. Almost two centuries later such comparisons remain current: a 2010 history of the U.S. Marine Corps "from Iwo Jima to Iraq" is called *American Spartans.* And it is not only in military contexts that the Spartans are venerated: seventeen U.S. states have municipalities named "Sparta," and eleven North American colleges (and countless high schools) have "Spartans" as the mascots of their athletic teams. The French historian François Ollier may have exposed what he termed *le mirage spartiate*, "the Spartan Mirage," in 1933, but the fantasy on which that mirage rests remains alive and well almost a century later. Some of those who have questioned this fantasy in high-profile venues have been harassed and have even received death threats.[17]

As Stephen Hodkinson has shown, professional scholars have contributed to the maintenance of this fantasy, partly out of admiration for Sparta and partly by playing up its harshness and military might in order to celebrate the supposedly more enlightened culture of Athens. This has even extended to propagating the story that Spartans practiced infanticide, for which there is very little direct evidence. Professional historians continue to produce books on Sparta that take Xenophon's and Plutarch's descriptions of Sparta at face value. Even those who approach ancient evidence critically find it hard to resist the allure of the fantasy: the title of the Cambridge University historian Paul Cartledge's book on Thermopylae celebrated it as "the battle that changed the world."[18] However much we might like to use historical research to complicate white nationalist conceptions of Sparta, the fact remains that those conceptions are dominant in both popular and even some scholarly treatments of that history. This is no small part of the reason that white nationalist intellectuals invoke Sparta so often, and why Spartan symbols appear so frequently at white nationalist gatherings.

One reaction to white nationalist appropriation of Sparta is to "point out the cultural and political flaws in Sparta," as one historian has argued, including "their use of enslaved labor and eugenics." But these are positive selling points for white nationalists, not complications to their idealization of Sparta. One might expect that the degree of influence and wealth that women in Sparta apparently enjoyed might offend patriarchal white nationalist sensibilities (it was enough to scandalize Aristotle, at least). But Plutarch's and Xenophon's accounts of Spartan women actually fit white nationalist politics very well because they emphasize the centrality of childbearing and motherhood to the Spartan woman's social role—precisely the values that white nationalists believe contemporary white women should hold.[19]

Even the homoerotic sexuality that clearly played an important role in the Spartan educational program does not complicate white nationalist admiration for Sparta as much as one might expect, even though homophobia is as central to many strands of white nationalism as is anti-Black racism or antisemitism. Let us say at the outset that those wishing to use this history to challenge white nationalist admiration for Spartan masculinity must beware of the danger of relying on the white nationalist equation of homosexuality with weakness in mounting this challenge. What is more, the same white nationalists who make that equation know that, despite the popular perception of ancient Greece as a liberated utopia for same-sex love, ancient sources frequently articulate modern-sounding disgust at sexual relationships between men. In an essay entitled "The Alt-Right and the Homosexual Question," for example, a contributor to AltRight.com can quote a character in Plato's *Laws* calling such sexuality "contrary to nature" and even the Spartan lawgiver Lycurgus designating it "very shameful." The interpretation of these and similar passages is controversial, but they have influenced modern homophobic activism: when an amendment to Colorado's state constitution that prevented cities from banning discrimination against gay people was challenged in court, the Australian legal philosopher John Finnis filed an affidavit defending the amendment. As he wrote in a later expansion of his argument, "All three of the greatest Greek philosophers, Socrates, Plato and Aristotle, regarded homosexual *conduct* as intrinsically shameful, immoral, and indeed depraved or depraving."[20] The Supreme Court of the United States eventually found this amendment to be unconstitutional, but Finnis's arguments were persuasive enough that a lower court upheld the constitutionality of the amendment.

As it turns out, white nationalist intellectuals can accommodate ancient homoerotic sexuality in their worldview. Greg Johnson at Counter-Currents has written that "some of the manliest men in history," including "Achilles and Alexander the Great," practiced what Johnson calls "homosexual pederasty" and "regarded homosexual relationships as completely consistent with marriage and family life." Even the white nationalist professor of classics Revilo Oliver, who contributed a "commentary" to a book that promoted a conspiracy theory about government-sponsored promotion of homosexuality via brainwashing, admitted that "it seems certain that in the Greek world there were homosexuals who were men—even men of honor," referring in particular to the "Sacred Band" of Thebes, which Plutarch says comprised pairs of male lovers.[21]

Within some circles of highbrow white nationalism, it seems, whom you sleep with is immaterial provided that you maintain the warrior ethos necessary to save the white race from extinction.

The Heroes of Hatred

Johnson's reference to the homoerotic relationships of Alexander and Achilles serves as a reminder that all the celebrated warriors of antiquity can be enlisted as models for white nationalist justifications of violence against effeminacy and immigrants. The Spartans of Thermopylae are only the most familiar ancient symbol of heroic masculinity among the many that white nationalists cite.

In 2018, Johnson spoke alongside other white nationalist intellectuals at an event in Helsinki that was billed as "the first ethnonationalist conference in Finland." His subject was what he described as the "crisis of manliness" among white people. He began his speech by quoting the opening lines of Homer's *Iliad*—"Sing, O Goddess, the destructive wrath of Achilles"—but devoted most of his discussion to the concept of *thumos*, which is one of the three parts of Plato's definition of the human soul, along with reason and desire. Johnson defines this term as "fighting spirit" and says it is what drives men to fight for "honor, family, and tribe." Johnson aims to inspire his audience to "be warriors and idealists, people who are willing to fight and die over matters of honor, principle, and patriotism." It is hard to imagine that Johnson, who holds a PhD in philosophy, does not know that Plato's Socrates says that the man whose soul is ruled primarily by *thumos* "does everything with savage violence, like a wild animal."[22] But it seems unlikely that Johnson, who praises Finland as "the land of Black Metal," is as interested in this speech in the details of Plato's argument as he may be in obtaining respectable philosophical cover for the idea that violence is an appropriate means of promoting white supremacy. Behind that respectable, authoritative veneer is an invitation to the audience to see themselves as Achilles and to turn their "fighting spirit," as Johnson says Achilles did, "to destructive wrath."

If anyone in Johnson's audience were familiar with the *Iliad*, they might recognize that the poem undermines the analogy Johnson seems to be drawing between his modern audience and the most famous Greek warrior. Homer specifies that Achilles' anger caused "countless woes" (in the words of the translation Johnson quotes) to the very people Achilles was supposed to be fighting for, the Greeks, making him a poor model for modern men who wish to see themselves as heroic defenders of Europe. But Johnson's real focus is on the familiar themes of effeminacy and the threat of invasion. He warns his audience that the "globalist Left" has "declared war on manliness by stigmatizing it and promoting feminism, androgyny, and confusion about sexual roles and identity." His evidence for the supposed "crisis of manliness" in "the West" is an image of "the words 'refugees welcome' on signs held up by soy-drinking, cuck-mouthed hipsters, man-purses dangling from their spindly arms."

This invective is saturated with a whole range of white nationalist conspiracy theories, but Johnson's emphasis on *thumos* has a more mainstream source. The political scientist Francis Fukuyama, who studied classics as an undergraduate at Cornell University, popularized the use of the concept of *thumos* in political science with his influential book *The End of History and the Last Man* (1992). Fukuyama viewed *thumos* as a threat to the stability of the modern liberal democratic order that he argued was the endpoint of human political evolution. This is not to say that Fukuyama and Johnson are fellow travelers: Fukuyama celebrates the moderation of *thumos* under contemporary liberalism, whereas Johnson seeks to undo that moderation to destabilize the modern order. But Fukuyama's promotion of *thumos* as an analytical term gives it an air of legitimacy it might not otherwise possess, and his much-criticized penchant for Eurocentrism and sanitization of the violence of European history makes his worldview palatable to white nationalist intellectuals. Indeed, Johnson's quotation in his speech of C. S. Lewis's complaint that modern education produces "men without chests" suggests that he had been reading Fukuyama's book, in which the same quotation provides a chapter title.[23]

Long before Plato analyzed *thumos* as a component of the human soul, that term had appeared in the poetry of Homer as the source not only of a warrior's life force but of his courage and his fury. Johnson is hardly alone among white nationalists in finding in the *Iliad* and the *Odyssey* inspiration for masculine heroism. A contributor to AltRight.com quotes the Greek warrior Diomedes' rebuttal to an advisor who urged caution—"Don't talk to me of retreat!"—as inspiration for the kind of relentless struggle he believes white men must undertake.[24] In a piece for Counter-Currents, the same essayist exhorts his readers to become "the tip of the spear and battle the degeneracy that characterizes the post-modern dystopia of the West," describing the objective of such a struggle with the Homeric term *doryktetos*, "spear won." A contributor to another white nationalist website uses more colorful language to articulate the relationship between heroic masculinity and degeneracy. He makes the "heroes of the *Iliad* and the *Odyssey*" "role models" for men seeking "more meaningful and fulfilling lives than the soy-guzzling, effeminate, sex-starved male consumers who inhabit . . . the decaying West."

Other white nationalist intellectuals make clear that Homeric heroism justifies violence. An essay on the *Occidental Observer* recommends the *Iliad* as "a poem about the tragedy of vital barbarism" (archaic Greece) "and decadent civilization" (Troy). Modern men who, the essay argues, "are of an unbearable and unheard of effeminacy" should read it to understand the threat of "being physically replaced by other peoples . . . who have kept that instinctive barbarian vigor" that the essayist claims the Homeric heroes embodied. The only way to prevent replacement by "barbarians," this reasoning goes, is to cultivate the same aptitude for violence. The same essayist understands the *Odyssey*, too, as a parable for modern men. In a piece entitled "The Return of the Father," he argues that the poem's description of Odysseus's adventures portrays a "trustless world" in which "strangers are synonymous with uncertainty and potential violence" and that when Odysseus returns home and slaughters the men who have taken residence in his house during his twenty-year absence this is intended to illustrate that "security . . . only exists by the strength of the family father, his domestic authority, and his willingness to use violence against hostile aliens." Odysseus's homecoming thus becomes a model for violent ethnic cleansing.

These understandings of Achilles and Odysseus grossly distort their portrayals in Homeric epic. The need to defend what Johnson calls "honor, family, and tribe" provides only the barest pretext for the Trojan War, in the form of Helen's departure for Troy with Paris. Achilles himself heaps contempt on Agamemnon for enriching himself in a war that saw the deaths of so many Greeks against whom the Trojans had committed no crime. Odysseus's violent homecoming does not reestablish him as lord of Ithaca: it leads to further violence that only the intervention of a god can arrest, and Odysseus himself must leave Ithaca again to atone for his crime against Poseidon. From that journey he will never return.[25] Hardly a ringing endorsement of the "strength of the family father" against "hostile aliens."

Despite the way these poems complicate simplistic understandings of heroism, popular understandings of the heroes of Homeric epic correspond to a large degree with those promoted in white nationalist thought. Although Achilles has received ambivalent and even villainous treatments in literature and on the stage—he is portrayed as an arrogant brute in Shakespeare's play *Troilus and Cressida* (1602), for example—modernity has adopted what one historian calls the "heroic archetype" as articulated in Greek myth, including the *Iliad* and *Odyssey*, as the "mode and model of masculine identity."[26] When white nationalists claim Achilles as a model for noble self-sacrifice in the name of honor, they may be simplifying his representation in the poem, but it is a simplification that is well established and widely accepted.

Already in 1939 the French Marxist and trade unionist Simone Weil had pointed out that the Homeric epics recognize that violent heroism—what Weil termed "force"—takes a toll not only on those on whom the hero inflicts it but on the heroes themselves, but this critical perspective on Homeric heroism has not displaced more celebratory perspectives. Elizabeth Vandiver has documented, for example, how the Trojan War, and Achilles in particular, was used by poets writing during and after the First World War primarily to "reinforce the belief in the nobility and essential validity of the modern soldiers' struggles," a comparison requiring "that the overall valor of the Homeric heroes was, in effect, a fixed point taken completely for granted." Wolfgang Petersen's 2004 film *Troy* all but guaranteed that contemporary audiences would see Achilles as an impressive and noble hero: the casting of sex symbol Brad Pitt in the role might have ensured this on its own, but the effect was heightened by the film's representation of the gods. Whereas the supreme power of the gods in the *Iliad* emphasizes human powerlessness and frailty, the film's secular portrayal of the gods has the effect of amplifying the heroism of the human characters. The *Iliad* makes clear in its opening lines that Achilles' rage inflicted as much pain and death on his fellow Greeks as it did on the Trojans, but he continues to be cited as a model of military heroism. In 2021, for example, a former U.S. National Security advisor published an essay in the *National Review* on the subject of "preserving the warrior ethos," which he wrote was characterized by "courage, honor, and self-sacrifice." The essay began by asserting, "The warrior ethos that emerged in the modern Western world has its origins in the warrior myth as embodied by Achilles, the hero of the Trojan War in the *Iliad*."[27]

Dominant understandings of Odysseus's heroism likewise emphasize his admirable qualities, such as resourcefulness and determination. This perspective on Odysseus minimizes his failures of leadership—not a single one of the men under his command survives the journey home from Troy—and justifies the violence he enacts at his homecoming, not only against his wife's suitors but against the enslaved women whose pragmatic accommodations to those men (themselves enslavers in their own households) are treated by Odysseus and Telemachus as a betrayal worthy of death. Only recently has Emily Wilson's best-selling translation of the *Odyssey* brought public attention to the poem's ambivalence toward its hero. In her translation, Odysseus is "a complicated man."[28]

This reorientation of our perspective on Odysseus allows us to take stock of the violence that uncritical admiration for his alleged heroism has authorized. Edith Hall has traced a variety of early modern and modern contexts in which such conceptions of Odysseus have justified and sanitized white supremacist understandings of the world. Odysseus became, for example, a kind of secular patron saint for the empire of Portugal, which initiated the transatlantic slave trade. European explorers viewed the indigenous people of the Americas as analogues to the Cyclops Polyphemus, accepting at face value the poem's description of his savagery even though it all comes from the mouth of his antagonist Odysseus in a section of the poem in which the character, attempting to convince the Phaeacians to take him home, has every incentive to paint his own actions in the most heroic light possible. The ideology of imperialism requires that violence be justified and glorified, and the violence of Odysseus's homecoming received the same treatment in the hands of English translators, who found in that passage a form of heroism congenial to nineteenth-century Victorian morals. As Hall notes, "The same he-man who can fight to the death to protect his property and assert sexual control over his women slaves is also an urbane gentleman."[29]

In the United States, which was preoccupied with the pacification and exploration of "the frontier," Odysseus likewise provided an attractive model for the lone individual's resourcefulness and determination in the face of the allegedly forbidding and hostile unknown. The work of Joseph Campbell in *The Hero with a Thousand Faces* (1949) and the subsequent PBS documentary *Joseph Campbell and the Power of Myth* (1988) did not so much invent as make explicit the centrality of this concept of heroism to American culture (though Campbell claimed to be describing a universal phenomenon). The iconic and popular 1984 film *The Natural*, which featured many references to the *Odyssey* (including a one-eyed antagonist), combined this concept of Odysseus with the American mythology of baseball. The film altered the tragic conclusion of the novel on which it was based and replaced it with a triumphalist ending that made the main character, as Hall argues, "a model for disaffected men seeking to rediscover their inner hero," which is as good a description as any for the rhetorical use to which white nationalist intellectuals put Homeric heroes. Similarly, the poet Robert Bly found Odysseus a useful source of inspiration in self-help workshops he offered to help men reconnect with warrior masculinity in the wake of the feminist movement. It's an ambition similar to the one that I have suggested Greg Johnson set for himself in his speech in Finland. Bly's *Iron John: A Book about Men* (1990) spent more than a year on the *New York Times* best-seller list.[30]

Scholars and educators have contributed to the celebration of concepts of heroism that lend themselves to white nationalist appropriation. The schools that educated future administrators of the British Empire promoted Odysseus as a model. In the United States, the Homeric epics were foundational in "Great Books" courses that celebrated the "rugged individualism" that virtuous Americans supposedly shared with both Achilles and Odysseus; one essay commonly assigned in such courses even compared Odysseus's revenge on the suitors in Ithaca to the "frontier justice" celebrated in the conclusions of movie westerns in which the virtuous "good guy" exacts violent justice on villains. When an interviewer asked Wolfgang Petersen, the director of *Troy*, how his education influenced his film, he responded that "Achilles was definitely my hero" when he read the *Iliad* in school, an experience that instilled in him "a quasi built-in love for heroes and their stories."[31] It is hard to believe that Petersen formed this admiration of Achilles in spite of a critical presentation of him and the war in school.

Influential scholarship and translations also promote concepts of heroism congenial to white nationalist thought. When the Harvard professor Bernard Knox argues, in the introduction to Robert Fagles's best-selling translation of the *Iliad*, that the poem suggests, "No civilization, no matter how rich, no matter how refined, can long survive once it loses the power to meet force with equal or superior force," he strikes a similar tone to the essay in the *Occidental Observer* that found in the *Iliad* a warning about "unheard of effeminacy" replacing "barbarian vigor." This glorification of "superior force" uses the nobility of the Homeric hero to justify violence. The University of Chicago's James Redfield describes Hector as "a martyr to loyalties" and "a hero ready to die for the precious imperfections of ordinary life." Speaking at the 2015 meeting of the London Forum conference, which has been described as "the home of the UK Alt-Right" for providing a venue for Holocaust deniers and British National Party activists, Tomislav Sunić praised Hector in similar terms, for his "sense of sacrifice, [and] the readiness to place the interest of his community above his own private and family interests." In the case of Odysseus, Stanford professor Hermann Fränkel's definition of the "new kind of heroism" that Odysseus supposedly represents (the "iron strength with which he masters feelings, resists seduction, and breaks attachments" in pursuit of the "high goal" of homecoming) exemplifies the same celebration of the violence of Odysseus's homecoming that white nationalists embrace. So too does the introduction to Walter Shrewing's Oxford

World Classics translation of the *Odyssey*, in which the Regius professor of Greek at Cambridge University, G. S. Kirk, writes that "Odysseus is a survivor who fights his way home to take up life again where it should be taken up after war."[32]

These scholars are not self-consciously making white nationalist claims and none has any connection to any white nationalist group. Bernard Knox's understanding of heroism transparently derives, for example, from his own experience fighting fascism in the Spanish Civil War and the Second World War.[33] Such descriptions of the poem indicate, rather, the prestige, familiarity, and popularity of the qualities that white nationalists celebrate in Homeric heroes. The prestige of these qualities obscures how such invocations give dignity to violent action intended to preserve white political and cultural dominance. It is striking that the mythological figure of Heracles does not receive nearly as much attention in white nationalist thought as Achilles and Odysseus do, because Heracles' deeds are undoubtedly heroic, and undoubtedly conform to concepts of masculinity that white nationalists embrace. But his heroism is not commonly understood as a form of service to a community, as Hector's, Diomedes', or Odysseus's is, or as a rejection of a corrupt ideology, as Achilles' is. White nationalists do not seek to recruit men whose only goal is self-aggrandizing glory. They seek men who will regard multiculturalism as dishonorable and white supremacy as a cause worthy of self-sacrifice.

The (Violent) Spirit of the Romans

For all their valor, both the Spartans and the heroes of Homeric epic provide only imperfect models for white nationalist theories of masculinity and violence, even if these imperfections usually go unmentioned in white nationalist publications. Leonidas and the Spartans were defeated at Thermopylae, after all, and the individualism of Achilles and Odysseus sits uneasily with the ideal of white racial solidarity. But in the "other half" of Greco-Roman antiquity, white nationalist intellectuals find a model that embodies both communal struggle and large-scale success. This model is the period of Roman history known as the Republic, running from the beginning of the fifth to the end of the first century BCE. During this four-hundred-year period the inhabitants of a small, apparently unremarkable city (Rome) conquered most of the lands surrounding the Mediterranean Sea, including Spain, Greece, Carthage, Gaul, and much of what is now Turkey, Syria, and Lebanon. The vast political entity known as "the Roman Empire" was in large part the product of the military campaigns of the Republic. Popular perception of this period of history minimizes the violent devastation wreaked by the Roman war machine in favor of an idealized portrait of Roman heroism. Alexander Hamilton wrote that the Roman Republic "attained the utmost heights of human greatness," and John Adams praised the Roman Republic for its "foundation" in "public virtue" and "positive passion for the public good, the public interest."[34] As is the case with Sparta, this aspect makes Rome a powerful reference point for those who seek to redefine political violence as noble heroism.

As with the heroes of the Greek tradition, white nationalists who set Roman heroes as models emphasize their masculinity and their bravery against outsiders and foreigners. When Counter-Currents published an essay by the University of New Brunswick professor of sociology Ricardo Duchesne entitled "There Is Nothing the Alt Right Can Do about the Effeminacy of White Men," the piece opened with an image of a marble bust commonly said to represent Cato the Elder, the Roman senator famous as the embodiment of traditional Roman morals. It is hard to imagine a figure whose legacy of violence and patriarchal masculinity is better suited to white nationalist admiration. Cato is best known for ending every one of his speeches in the Senate, no matter what the topic, with a particular recommendation concerning Rome's regional rival Carthage: "I declare that Carthage must be destroyed." The popularity and familiarity of this phrase in both English and Latin (*Carthago delenda est*) somewhat obscures that it represents, according to the professor of genocide studies Ben Kieran, "the first recorded incitement to genocide." Along with this insistence on the necessity of political violence, Cato's condemnation of the supposed effeminacy of his age bears a striking resemblance to misogynist "Men's Rights" advocates who claim that feminism has led to widespread discrimination against men: "All other men rule their wives," Plutarch says Cato remarked. "We rule all other men, and our wives rule us."[35] For his part, Duchesne celebrates Cato's Rome as "a civilization at its peak," one that demonstrates the desirability of "a very patriarchal culture that [has] harsh laws and expectations" and in which "intense military training and warfare" are the norm. As his essay's title suggests, Duchesne does not see much chance to arrest contemporary effeminacy: "Only out of the coming chaos and violence," he writes, "will strong white men rise to resurrect the West."

It is difficult to estimate how many people Duchesne's complaint about contemporary effeminacy on Counter-Currents might have reached, but Elon Musk, one of the richest men in the world, tweeted a meme to his 200 million followers on X (formerly Twitter) that invoked the example of Rome to make a similar point. Against a background composed of a sequence of neoclassical paintings portraying the Roman military, the city of Rome in majestic splendor, a decadent Roman banquet, and the city in flames, the meme's text reads, "Hard times create Strong men. Strong men create good times. Good times create weak men. Weak men create hard times." "You are here" is superimposed over the final image. As of the time I am writing this, his post has been liked by more than 1.3 million readers.[36]

Somewhat more optimistic is an essay at Counter-Currents entitled "The Roman Way." Its author finds in "the wisdom of the ancients" a set of "aristocratic virtues like honor, duty, and loyalty" that he believes white nationalist men should cultivate. And his models for these virtues are the heroes of the Roman Republic: Publius Horatius, who, according to Roman myth, singlehandedly defeated the three Curiatii brothers to end Rome's war with Alba Longa; Publius Decius Mus, who ritually sacrificed himself during the Latin War in order to secure victory for Rome; and Horatius Cocles, who, at the cost of his own life, delayed an invading Etruscan army at a bridge, enabling the Romans to retreat.[37] This last story, according to Counter-Currents, "glorifies a heroic sacrifice made in defeat that secured a greater victory." Although the essayist does not compare Horatius to Leonidas, such language makes it clear that the same concept of heroism is in play.

This turn to the heroes of the Roman Republic as models has an ancient pedigree. The stories of Decius Mus, Publius Horatius, and Horatius Cocles are recorded by the ancient Roman historian Livy, who composed a 142-book history of Rome in the early first century CE. Livy begins this monumental work by saying that his history provides evidence of models for imitation and avoidance. He invites his reader to "note how, with the gradual relaxation of discipline, morals first gave way, as it were, then sank lower and lower, and finally began the downward plunge which has brought us to our present time, when we can endure neither vices nor their cure."[38] This is precisely the use to which the Counter-Currents essayist has put them. For Livy, as for white nationalist intellectuals, the heroism of the past should inspire urgent attention to contemporary threats. "If the Alt Right is to reverse the course of the West," the essayist in Counter-Currents writes, "then we will need to revive the Spirit of the West: the Spirit of the Romans."

Publius Decius Mus and Horatius Cocles are not as well known as Leonidas and the Spartans, but Michael Anton, who would later serve on Donald Trump's National Security Council during his first term as president, used the pseudonym Publius Decius Mus when he wrote an influential essay in 2016 arguing that American conservatives should support Donald Trump's candidacy for president. The pseudonym was appropriate because Anton argued that even if supporting Trump seemed reckless—just as, he implied, Decius Mus's self-sacrifice in battle must have—it was the only act that had a chance of arresting what Anton described as "the trajectory" of "America and the West . . . toward something bad." Later in the essay Anton revealed that "something bad" involved the presence of immigrants in the United States. Openness to immigration, he wrote, was "the mark of a party, a society, a people, a civilization that wants to die."[39] The Roman hero thus becomes a mouthpiece for the same anxieties that inform the essay on Roman models in Counter-Currents.

Anton may not have elaborated on the role of masculine heroism in resisting this alleged threat, but another prominent political commentator has. Michelle Malkin built a journalistic career devoted to promoting anti-immigrant policies by leveraging her identity as a Filipino American (she distinguishes her parents, who immigrated to the United States on employer-sponsored visas, from immigrants who lack such documents). Throughout this career she has contributed to white nationalist publications, writing a weekly column for VDARE for twenty years as well as appearing at the *American Renaissance* conference in 2021 and writing several pieces for that site, even as her numerous books were listed on the *New York Times*'s best-seller list, her columns were published in major newspapers, and she appeared as a commentator on Fox News.[40] Malkin linked Roman heroism and immigration at one such mainstream appearance at the 2019 Conservative Political Action Conference (CPAC), which describes itself as "the largest and most influential gathering of conservatives in the world." In her speech, she characterized immigration to the United States as an "invasion" and declared that she and other CPAC members must "stand at the bridge as Horatius stood at the narrow bridge over the Tiber River alone facing fearful odds as hordes of Etruscans marched toward him and cowards cut and run behind him." Never mind that the heavily armed and militarily organized Etruscans that Horatius faced were nothing like the downtrodden refugees who come to the United States seeking economic opportunity: the Roman model provides Malkin a link between the imagined threat posed by immigration and the kind of heroism for which she believes the Roman Republic provides a model.

Malkin does not claim originality for her invocation of Horatius Cocles. To illustrate his heroism, she quotes a passage from the poem "Horatius," published in 1842 by Thomas Macaulay in his collection *Lays of Ancient Rome*. Malkin's quotation of this particular work reveals the long-standing entanglement between admiration for Roman republican heroism and white supremacy. Macaulay was a member of the Supreme Council of India under British rule. In campaigning for the 1835 English Education Act that ended support for Muslim and Hindu education in India and replaced it with an English-language British curriculum, Macaulay argued that "a single shelf of a good European library was worth the whole native literature of India and Arabia." Macaulay's book of poems celebrating the virtues of the Romans sold well, but attained the status of what Robert Sullivan called a "surrogate national epic" for Britain after the repression of the first major rebellion of colonized Indians in 1858. A study of vestiges of colonial education in India published in 1971 found that his poem "Horatius at the

Bridge" was still being taught there almost twenty-five years after Indian independence.[41] However inflammatory it may have been, Malkin's speech is only the latest invocation of Horatius by an advocate of European superiority.

A History of Violence

Self-sacrifice, honor, dedication to duty: these are virtues most people would not want to cede to white nationalists. The deployment of ancient models of heroism to attach these virtues to white nationalist conspiracy theories, however, brings into focus how the idealization of these virtues, especially when they are connected to military valor, sanctions and even glorifies violence. Certainly, the glorification of violence is inseparable from popular representations of the Roman military. There is, for example, no shortage of representations of the Roman Republic as the consummate war machine in popular video games that simulate ancient battles and empire-building. The titles of popular franchises alone (including *Rome: Total War* and *Imperator: Rome*) signal that in such games, winning usually requires "military dominance . . . at the expense of a rival society or civilization," reproducing and naturalizing an association between Roman history and what Ross Clare has described as "empire-building, forceful acquirement of space, and [the] masculinization of history." Even if one avoids games that engage in colonialist representations of foreigners as barbaric and homogeneous, as some do, to play this genre of Roman strategy game is to celebrate Roman military valor and the imperialism that came with it, just as white nationalists do. Add to this books published by academic presses, like Steele Brand's *Killing for the Republic* (2019), that paint simplistic and idealized pictures of the Roman army in order to condemn the supposed lack of civic virtue in the modern American military—there's that theme of declining masculinity again—and it is easy to see why notions of Roman republican heroism that are congenial to white nationalist interpretation persist. The white man who murdered sixty-six-year-old Timothy Caughman told an interviewer that he committed this crime in order "to deter white women from interracial relationships." The *Washington Post* reported that the murderer, who had studied Latin in high school, stabbed Caughman to death with "a Roman-style 'Gladius' sword purchased on Amazon for $56."[42]

This is only the most gruesome example of how such attitudes toward the heroes of ancient Greece and Rome provide the foundations for real-world violence by making violent masculinity glorious and white nationalist activism a form of noble self-sacrifice. At the 2021 attack on the U.S. Capitol, journalist Mark Danner interviewed a rioter who told him that "it's time to sweep all of them away," referring to the members of the U.S. Congress. "We can't do it by voting." This rioter came to Danner's attention because of the flag he was carrying, which read, "Lead us across the Rubicon!" This flag casts Trump as a modern-day Julius Caesar. It likens the president's refusal to concede electoral defeat to the Roman general's decision in 49 BCE to lead his army into Rome, defying the Roman Senate's lawful order to relinquish his command following the end of his term as governor of the Roman provinces north and east of Italy. It should be an unpalatable analogy. Caesar had just returned from a campaign in Gaul, about which Kurt Raaflaub has argued, "Caesar can rightfully be accused of multiple cases of genocide."[43] His march upon Rome after crossing the Rubicon precipitated a civil war that established authoritarian rule in Rome for the next four centuries. But for the rioters at the Capitol this is the kind of leadership worth fighting for.

And why shouldn't they think that? Julius Caesar routinely appears on lists of the greatest military leaders in history. A cultural milieu like this, which glorifies Greco-Roman antiquity and sanitizes and even celebrates violence as a means for men to earn honor, is fertile ground for white nationalist ideas about heroism to take root. It does not matter if the historical Spartans or Romans were actually praiseworthy or blameworthy: that determination has already been made by centuries of historians praising them and countless popular representations perpetuating that view. White nationalist intellectuals have only to call attention to these representations to cast hatred as heroism, recognizing that this reframing may convince at least a few of their supporters to translate their fear and resentment into real-world violence.

CHAPTER THREE

Predicting the New Dark Ages

IN THE FALL OF 2023, everyone, at least on social media, was talking about how often they thought about the Roman Empire. A consensus emerged that men in particular think about Rome very frequently, and the whole issue went viral. The *New York Times* reported it. *Saturday Night Live* did a skit about it. Various media outlets interviewed men about why they thought about Rome so often. Large numbers of people believing that ancient history is important might seem to be good news for historians. But as critical observers pointed out, all this media attention reinforced the conceptual link that many people (usually unconsciously) make between Rome and masculinity. Such a link grossly simplifies ancient gender politics but is endlessly reinforced in popular representations of ancient Rome. Think, for example, of Russell Crowe's character in the 2000 film *Gladiator*, of "grand strategy" video games such as *Imperator: Rome*, in which players take on the role of generals of Roman legions, and of the modern popularity of Roman Stoicism—complete with its gendered focus on the production of the perfectly rational "wise man."[1] Perhaps it's not so surprising after all if men surrounded by such media think about Rome so frequently.

Many people may be familiar with the story that the Roman military conquered and subjugated vast stretches of land, but just as many people, if not more, are familiar with the story that in spite of its size, grandeur, and strength, the Roman Empire collapsed and fell. Part of Maximus's heroism in *Gladiator* derives from his honorable opposition to and critique of the decadent and declining society around him. Part of the appeal of playing as Rome in a video game is the prospect of staving off the decline that the historical Roman Empire supposedly suffered. Rome provides not just a source of inspiration but also a warning. Many men who were interviewed for their thoughts about Rome emphasized the greatness of Rome and its supposed influence on the modern world. But the specter of decline haunted reporting about this viral meme as well. As a man interviewed by the *Huffington Post* put it, "The fall of Rome is comparable to the fall of our entire civilization, so perhaps there is no better culture to learn from and reflect upon."[2] This specter of decline haunts white nationalist thought about Rome as well.

As we have seen, the themes of heroism and glorified violence that are popularly associated with Rome form the basis of white nationalist calls for white men to oppose the alleged threats of creeping effeminacy and immigration. But white nationalist commentary on the viral "men thinking about the Roman Empire" meme reveals an ambivalence about Rome as a model similar to that felt by the general public. A contributor to the anti-immigrant website VDARE, for example, wrote that the reason he thinks about the Roman Empire frequently is that "Rome fell because its people were becoming less intelligent. And the same thing is happening today." The viral meme was well timed for this essayist, who used it to promote an academic paper he had recently published purporting to demonstrate this ancient decline in intelligence using genetic data. The journal in which he published this paper, *OpenPsych*, is nominally peer reviewed but primarily provides a respectable-looking platform for practitioners of race pseudoscience whose work most traditional academic journals would refuse to publish.[3] Informed readers should thus take this author's conclusions about the reason for Rome's decline for what they're worth.

We may chafe or scoff at this attempt to harness the prestige of scientific inquiry to promote a pseudoscientific understanding of ancient history, but his choice of the Roman Empire to illustrate his eugenic and xenophobic theories about the contemporary world partakes in a popular and mainstream mode of comparison. A look at headlines from 2017 to 2023 reveals not only the frequency of comparisons between the contemporary world and Rome but the prominence of narratives of decline in such comparison. Apocalyptic language abounds: "Rome's Slow Motion Catastrophe—And Ours." "The Roman Republic Destroyed Itself: Are We on a Similar Path?" "America Is Eerily Retracing Rome's Steps to a Fall: Will It Turn around Before It Is Too Late?" This steady drumbeat of declinist comparisons is accompanied by an equally steady stream of books with similar focuses. Some of these make the comparison between Rome and the United States explicit, such as Thomas Strunk's *On the Fall of the Roman Republic* with its subtitle "Lessons for the American People" or Cullen Murphy's older book *Are We Rome? The Fall of an Empire and the Fate of America.* Others invite readers to come to their own conclusions, like Mike Duncan's *Storm before the Storm: The Beginning of the End of the Roman Republic.* Duncan has perhaps done more than anyone to keep people thinking about the Roman Empire: the episodes of his History of Rome podcast have been downloaded more than 100 million times. In the introduction to his book, he notes the "historical echoes" that he expects readers to notice in his narrative. "It at least behooves us," writes Duncan, "to identify where in the thousand-year history of the Roman empire we might find an analogous historical setting" to our own. Duncan does not offer further guidance on this point, but the title of his book makes clear that whatever analogy is found will be one involving decline.[4]

Many of the examples cited above focused on President Donald Trump's perceived erosion of political norms and democratic institutions, drawing comparisons between modern America and the end of the period of Roman history conventionally known as "republican," which saw the rise of autocratic strongmen, culminating in the regime of the emperor Augustus. But this does not mean such narratives are to be found only on the political left. When JD Vance, who would eventually be elected vice president of the United States in 2024, was running for election to the Senate from Ohio in 2021, he, too, described the United States as being "in a late republican period" during which there is a risk that "this whole thing is going to fall in on itself." And in 2022 Hillsdale College, which a *New York Times* headline described as a "shining city on a hill for conservatives," offered an online course entitled "The Rise and Fall of the Roman Republic." Its promise to teach students how the decisions of "great men . . . led to triumph or disaster" reveals a similar preoccupation with decline.[5]

These recent examples continue a conservative strain of Roman Empire comparisons. The historian Niall Ferguson's *Colossus: The Rise and Fall of the American Empire* stands as an earlier example, with its declaration that "The United States is perhaps more like a 'new Rome' than any previous empire."[6] But no single political party owns the comparison with Rome. A look at the recent history of these comparisons also reveals how they are transparently shaped by present-day concerns. During America's interventionist war in Iraq, commentators sought analogies between the imperial ambitions of the United States and the Roman Empire. During the divisive first presidency of Donald Trump, the focus fell more squarely on the civil strife of the late Roman Republic. Whatever the preoccupation of the present, a parallel can be found, it seems, in the Roman past.

The evergreen popularity of such comparisons is a source of frustration for Roman historians, for whom the difficulty of defining what is meant by the "fall of Rome" renders all such comparisons faulty.[7] For one thing, they inevitably require cherry-picking sources and simplifying complex cause-and-effect relationships in order to produce predetermined analogies and conclusions. Narratives about the fall of Rome that begin with the political turmoil of the first century BCE have to minimize that Rome maintained and even expanded its influence for at least three more centuries after that decline supposedly began. Explanations that blame "barbarian invasions" for the fall of Rome tend to ignore the long period during which the Roman military successfully and effectively employed troops drawn from outside the boundaries of the empire. And most narratives of the fall of Rome avoid grappling with the fact that the eastern capital of the empire, Constantinople, maintained its influence for another thousand years.[8]

But even these caveats don't do justice to the state of the question in academic circles. The popular idea that the collapse of centralized Roman political power in western Europe ushered in a "dark ages" is now recognized as an erasure of a thousand years of intellectual and artistic activity, both in Europe and elsewhere. And some historians even argue that the Roman Empire never "fell" at all. The idea of a violent and cataclysmic fall of the Roman Empire can be found in ancient Roman texts, it's true, but other evidence, whether from outside the empire or in the form of archaeological remains, suggests instead a period of political transformation and cultural blending that was peaceful at least as often as it was violent.[9] This version of history doesn't suit the modern prophets of decline, so it isn't nearly so familiar.

Comparisons between modern America and Roman decline have remained popular despite their flaws and inaccuracies. When considering the fall of Rome, we are asking the wrong questions if we focus on what "really" happened, whether Rome "really" fell, and if it did, what the "real" causes were. We should be asking instead why these comparisons remain so persistently attractive to popular audiences and white nationalist publications. Scholars who have studied the history of analogies between the Roman and British Empires, such as Phiroze Vasunia and Javed Majeed, argue that although such comparisons don't tell us much about the future of the nation, they tell us everything about the political anxieties of the present.[10]

In this sense, the idea of Rome declining and falling has transcended history to become a shared myth. As Jonathan Theodore has argued in his study of nineteenth- and twentieth-century perceptions of the fall of Rome, this does not mean it is "false" in the sense that most people use the word *myth*.[11] All discussions of the fall are based, however selectively, on historical facts that are believed to be true with as much confidence as can be had about things that happened more than a thousand years ago. Rather, it is a myth in the sense that myths are narratives that a culture shares because they perform important ideological work for the participants in that culture. To study such myths is to consider what that ideological work is, and why it is important to those who share these myths.

The myth of the decline and fall of the Roman Empire is very important to white nationalist intellectuals. This importance derives in part from the explanatory power that mainstream and popular culture attaches to this myth, from the widespread acceptance of the idea that the majestic, impressive, and admirable Roman Empire eventually declined and collapsed. White nationalists are attracted to any historical narrative that large numbers of people accept in an unreflective way. But this historical narrative in particular attracts their special attention because it provides scope for promoting the white nationalist belief that forms the basis of this chapter: that the contemporary world has declined to the point that it is on the brink of cataclysmic collapse.

One of the most influential theorists of fascism, Roger Griffin, has argued that "the currency of a myth of national decadence" is one of the "catalysts" necessary for the appearance of fascist politics. Fascist movements promise national rebirth and regeneration, which appear necessary or desirable only if the present is perceived to be degenerate. Something akin to this rhetoric can be felt in the popularity of the slogan "Make America Great Again." To my knowledge that slogan has never been paired with a comparison to the Roman Empire, but it hardly needs to be when, as we have seen, ancient Rome is already so frequently invoked as the harbinger of America's own decline. It is the pervasiveness of such comparisons in American culture, not a single candidate's slogan, that should prompt us to reflect on the implicit politics of all such comparisons, given the centrality of decline to fascist thought. Nor is this pervasiveness a recent phenomenon: ancient Rome has been invoked as a warning about American decline at least since the beginning of the nineteenth century, when America's own imperial ambitions began to emerge.[12] Whatever the popularity of declinist thinking reveals about the contemporary United States, its popularity throughout this nation's history also may reveal xenophobic and authoritarian tendencies lurking in the national consciousness. It is this that white nationalists tap into when they turn to the example of ancient Rome to promote their hateful politics. And they do this with startling regularity.

White Nationalist Narratives of Decline

Predictions or diagnoses of the decline of the United States that refer to ancient Rome are at least as common in white nationalist thought as they are in mainstream media. Like those in the popular press, these comparisons reveal more about the anxieties of those making them than about historical or present reality. Therefore, white nationalist anxieties about the Great Replacement of white people feature prominently in their comparisons between the United States and Rome.

Chief among these is the fear that immigration exacerbates decline by eroding the white demographic majority of the nation. An essayist for *Breitbart* who used the classical pseudonym Virgil wrote, "America is under threat, not least from the same sort of demographic transformation—some might call it invasion—that toppled Rome."[13] To substantiate this, white nationalists force an analogy between current patterns of migration and the military conflicts of the fourth and fifth centuries CE between the Roman state and migrating Germanic tribes. White nationalists claim, for example, that the increasing proportion of Black and Latino soldiers within the ranks of the U.S. military parallels the Roman army's inclusion of foreign-born and noncitizen soldiers as auxiliary troops, recruited from groups that Roman emperors had allowed to settle within the boundaries of the empire. "The fall of the Roman Empire," wrote a contributor to VDARE, "was enabled when the Romans no longer took responsibility for their own defense . . . [and] turned it over to foreign barbarians," suggesting that a more diverse military threatens the security of the United States in the same way. And it is true that the Gothic mercenaries who served in the Roman Empire eventually joined rebellions against the empire: for white nationalists this is evidence that immigrants are always and everywhere ungrateful and disloyal, but the historical situation is more complex than that. These migrants were refugees, forced from their homelands by the violent invasions of the Huns farther to the east, a trauma compounded by the starvation and mistreatment they met with in the Roman Empire. Surely the rebellions had more to do with these experiences than any other factor.

Furthermore, the status of the Gothic mercenaries is not like that of the American enlistees that white nationalists claim pose a similar threat to the United States: all modern service branches require that enlistees be citizens or green card holders, and the demographic changes within the military match those of the overall population of the United States. The flaws in this analogy reveal the racist assumptions that inform white nationalist assessments of an increasingly diverse U.S. military: that nonwhite immigrants pose a threat to national security because they are necessarily disloyal. An essayist for VDARE doesn't feel the need to conceal these assumptions for his audience, and neither, apparently, does Elon Musk. When the Minneapolis Police Department, which had employed the officer who was convicted of murdering George Floyd in 2020, announced that its 2024 class of new officers included its first Somali American woman and its first noncitizen—a legal permanent resident who has lived in Minneapolis since she was four years old—Musk commented to his 200 million followers that "near the fall of the Roman Empire, the Roman Army also increasingly relied on non-citizens."[14]

The racist assumptions underlying such fear-mongering about the supposed disloyalty of foreigners emerge more explicitly in other aspects of white nationalist understandings of Roman decline. The mere presence of foreigners within the nation, according to a contributor to the *Occidental Observer*, fosters a "deviation from the racio-cultural values unique to our Indo-European nature" that inevitably "causes civilizational decline." The evolutionary psychologist and notorious antisemite Kevin MacDonald applies this thinking to the context of ancient Rome. "So long as the incorporated peoples were closely related to the original founding stock" of Rome, MacDonald writes about the Roman conquest of regions in western Europe, the Roman state remained strong. But once Roman conquest reached further east and the empire began incorporating non-Europeans, he argues, "Rome [lost] its ethnic homogeneity, which likely contributed to a decline in the qualities that established and maintained Roman power." Immigration by white people, this analogy suggests, is acceptable, but contemporary immigration to the United States from South and Central America, Asia, Africa, and the Middle East is different—and worse. As the French white nationalist Guillaume Faye wrote in his book *Ethnic Apocalypse*, published in English by Arktos, the "slow dismemberment of the Roman identity in favor of independent kingdoms" should serve as a reminder of this "ruthless logic." His advice to the United States is for "states inhabited by a mostly Hispanic population" to "embrace secession" along with the creation of "relatively independent African-American enclaves."[15]

Immigration is only one factor driving the demographic changes that white nationalists interpret as decline. The other is declining birth rates among citizens who are designated as "white" by the U.S. Census Bureau. White nationalists blame this phenomenon on the availability of contraception and cultural acceptance of women choosing not to have children. A contributor to VDARE invokes Rome as evidence for this perspective as well: in any declining society, he claims, "you see the rise of feminism, with women abandoning traditional roles and achieving relative independence, as had long been the case in Rome by the first century." At the same time, he adds, "sexual morality breaks down and homosexuality becomes more acceptable." For the most part, white nationalist analyses like these treat the civilizational decline that such factors allegedly predict as inevitable, both in antiquity and in the present, but occasionally such discussions reveal why these narratives are so integral to fascist politics. This same essay at VDARE finds "hope" for America in the fact that "the Roman Republic reinvented itself as an authoritarian empire."

These analogies, however offensive or outlandish they may seem, are not produced out of thin air. All of them find at least some basis in ancient evidence that both white nationalists and mainstream commentators invoke in rhetorically similar ways: both believe it gives their narratives of decline credibility. At first glance, I admit, that may seem to be where the similarities between these discussions end. It is hard to imagine finding anything on mainstream sites like *Vox* or in the *Atlantic* as explicitly hateful as, for example, an essay in the *Occidental Observer* about how "comparisons with the Fall of Rome" explain the "New Dark Ages in Western Europe and North America." In that piece, the antisemitic paranoia of the white genocide conspiracy theory is on full display, with claims that the "hostile Jewish-dominated globalist elite" promote "prostitution" of white women to foreigners as a means of bringing about "white racial suicide." And yet, both the historical assumptions and the racist conspiracy theories that inform this essay have found much more prominent platforms. At the peak of its influence, *Breitbart*, which published "Virgil's" similar comparison between America and Rome, had a larger readership than all Web-based political news outlets combined. The host of the most-watched show on Fox News promoted the same conspiracy theories about population decline as those found on overtly white nationalist sites.[16] White nationalist and mainstream comparisons to the fall of Rome may not be as different as we hope.

Mainstream Declinism

The similarities between popular analyses of Roman decline and those found in white nationalist publications are evident, first, in each's rhetorical orientation to the subject. The "obvious and disturbing parallels" noted in a review of Murphy's *Are We Rome?* echoes the "grim parallel" with ancient Rome that an essay at Alt-Right.com finds. The same essay diagnosed the "moribund death spiral" of modernity with the same metaphor that Dan Rather employed after the first presidential debate between Donald Trump and Hillary Clinton. The celebrated news anchor worried in a Facebook post about America falling into a "downward spiral" toward what he called "the savagery of the Coliseum." *Destruction*, the nineteenth-century painting by Thomas Cole that warned Americans of the dangers of empire-building by blending Roman and American imagery in a scene of violent cataclysm, can be found illustrating proclamations of civilizational decline at *American Renaissance*, VDARE, Counter-Currents, and *Breitbart*.[17]

Beneath these similarities of language we find similar anxieties. In 1995, the journalist Peter Brimelow published a book called *Alien Nation: Common Sense about America's Immigration Disaster*. The fifth century, Brimelow wrote, when "Germanic tribes overr[a]n the Western Roman Empire," is the "nearest thing to a precedent for today's world." This comparison appears in an eminently mainstream book published by one of the "Big Five" English-language publishing houses (Harper Collins) by an author with all the marks of mainstream credibility: Brimelow has an MBA from Stanford, has written for financial publications like *Fortune* and *Barron's*, and was an editor at *Forbes*, where he won a George Loeb award for business journalism. Reviews in both the *Atlantic* and *Foreign Affairs* called his arguments against American immigration policy "powerful." The *National Review*, where Brimelow had also previously been an editor, invited conservative intellectuals to engage with the book and allowed Brimelow to publish a rebuttal to critics. But many aspects of Brimelow's argument reveal the similarities between his positions and those of the white nationalists catalogued above. He is preoccupied with declining birth rates among native-born citizens. When he writes that immigration in Rome, as in the present, "was connived at, to some extent, by the authorities," he gestures toward white nationalist conspiracy theories about governments seeking the dilution of the white race. His criticism of the 1965 Immigration and Nationality Act constitutes an implicit endorsement of early twentieth-century federal immigration laws such as the 1924 Asian Exclusion Act, which, as the *New York Times* reported at the time, sought "to preserve racial type as it exists here today." This is the same reasoning as that found in Kevin MacDonald's claim that immigration posed no threat to Rome until it extended beyond western Europe. Brimelow promoted *Alien Nation* with an essay in *Commentary Magazine* in which he warned that "unless there is another pause for assimilation ... immigration will add to America's latent sectionalism and ultimately break the country up like the late Roman Empire."[18] It's the same prediction Guillaume Faye has made. Four years after the publication of *Alien Nation*, Brimelow launched the anti-immigration website VDARE.

One notable characteristic of Brimelow's site is that many of its contributors are nationally recognized and syndicated political commentators. One of these is the journalist Michelle Malkin, whose invocation of the Roman hero Horatius at the 2019 Conservative Political Action Conference cast opposition to immigration as a form of heroism worthy of Roman myth. The following year, Malkin referred to Rome again, this time at the America First Political Action Conference (AFPAC), where she shared the podium with prominent white nationalist activists. If at CPAC she espoused the tradition of seeing Rome as a model for emulation, at AFPAC she cast it as a model to avoid, comparing "end-stage America" to "end-stage Rome" where, according to a passage from the ancient historian Cassius Dio that Malkin quoted, "you could get citizenship for a piece of glass."[19] Another prominent contributor to

VDARE is Ann Coulter, who has appeared on one of *Time*'s lists of the hundred most influential people in the world. Writing for VDARE in 2019, Coulter warned, "We're becoming Rome." Coulter's discussion reproduces Kevin MacDonald's argument that Rome was strong until it admitted nonwhite foreigners. For hundreds of years, Coulter wrote, "the U.S. was demographically stable," but "in a generation, the white majority has nearly disappeared." Coulter predicts that this change will destroy an American culture that "is the envy of the world" and usher in a new "dark ages" like those she claims the Roman Empire experienced.

Malkin and Coulter are political commentators, but VDARE also hosts the work of Patrick J. Buchanan, who has not only observed American politics but participated actively in them as a staffer for three U.S. presidents and as a presidential candidate in his own right during the 1990s. The Roman Empire has been a recurring touchstone in Buchanan's many books (all published by reputable mainstream presses), most prominently in his 2006 book *State of Emergency: The Third World Invasion and Conquest of America.* "What the Danube and the Rhine were to Rome," this book begins, "the Rio Grande and Mediterranean are to America and Europe." Roman history proves, Buchanan claims, that movement across these borders threatens the nation. "As Rome had conquered the barbarians," he writes, "the barbarians conquered Rome [and] . . . the Dark Ages descended."[20]

In other books, Buchanan expands his comparison to include the misogynistic themes of reproductive and moral decline. In *The Death of the West* (2002), Buchanan compares modern women to the Roman women whom the white nationalists quoted above said "abandon[ed] traditional roles," equating a decision to have fewer children to a "No" vote on the question of whether "Western nations will even be around in a century." But Buchanan didn't need to formulate this theory of decline himself: the conservative organizer Phyllis Schlafly had already argued much the same thing in the 1970s. Schlafly compared "the liberated Roman matron" to "the present day feminist" and accused her of "help[ing] bring about the fall of Rome through her unnatural emulation of masculine qualities, which resulted in a large-scale breakdown of the family and ultimately of the empire." Buchanan and Schlafly illustrate that it's not just the observers of American politics who trade in these decline-focused comparisons between the United States and Rome: they animate the thinking of those who take an active and consequential role in the political life of our nation. More than anyone else, Schlafly was responsible for the defeat of a popular constitutional amendment that would have guaranteed equal rights for men and women in the United States. Buchanan's failed campaign strategy of appealing to white resentment against immigrants and neoliberal economic policy was adopted successfully by Donald Trump in 2016.[21]

The same can be said of the white nationalist designation of homosexuality as a cause of the decline of Rome. Already in 1969 Ronald Reagan told an audience at Eisenhower College that the Roman Empire declined because men became effeminate. As president, Richard Nixon asked his advisors, "Do you know what happened to the Romans? The last six Roman emperors were fags." Presidential candidate and eventual Trump cabinet member Ben Carson wrote in 2012 that same-sex marriage was the first step down "a slippery slope with a disastrous ending, as witnessed in the dramatic fall of the Roman Empire," and Mike Johnson, the Speaker of the United States House of Representatives, said something similar in an interview.[22] Considered alongside these men who have occupied positions at the highest levels of the U.S. government, Pat Buchanan turns out to be one of the *less* prominent and influential figures whose comparisons between America and Rome reproduce white nationalist explanations for decline.

I noted above that many professional historians argue that "decline" is the wrong concept to describe the transformations that took place in the Roman world of late antiquity. But such is the power of this myth that even professional academics who venture into political commentary reproduce it, and in doing so often end up striking similar notes to those found among white nationalists. One example is Samuel Huntington, the Harvard professor of political science who rose to prominence for his theory that a "Clash of Civilizations" would define post–Cold War geopolitics. Huntington's last book, *Who Are We? The Challenges to America's National Identity* (2004), argues that Spanish-speaking Latino immigrants pose a threat to the coherence of the "Anglo-Protestant" culture without which, Huntington believes, America cannot exist. It's the same line of thinking that many white nationalists promote: immigrants must not be too "foreign." And like them, Huntington takes ancient Rome as an important illustration of the rightness of this claim: "In the end," he writes, "America will suffer the fate of Sparta, Rome, and other communities" because "the racial and ethnic Americans are no more" and "cultural America is under siege."[23]

Niall Ferguson is in some respects a successor to Huntington as a political and cultural commentator. A few years after the publication of his *Colossus: The Decline and Fall of the American Empire*, Ferguson wrote an essay in *Vanity Fair* that elaborated an extensive comparison between ancient Rome and the United States and Europe. As in his other work, decline was a prominent theme. His discussion of America's supposed "inner decadence" struck a note similar to that of Buchanan or Schlafly. "The demographic transformation of the West has its roots in feminism," wrote Ferguson, complaining that "girls no longer play with dolls." Ferguson's diagnosis of the "perplexing vulnerability" of Western culture compares "pornography and NASCAR" to the supposedly decadent "orgies and circuses" of Rome. Here Ferguson modifies the Roman satirist Juvenal's description of the "bread and circuses" that has always been taken as the prime illustration of Roman decadence. The same line is frequently quoted to illustrate contemporary decline in white nationalist publications.[24]

Just as comparisons between Rome and America transcend political divides, so do the anxieties they reflect. Cullen Murphy's *Are We Rome?* has been described as "a more dispassionate view in the manner of the liberal journalistic observer." Noting that "many millions of barbarians were incorporated into Roman society as a matter of routine," Murphy eschews the xenophobic nativism of many such comparisons. But even Murphy seems unable to avoid employing language reminiscent of white nationalist narratives of decline: his section about the U.S. military's increasing recruitment of "outsiders" and "illegal aliens" is called "The New Barbarians." He writes of a "Hispanic tide" and "immigrant hordes." He describes the cultural borders of America as "infinitely porous, open to invasive influences," and repeats an army recruiter's lament that "there's just a lot of kids sitting around playing Xbox and eating junk food," appearing to echo the declinist theme of internal degeneracy.[25] It seems that whatever your political persuasion, and whatever your attitude toward white nationalist politics, such framing is inescapable when you compare America to Rome.

The Long Shadow of Edward Gibbon

If themes of immigrant invasions and cultural decay feel inescapable, it is because they have been central to historical analyses of the end of Roman political power for as long as those analyses have been performed. The name that looms the largest in this tradition is that of Edward Gibbon, whose six-volume *Decline and Fall of the Roman Empire* was published at the end of the eighteenth century. Many others had treated this subject before Gibbon, including such well-known figures as Montesquieu and Machiavelli, but it was Gibbon who established "decline" as the primary lens through which the sweep of Roman history would be understood, and it is his version of history that informs, whether it is acknowledged or not, nearly all analyses of contemporary decline that take Rome as a model. Ferguson's essay in *Vanity Fair* invoked "the long lens of Edward Gibbon's history" as its source, but he's hardly the first to consider Gibbon essential reading. George Washington owned a copy of Gibbon's history, Aaron Burr compelled his daughter to read it, Thomas Jefferson called it the best book of its kind, and Daniel Webster predicted that as long as America stayed a republic and maintained its Christian faith, "it will afford no topic for a Gibbon."[26]

Like nearly everything written three centuries ago, almost none of Gibbon's methods or findings are still accepted by those who study Roman history critically. With that much hindsight, his apocalyptic understanding of the dissolution of the Roman Empire looks very much like a response to the crumbling of imperial and monarchical political structures during the period in which he was writing: he published his first volume the same year that the American Revolution began and his last as the French Revolution was beginning. So it should come as no surprise that later scholars have demonstrated that Gibbon exaggerated ancient sources or took them at face value when doing so served the narrative he wanted to construct.[27]

Despite this, Gibbon's influence has been as durable as the belief that Rome declined and fell. No other work written in the 1700s can be said to have influenced everyone from the framers of the U.S. Constitution to *Breitbart* editor and Trump White House advisor Steve Bannon, who named it one of the books most important to his thinking, to the Rock & Roll Hall of Fame inductee and "Godfather of Punk" Iggy Pop, who described his love of Gibbon's *Decline and Fall* in an essay published in the academic journal *Classics Ireland.* The 2017 book *The Darkening Age: The Christian Destruction of the Classical World* reproduced Gibbon's claim that the adoption of Christianity brought about the collapse of the empire in a form that proved attractive to modern secular readers. It has been translated into twelve languages. Even though it seems unlikely that very many people have read Gibbon's thousand-plus-page work—Iggy Pop says he read an abridged version—the title alone has proven definitive for the popular perception of the ancient world. "Because of it," Edward Watts has written, "a huge portion of the English speaking world knows that the Roman Empire declined and fell."[28]

White nationalist intellectuals know this. And they expect that the familiarity of this narrative among a broader public provides fruitful ground for cultivating the narratives of decline that are integral to fascist politics. Iggy Pop provides but one mainstream example of how Gibbon might influence the ways those not otherwise connected to white nationalist groups perceive the contemporary significance of Roman history. He writes that reading Gibbon convinced him that "America is Rome." That was in 1982, two years into the presidency of Ronald Reagan, whom Pop later praised for "communicat[ing] the joys of liberty as compared to the joys of equality."[29] It is impossible to say whether reading Gibbon informed this political position, which would be at home in most highbrow white nationalist publications, but it illustrates that white nationalist intellectuals may not be far off base in granting Gibbon pride of place in their list of historians who provide legitimacy for their positions.

And so, although white nationalists invoke other narratives of Roman decline, such as those of Machiavelli and Montesquieu, it is Gibbon's narrative that sets the agenda for the most prominent thinkers. Patrick Buchanan listed Gibbon first in his list of scholars who recognized and delineated "the symptoms of dying civilizations." And William Pierce, the author of the apocalyptic novel that inspired several acts of terrorism, including the 1995 Oklahoma City bombing, said that Gibbon was the second book he read when he decided he wanted to learn about the relationship between race and history. The VDARE columnist Steve Sailer, a major figure in the popularization of race pseudoscience, is fond of quoting sections of Gibbon that he believes illuminate contemporary decline. For example, Sailer reported on George W. Bush's efforts as president to create a guest-worker program with a passage from Gibbon describing the Gothic tribes that were allowed to settle within the empire as "secret enemies." During the 2015 European migrant crisis, Sailer returned to Gibbon's discussion of this same period of history, during which the emperor who had allowed entry to these tribes would, two years later, die in a battle against armies in which many of these migrants fought.[30] Few could fail to understand Sailer's implicit prediction of a similar cataclysm in contemporary Europe, but what is striking is the similarity between Sailer's method of using Gibbon at VDARE and that of Ferguson in the popular journal *Vanity Fair*. Both of them alternated between quoting Gibbon and offering their own analysis of contemporary parallels.

Gibbon's analysis is attractive to white nationalists like Pierce, Buchanan, or Sailer because it articulates so many attitudes that are congenial to their way of thinking. The very term *barbarian*, to say nothing of recurring expressions such as "deluge of barbarians," "swarms of barbarians," and the language of the "horde," conform well to the white nationalist equation of foreignness with violence. When contemporary journalists use that term, the very familiarity that Gibbon's treatment has given the word disguises that association. More pointedly, Gibbon describes Jews as "a race of fanatics . . . [who are] the implacable enemies not only of the Roman government, but also of mankind"—a passage that Kevin MacDonald quotes to make antisemitism respectable—and calls homosexuality an "odious vice," a "sin against nature," and a "disease." Of the Ethiopians, Gibbon wrote that they "slept near a thousand years, forgetful of the world" until "they were awakened by the Portuguese," a formulation that erases African history before the supposedly civilizing arrival of their European enslavers.[31] To be sure, Gibbon shared these views with many of his contemporaries, but his narrative remains influential, imparting lasting respectability to perspectives that deserve to have been abandoned centuries ago.

Gibbon was a product of the European Enlightenment, as J.G.A. Pocock's monumental study of the intellectual context of his work has shown. This was the same period that saw the invention of the category of "race" as a means to justify the enslavement and colonization of people living outside Europe. Although Gibbon himself did not incorporate this nascent concept into his argument, his narrative of Roman history proved attractive to notorious exponents of racist pseudoscience such as Arthur de Gobineau, Madison Grant, and Lothrop Stoddard, all of whom treated the "decline of the Roman Empire" in their works. To Gibbon's inchoate and implicit theory of race, which held that the "barbarian" was essentially and inescapably violent and uncultured, or that the Christian was necessarily meek and unwilling to defend himself from invasion, these men added the idea that Rome had been weakened by racial degeneration as a result of the intermarriage of Italians with immigrants and freed slaves from other, allegedly inferior, populations. We must remember that this was not a fringe intellectual movement: the Massachusetts senator Henry Cabot Lodge, who campaigned actively and successfully for federal immigration restrictions based on racist pseudoscience, told President Theodore Roosevelt that "in all the great essentials Gibbon is as right now as he was when he wrote." For his part, Roosevelt was preoccupied with the threat of "race suicide" throughout his life. He wrote in a letter to the owner of the *New York Daily Tribune* about the "unpleasant resemblances between the occidental civilization of the present day" and "the civilization of the Roman world," calling special attention to "the decline in the birth rate."[32]

Such openly expressed racism became taboo following the Second World War, but belief in the racial degeneration of the Roman Empire retained currency in, for example, the popular historical works of Will and Ariel Durant. Their prize-winning *Story of Civilization* (1935–75), whose eleven volumes have sold more than 2 million copies in nine languages, is a favorite source for Patrick

Buchanan. He quotes the Durants' account of how "biological factors" hastened the fall of Rome: "The population of Italy had long been mingled with Oriental strains physically inferior," they wrote, who were "mostly of a mind to destroy" Roman culture, while the "rapidly breeding Germans could not understand" that culture. This is a repackaging for middlebrow readers of white nationalist perspectives on the threats of miscegenation and hostile foreigners. After the Durants had completed ten volumes of their survey, they published a short retrospective entitled *The Lessons of History*. Among these "lessons" was their finding that "utopias of equality are biologically doomed."[33] It was published in the same year as the passage of the Civil Rights Act.

Professional historians have been no more innocent of perpetuating this narrative of Rome's decline than have been those whose more popular accounts are derived from scholarship. A white nationalist press that issued a "centenary edition" of Madison Grant's *Passing of the Great Race* has even published a collection of passages from the works of classical scholars that support white nationalist politics. Chief among these is the article "Race Mixture in the Roman Empire," written by Johns Hopkins University professor Tenney Frank and published in the *American Historical Review* in 1916, the same year that Grant published his book. Frank argued that "the orientalization of Rome's populace" led to "the failure of foresight and common sense, the weakening of moral and political stamina" that Frank suggests had characterized the Romans of earlier ages. Alongside this article, the collection includes passages from other prominent scholars including, for example, the Nobel Prize–winning historian Theodor Mommsen describing "parasitic immigrants" in the provinces of Rome, and the Swedish historian Martin Nilsson, who was an honorary member of the American Academy of Arts and Sciences, claiming that "race-blending . . . was the most active cause of the decay of ancient culture and the fall of the Roman Empire" and making the same argument we have seen Kevin MacDonald make, that "as long as the peoples of Western Europe lived in their old primitive and independent condition the status was rather stable." "What of the enormous change in the intellectual outlook and atmosphere between Augustus and Constantine?" asked the compilers of *The Cambridge Ancient History* in another passage collected in this volume. "Is not the result something more Oriental than Greek or Roman in type or character?"[34]

You would be hard-pressed to find such explicitly xenophobic analyses in twenty-first-century scholarship, but the very datedness of these historians, paradoxically, is the source of their authority for white nationalist thinkers. "The modern era's censorship of the issue of race as a determining factor has led to the deliberate suppression of the work of Frank (and others)," claims the editor in his introduction to the collection that reprints their essays. What may seem a paranoid attitude should in fact be understood (also) as a component of neofascist narratives of decline: a degenerate age, this reasoning goes, will produce degenerate understandings of the past. It holds that it is only by looking back to historical work that was composed before such degeneracy supposedly set in that history can be objectively understood. When Mike Johnson argued that homosexuality caused the "fall of Rome," he claimed he was basing his argument on the claims of "objective" historians.[35] With this remark he is simultaneously elevating the discarded theories of bygone ages and dismissing contemporary perspectives as symptomatic of what he believes are the corrupt morals of today.

This doesn't prevent white nationalists from embracing and promoting modern scholarship that they believe gives fresh legitimacy to their outdated interpretations of Roman history. A book by Peter Heather of King's College London, *The Fall of the Roman Empire: A New History of Rome and the Barbarians* (2006), is a much-cited text in white nationalist circles. The influence of Gibbon is evident from Heather's invocation in the first chapter of the book. And even though Heather shifts the blame for the "destruction" of Rome away from foreign invaders onto the Romans themselves and their "unbounded aggression" toward others, his use of the term *barbarian* without critical reflection on its connotations (ancient or modern) and his overall project of restoring the centrality of these "barbarians" to narratives describing the political transformations of the fourth and fifth centuries explains why his book has attracted this audience in particular. "We do not at present," wrote the historian Michael Kulikowski in a review of Heather's book, "lack for prophets declaring that the empire of western civilization is besieged by advancing hordes of barbarians. This book will appeal to them."

Heather has criticized those who make a "simple equation of the role of migration in Rome's unraveling and the travails of the modern West," but Kulikowski's prediction proved to be correct. Patrick Buchanan began his book *State of Emergency: The Third World Invasion and Conquest of America* (2006) with a reference to Heather's work.[36]

Even more attractive to white nationalists is when classical scholars invoke ancient Rome to predict contemporary decline. *American Renaissance*, for example, reprinted an article written by Peter Jones, whose weekly column in the *Spectator* made him one of the most prominent classical scholars in Britain, entitled "It was Tribalism That Finished Rome, and It Will Finish Brussels Too." And the *Occidental Observer* published a two-part review of the Belgian historian David Engels's 2012 book *Le déclin: La crise de l'Union européenne et la chute de la République romaine* (Decline: The Crisis of the European Union and the Fall of the Roman Republic), a book that, like Heather's, quotes Gibbon on its first page. This provocative book earned Engels more than seventy reviews and interviews in academic journals and in the mainstream press, including English-language reviews in well-regarded classics journals that described its discussions of Rome and the European Union as "equally insightful" and expressed hope that the book would "serve as a timely wake-up call." At least in the case of Engels, the attention his book received from white nationalists cannot be attributed solely to their opportunism. The book itself gestures toward a white nationalist conspiracy theory concerning a governmental plot to "Islamize" Europe, calling "Eurabia"—the same term white nationalists use to describe this alleged conspiracy's objective—a "perfectly credible prediction." After his book was translated into Hungarian, Engels said in an interview for the conservative *Magyar Hírlap* newspaper that he had plans to move to Viktor Orbán's authoritarian Hungary because it "reminds me much of the Belgium I grew up in." He praised it for "show[ing] an example in protecting traditional values."[37]

Decline through the Eyes of the Romans

The perspectives on Roman history that white nationalist thinking feeds on remain current in large part because ancient observers showed an obsession with decline to rival that of the most committed neofascist. We have already noted Ricardo Duchesne's quotations at Counter-Currents of the harangues of Cato the Elder against luxury, and the historian Livy's hope that his history would provide readers with an understanding of how, "with the gradual relaxation of discipline, morals . . . finally began the downward plunge" in the period before Augustus's reign. Livy was not the first or last Roman historian to comment on alleged decline. Before Livy, Sallust had written that "avarice subverted trustworthiness, integrity, and other virtuous practices" in Rome, and one of the speakers in Tacitus's *Dialogue on Orators*, written a hundred years after Livy's death, complains about the "decay of old-fashioned virtue" in Rome. Three centuries later, the Roman soldier and historian Ammianus Marcellinus wrote that Rome was "declining into old age" and decried the "sluggish indolence" of patrician families "that were formerly famed for devotion to serious pursuits." And the fifth-century bishop Salvian, who cast Roman decline as a divine punishment, claimed that "the barbarians themselves are offended by our vices."[38] These passages come from every period of Roman history: Cato lived a full four centuries before any modern historian seriously argues that Rome fell. So even though Ammianus wrote in a period that Gibbon defines as one of decline, we might well wonder whether he is accurately diagnosing the ills of his time or merely repeating a timeworn trope of Roman historiography. But this is not a question ever asked by the white nationalists who quote these passages at the *Occidental Observer* and the Daily Stormer to prove that modern America is on the brink of social, racial, and moral collapse.

Roman authors don't just emphasize the theme of decline but attribute it to factors strikingly similar to those that contemporary white nationalists do. The "barbarian" that has animated historical narratives from Gibbon to Heather to Engels as well as the xenophobic rhetoric of white nationalists is a product of Roman sources that are well known to white nationalist intellectuals. The philosopher Seneca claimed that "barbarians" showed special "ferocity" because they had "no contact with learning of the culture of letters," an ancient version of the claim that foreigners cannot and will never value the culture to which they are immigrating. Both Jerome, whose translation of the Hebrew Bible into Latin became the standard translation of the Middle Ages, and his contemporary Libanius, a prominent pagan professor of rhetoric, described them as "wild beasts." In both cases it is easy to perceive why these men found it expedient to represent foreigners in this way: Jerome, writing to console a friend whose nephew had died, was exaggerating the suffering of their present in order to emphasize the bliss he and his correspondent expected from eternal life with God; Libanius was trying to convince the emperor Theodosius to spare the inhabitants of Antioch, who had recently rioted, by arguing that only "barbarians" would seek revenge. Attention to the historical context in which ancient historians wrote about "barbarians" can similarly complicate the argument, found in both Gibbon and an essay published by the anti-Muslim blog *Gates of Vienna*, that the Goths whom the emperor Valens allowed to settle within the Roman Empire were predestined to betray the hospitality of the Romans. Both Gibbon and the *Gates of Vienna* essayist cite Ammianus Marcellinus, who remarked that "diligent care was taken [by the Romans] that no future destroyer of the Roman state should be left behind, even if he was smitten by a fatal disease."[39] Ammianus served as an officer in a military division that suffered several humiliating defeats at the hands of the Persians, making him anything but an unbiased source for the period he described in his history.

White nationalists identify the corrupting influence of foreigners as one of the engines of internal decline: when the speaker of Juvenal's third satire complains that first Greeks and later Syrians have made Rome unrecognizable to the traditional Roman, his mention of alien-sounding music and the allegedly promiscuous sexuality of Syrian women precedes by several thousand years the familiar complaints of the modern nativist. So too do other ancient attacks on women as complicit in civilizational decline. The poet Propertius complains that contemporary women care too much for luxury and that they refuse to emulate mythological models of female chastity such as Penelope. To cite the poetry of this embittered loner, as David Engels does, as evidence of the decline of sexual morality in Rome is like lending credibility on such topics to a member of the misogynistic "incel" community of today. Nor should we take at face value the sensationalist invective found in ancient biographers who vilified previous emperors in order to celebrate those of their own time. That's what the neo-Confederate site *Occidental Dissent* did when it quoted Suetonius's description of

Nero's "marriage" to the eunuch Sporus just weeks before the U.S. Supreme Court heard oral arguments concerning the legality of same-sex marriage bans.[40]

Even the anxieties that might seem to be the province only of committed white nationalists—obsession with birth rates and racial purity—find expression in ancient texts. The historian Polybius, for example, claims that Roman "men [became] perverted to a passion for show and money and the pleasures of an idle life" and uninterested in having children, with the result that "the houses must be left heirless" and "the cities become sparsely inhabited and weak." White nationalists pair citations of this passage with complaints about childlessness from both well-known Roman authors such as Ovid, Tacitus, and Pliny the Younger and also from more obscure sources like Petronius, the Theodosian Law Codes, or a philosopher whose work only survives in fragments, Hierocles. Setting aside that there was no way in antiquity to measure birth rates accurately, no less a figure than the emperor Augustus is said to have warned the Romans that their families were in danger of dying out even as the city was "be[ing] given over to foreigners." According to the biographer Suetonius, Augustus limited citizenship and the manumission of slaves out of concern for "keep[ing] the people pure and unsullied by any taint of foreign or enslaved blood," making him a hero to white nationalists not only as an authoritarian leader but as a defender of the racial purity of his state.[41] If modern historians have argued that the Roman Empire declined because of race-mixing, this is as much a product of the perspectives they found in ancient sources as it is of their own embrace of white supremacy.

Some of these ancient writers, like Cato or Ammianus, had a lot to lose from political change and so cast it in apocalyptic terms. Others, like Sallust, wanted to justify a contemporary revolution by highlighting the supposed degeneracy of the past. Today's white nationalists find themselves in both of these positions, losing political and social power in a world where white supremacist racial hierarchies are being questioned and, ever so slowly and with tremendous resistance from entrenched power, abolished, but also promoting a revolution in white consciousness against a world that they claim discriminates against them to the point of extermination. The argument is no more coherent than that of the Romans themselves, but it reflects analogous political investments and anxieties. So white nationalists see ancient sources as providing proof that their denunciations of past, present, and future degeneracy belong to a prestigious tradition of truth-telling. What they really illustrate is that narratives of decline are one of the timeless rhetorical tools that those who benefit from unjust and unequal political systems use to attempt to justify and maintain that power.

Rejecting Declinism

The proof that these rhetorical tools are effective lies in the extent to which large numbers of Americans share white nationalist anxieties about immigration, birth rates, and morality. When a candidate for the presidency of the United States runs his campaign on anti-immigrant rhetoric and, upon election, makes it among his first acts to sign an executive order that he himself referred to as a "Muslim Ban," it should need little argument that many Americans regard foreigners as a threat to our nation. But it is nevertheless worth noting that research suggests that President Trump's campaign rhetoric in 2016 did not create these xenophobic attitudes but rather capitalized on those that large numbers of Americans already held. And although public discourse about immigration often focuses on economic issues, surveys suggest that individual citizens worry more about the symbolic and cultural factors that white nationalist commentators emphasize, including the integrity of the national identity of the United States.[42]

Fear of moral decline and low birth rates is also widespread. A 2023 analysis published in the journal *Nature* examined seven decades of public opinion surveys and found that throughout this period people in sixty nations worldwide have claimed that morality is declining. This does not mean that morality really *is* declining: "Our studies show," wrote the authors, "that the perception of moral decline is pervasive, perdurable, unfounded and easily produced." What it means is that the American, and indeed international, public already holds beliefs that prime them to accept white nationalist claims of moral degeneracy. Similarly, the U.S. Census Bureau's prediction that the United States will soon become a "minority majority" nation, in which no racial group has a demographic majority, has been widely reported in the mainstream press. Research has shown that just hearing this stated prompts white Americans to develop hostile attitudes toward other races, when the actual demographic "threat" is every bit as illusory as that of moral decline. As demographer Richard Alba has argued at length, the very idea of a "minority majority" nation is an artifact of the arbitrary ways that the Census Bureau categorizes citizens.[43] But Americans trust the census, and they trust their instincts and perceptions about population and moral decline. Could this, at least in part, be because we are so inundated by narratives of decline, including those that make the Roman Empire their touchstone?

One of the most distinguished historians of late antiquity, Glen Bowersock, told the American Academy of Arts and Sciences in 1996 that "the fall of Rome is no longer needed" because "we live today in a shrunken world in which the Gibbonian categories of religion and alien cultures . . . have become positive components of late twentieth-century civilization." Hardly anyone was more perceptive about the tendentiousness of Gibbon's historiography than Bowersock, but hindsight makes his optimism about what our "civilization" considers "positive components" seem downright naive. The truth is that narratives of decline have remained pervasive because they serve the maintenance of the status quo very well. They paint change as degeneration, and in particular any attempt at progress—whether racial, economic, or environmental—as a dangerous deviation from the values that supposedly made the nation-state strong. And since it is often through violence and oppression that nations become "strong" in the conventional sense of the word, narratives of decline, as Jed Esty has argued recently, will continue to serve a whole range of supremacist ideologies.[44] This is partly because they blame marginalized groups—immigrants, foreign-born citizens, women, gay people—for whatever crises our society faces rather than the wealthy and powerful, whose interests are served by directing attention away from income inequality and the climate crisis. If America's dominant culture shares with fascist ideology a fascination with narratives of decline, this is why.

Another perspective is possible. There are analyses of the transformation of the Roman world in late antiquity that attribute the collapse of Roman political power not to any human factor but to environmental ones. There are even analyses that make the fall of the Roman Empire the best thing ever to happen to Europe.[45] You learn a different lesson than the one white nationalists are pushing about history if barbarians, ethnic diversity, and the moral degeneracy of the elites are only incidental to the fate of nations. You learn a different lesson if giving up political and military supremacy actually turns out to be beneficial. Few would deny that we live today in a time of crisis, whether political, economic, or environmental. We have seen that white nationalist intellectuals claim that comparisons to ancient Rome will save us. Do we agree?

CHAPTER FOUR

The Descendants of Achilles

As 2015 drew to a close, Richard B. Spencer's fortunes were on the rise. Seven years earlier he had left a PhD program at Duke University where immigration hardliner Stephen Miller, who would become Donald Trump's senior advisor for policy during his first presidency and his homeland security advisor during his second, was a fellow student. After working in conservative journalism for a few years, Spencer founded a website to promote what he described as an "alternative" to the mainstream American conservatism of the early twenty-first century. He believed that George W. Bush and the "neoconservatives" who dominated the Republican Party were too interventionist, too much in thrall to corporations and wealthy oligarchs, and above all too soft on immigration. He named his site AlternativeRight.com.[1]

Spencer's wasn't the only white nationalist website on the internet in 2010: Greg Johnson launched Counter-Currents that same year, the *Occidental Observer* had started publishing shorter articles online in 2008 to complement those in the print-only *Occidental Quarterly*, and *American Renaissance*, which published its first print issue in 1990, had begun establishing a presence online. Stormfront had been online since 1994. But the clean-cut and articulate thirty-two-year-old Spencer proved particularly adept at packaging white nationalist ideas for the internet age. He attracted the attention of the behind-the-scenes figures that fund the movement, including one of the heirs to the Regnery publishing fortune, William Regnery II.[2] With Regnery's support, Spencer became the director of the National Policy Institute think tank, whose logo features classical columns, and president of Washington Summit Publishers, a press devoted to distributing white nationalist works. He published a collection of essays by prominent white nationalists entitled *The Great Erasure* focused, in the words of Spencer's introduction, on "the worldwide status of the White man" in an age he claimed was bent on "the destruction of Europeans as a unique biological entity." Within a few years Spencer had further refined and popularized his concept of an "Alternative Right." He closed down his old website and launched a new one with a sharper name that would come to define Spencer's movement: AltRight.com.

Today, Spencer is a marginal figure. His reputation has been tarnished by videos showing him leading a crowd of white nationalists in a Hitler salute and recordings of his use of racial slurs quite at odds with his highbrow public persona. More significant, his ability to organize has been neutralized by ongoing civil lawsuits related to his participation in the 2017 gathering of white nationalist activists known as the Unite the Right rally, where a participant killed Heather Heyer and injured thirty-five other counterprotestors. But in December 2015, he was nearing the height of his influence. He was still a regular speaker on college campuses, and media outlets had not yet seen past his slick repackaging of the antisemitism, racism, and misogyny of earlier generations of neofascists. Presidential candidate Donald Trump had recently called for a temporary ban on Muslims entering the United States, a proposal that seemed to indicate that Spencer's brand of nativist conservatism was entering the mainstream. The "Great Meme War" was in full swing, as large numbers of anonymous individuals online marshaled ironic humor to vilify Trump's opponents in the presidential race. Spencer sensed an opportunity to expand his organization's already substantial online reach. "In 2016," he announced on his *Radix* website, "we are going to explore video."

That exploration began with a video that used Greco-Roman antiquity to define the concept of white identity that Spencer had claimed in *The Great Erasure* was in danger of being destroyed. The video begins with a scene in which a white man stands still while a crowd of people swirls around him and Spencer's voice-over asks, "Who are you?" As the video progresses through more scenes intended to evoke loneliness, Spencer offers viewers a "connection to a culture, a history, a destiny" and "an identity that stretches back, and flows forward, for centuries."

Then the tone shifts as Spencer contrasts the "rootless" modern man with "our ancestors" who, he says, "had a strong sense of identity." And as the message changes, the visual tone does too: scenes of modern alienation are replaced by images taken from European history, in particular from Greco-Roman antiquity: the Parthenon, the Temple of Olympian Zeus, busts of Plato and the Roman emperor Augustus, a mosaic portraying Alexander of Macedon, a sculpture of the Spartan general Leonidas. This sequence brings together the white nationalist belief in the decadence of the contemporary world, as represented by the lonely man in the swirling crowd, and the related belief, represented by the increasingly martial images of ancient scenes, that masculine heroism provides an antidote to this decline. Spencer's narration only hints at the conspiracy theory that is at the center of the essays collected in *The Great Erasure:* "So long as we avoid and deny our identity . . . we will have no chance to resist our dispossession." The images make clear that Spencer believes that a sense of connection with the Greco-Roman past will provide inspiration for such resistance: "What our ancestors took for granted, we must discover, we must renew."

Spencer's choice of affirmative terms like *identity* and *ancestors* was typical of his media-savvy avoidance of language associated with fascist politics. He does not say the word *race.* He even goes so far in the video as to dismiss "white" as "a checkbox on a census form." Instead, metaphors of ancestry and inheritance abound, as in other white nationalist discussions of the value of Greco-Roman antiquity. A contributor to Spencer's AltRight.com described members of their movement as "heirs" of Seneca, "the ancient Romans," "the Greeks," and "the Germanic founders of modern Europe," concluding that "a healthy and robust Europe is alive inside us." A contributor to Spencer's *Radix* website similarly crowed that "we are the descendants of Achilles and Odysseus, Aeneas and Caesar, Charlemagne and Dante, and yes even John Smith and Hernán Cortés," embracing not only the militaristic masculinity of ancient warriors but the violent colonization of the Americas as sources of inspiration. And the white nationalist organization Identity Evropa made the notion of Greco-Roman ancestry central to a recruitment campaign in which they plastered college campuses nationwide with flyers showing images of classical art. One featured an image of a sculpture of Heracles from the collection of the Metropolitan Museum in New York together with the slogan "Protect Your Heritage," while another showed the bust of the Vatican Museum's Apollo Belvedere with the caption "Our Future Belongs to Us." These images were likely selected to provide a veneer of gentility and intellectualism to Identity Evropa's racial politics, producing posters that would not, at first glance, seem out of place on a bulletin board advertising college lectures, art exhibitions, and student organizations. The Anti-Defamation League documented Identity Evropa flyers on thirty-six college campuses in 2017 alone.[3]

These flyers distilled into brief slogans the more extensive claims about a racial connection between modern white people and the ancient Greeks and Romans that Spencer and others were making in their publications. In *The Great Erasure*, Spencer had described Europeans as "a unique biological entity." Two years after producing his *Who Are We?* video, Spencer asserted in a manifesto entitled "The Charlottesville Statement" that "race is the foundation of identity." Both of these remarks link Spencer's concepts of identity and ancestry to a concept of race that is biological, and as such, inherited from generation to generation. It's a link that makes the "inheritance" of Greco-Roman antiquity a source not only of racial identity but of racial pride. Spencer's message to white people is that they should be proud to be white because they can be proud of their ancestral, and indeed racial, link to the Greco-Roman past. Achilles, the reasoning goes, was a great warrior, Odysseus a cunning strategist and resourceful survivor. Because you are white, suggests Spencer, these are your ancestors. You are like them. Be proud.

Such calls to derive racial pride from a supposed ancestral connection with the ancient Greeks can be described as acts of "racialization." That is, Spencer and his ilk assign a white racial identity to the ancient Greeks in order to create a racial connection with modern people who identify as white. To make such a connection requires an understanding of race that makes not only skin color but all manner of group-level characteristics—in this case, anything one might be proud of—genetic and ancestral. Such an understanding of race is fundamental to all white nationalist politics and integral to the value they place on the Greco-Roman world. And even though the linking of racial identities with ancestry has no basis in genetic science, this understanding of race enjoys currency far beyond the audience for Spencer's video.[4]

Looking for Whiteness in the Ancient World

It is possible to abhor or deride the conspiracy theory that a small group of global "elites" is plotting the extermination of the white race but nevertheless consider it self-evident that we should regard the ancient Greeks as white. After all, this line of thinking goes, they lived in Europe before mechanized transportation made large-scale migration from other parts of the world possible. The association of Europe with whiteness is so widespread as to be practically invisible: no less an institution than the U.S. Census designates "a person having origins in any of the original peoples of Europe" as "white." What are the ancient Greeks if not one "of the original peoples of Europe"? When the federal government employs such categories, one does not have to be an avowed white nationalist to assume that the ancient Greeks were white.[5]

Two aspects of this conception of race bear further scrutiny in relation to white nationalist claims about the racial identity of the ancient Greeks. One is the focus on "origins," which is recognizably related to the claims of "ancestry" that we have seen white nationalists make to link modern white people with the Greeks and Romans. The other is the focus on skin color. The two aspects are interrelated, because genetic ancestry does affect physical appearance. In this limited sense, modern racial categories can be said to reflect genetics, and in the same limited sense it may be fair to say that the Greeks were white, if by this you mean nothing more than that many of them likely had lighter-colored skin than black Africans. But almost no one means *only* this when they racialize someone, because so many of us engage in what the philosopher Paul C. Taylor calls "race-thinking." That is, so many of us, on some level, have been acculturated to accept a set of muddled, self-contradictory, and, from a historical point of view, arbitrary ideas about human difference. Race-thinking, for example, assumes that the genetics that produce differences in skin color also produce differences in intelligence, morality, strength, and dexterity, such that skin color becomes a predictor of those other qualities. Genetic science has roundly disproven this assumption, which has become known as "biological determinism": not only is there no connection between the genetics of skin color and the genetics of any other quality, there is more genetic variation among people who share a particular skin color than there is between them and members of a group with different-colored skin. Even though there may be large variations between individuals in intelligence or other qualities, genetics do not predict any kind of meaningful differences between groups.[6]

White nationalists know that the reality of genetics obliterates their claim to share a racial identity with the ancient Greeks. But they also know that most people continue to believe in the reality of race. They know that the census, media, and institutions perpetuate such beliefs.[7] And they know that the genetic reality of differences in skin color is easily confused with the genetic unreality of the group-level differences that race-thinking assigns to differences in skin color. So they play on this confusion and attempt to cast scientific refutations of the reality of race as absurd, counterintuitive, and out of step with human history.

To do this, contributors to a whole range of white nationalist publications, including *American Renaissance*, the *Occidental Observer*, and the *Occidental Quarterly*, turn to the Greeks. Their essays collect references to white skin, blond or red hair, and blue eyes in ancient texts in order to demonstrate, they believe conclusively, that the ancient Greeks were white. They point out that the Homeric epics mention the blond hair not only of central figures like Achilles, Helen, and Apollo, but also of heroes from other ages, such as Meleager, and even people who are hardly mentioned, such as Agamede, the wife of a warrior Nestor remembers killing years before the action of the poem. This suggests, they argue, that blond hair characterized the majority of Greeks of the Homeric period, or at least those of the aristocratic class. They note that in the *Odyssey* Penelope's cheeks are compared to snow, and that Menelaus is repeatedly called "red-haired." They collect references to blond hair in the odes of Pindar and Bacchylides, which were written to celebrate victors in athletic competitions; in the hymns of Alcman, which groups of young women performed in archaic Sparta; and in the fragmentary remains—unknown even to most professional historians—of the observations of Heracleides Criticus, who commented on the yellow hair of the women of Thebes. The biographer Plutarch provides descriptions of many famous Romans whom white nationalists cite to racialize the Romans, too, as white: Cato the Elder had red hair and light-colored eyes; Sulla had blue eyes and blond hair; so, too, the emperor Augustus. Suetonius adds that Nero had blue eyes and blond hair; a sixth-century Byzantine historian mentions the blue eyes of the second-century emperor Hadrian. The poets Horace and Ovid sometimes describe their sexual partners as blond.[8]

If the range and obscurity of sources seems impressive it is because generations of scholars have invested their energy in affirming the whiteness of the ancient Greeks. Some of these are notorious white supremacists, such as the man known as the Nazis' "Race Pope," Hans F. K. Günther, whose *Racial Elements of European History* (published in German in 1924) collected many of these passages. But the impulse to create this ancestral connection was much more widespread than that due to the way it supported the idea of European exceptionalism. The ideas that men like Günther made notorious were not always taboo: the English translation of his book was published in 1927 by Methuen, the same publisher that published *Winnie-the-Pooh* and the celebrated Arden edition of Shakespeare's plays.

Nor did Günther, who continued to publish work advocating for eugenics even after the Second World War, originate this link. He simply expanded a racial theory concerning the Greeks that was already widely accepted in his time. This held that the "classical" age of Greece was ushered in by blond-haired "Dorian invaders" from northern Europe. This theory of the origin of the Greeks was an expansion of a Greek mythological story that the children of Heracles were exiled from a region of Greece (the Peloponnese) to which their descendants returned and took political power. This is a far cry from the claim that these people came to Greece from as far away as modern Germany. Furthermore, Jonathan Hall has demonstrated that this mythology reflects a desire to define a Dorian sub-identity within Greekness rather than a memory of historical migration. But nineteenth-century historians developed and perpetuated this theory in order to make the same racial link between the Europe of their day and the ancient Greeks that contemporary white nationalists seek to make. It was so widely disseminated and accepted that an essayist for *American Renaissance* can point to the 1911 edition of the *Encyclopedia Britannica*, as well as a popular 1939 book by the Harvard professor Werner Jaeger, as evidence that modern skepticism about the whiteness of the Greeks is an ideologically driven deviation from what has been the mainstream scholarly position.[9]

Few people nowadays consult the 1911 *Encyclopedia Britannica*, although early editions of Wikipedia used its public domain entries as the basis for numerous articles. Fewer still read the scholarship of Werner Jaeger. But the ideas about the supposed racial identity of the ancient Greeks and Romans that they espoused live on. In 2004 Vincent Sarich and Frank Miele published *Race: The Reality of Human Differences.* The authors—one a University of California–Berkeley anthropology professor, and the other the editor in chief of *Skeptic* magazine, which claims to "promote critical thinking" about "pseudoscience"—intended their book to refute the 2003 PBS documentary *Race: The Power of an Illusion*, which attempted to raise Americans' awareness about the unscientific and arbitrary nature of familiar racial designations. In response, the book argued for the reality of race on both scientific and historical grounds. The endnotes of the chapters on genetics are filled with references to notorious figures such as Carleton Coon, J. Philippe Rushton, and Arthur Jensen. And the book's chapters on history reproduce white nationalist thought as well: they begin with a catalogue of references to white skin from ancient Greek sources similar to the one found in *American Renaissance.* Neither of these features prevented the American Library Association from publishing a review in a section of its journal *Booklist* entitled "Spotlight on Black History" that called the book "an important work, despite its conservative inferences, that challenges both the existence and the value of America's obsession with color blindness."[10]

That pseudoscientific theories of race have permeated the consciousness of the wider public is evident from the public outrage whenever a Black actor is cast to play a symbolically significant figure from Greco-Roman antiquity, particularly the Egyptian queen Cleopatra. The most recent backlash came when Netflix cast Adele James to play her in *Queen Cleopatra* (2023). This casting prompted the former head of Egypt's Supreme Antiquities Council to accuse Netflix of promoting a "falsification of Egyptian history," and James reported that she endured harassment and even death threats for her role in the show. Similar denunciations of the "blackwashing" of history and of "political correctness" met the casting of David Gyasi and Hakeem Kae-Kazim to play Achilles and Zeus in the BBC's *Troy: Fall of a City* (2018).[11] The vitriol and violence these productions provoked—involving, it should be noted, a character who never really existed (Achilles)—reveal the strength of the public's belief that figures associated with ancient Greece were, and should be, white in modern racial terms.

That such reactions have been particularly strong in Egypt and Greece—both countries claim Cleopatra as a historical icon of their culture—reveals the belief that Black skin somehow diminishes the dignity of these figures. Attempting to cloak this belief in an appeal to "historical accuracy" rings false, since few complained that a forty-year-old Brad Pitt was cast to play Achilles (who was likely half that age during the Trojan War), or that Adele James is somewhat taller than some evidence indicates the historical Cleopatra was. Of all these physical differences it is only skin color that provokes controversy, because only skin color has been embedded in an implicit hierarchy of races. Most scholarly discussions of Cleopatra's racial identity have done little more than perpetuate this logic, focused as they have been on whether her ancestry is entirely Greek or not. As Shelley Haley has pointed out, attempting to determine Cleopatra's racial identity with reference to her ancestry depends on the same logic as the patently racist "one-drop rule" of American segregation, which held that if a person had any African ancestry, no matter how distant, they should be classified as "Black" and deprived of various civic rights.[12]

Ever more refined inquiries into Cleopatra's ancestry are only one example of how historical scholarship does not really disrupt white nationalist appropriation of history unless it engages with the underlying theories of race that inform that appropriation. Similarly, it does not really suffice to point out that the sculptures that Identity Evropa used to represent ancient whiteness were originally painted with colors that modern viewers would probably find gaudy or absurd. All available evidence suggests that the skin on the figures portrayed in these sculptures was painted in colors that modern race-thinking analyzes as white and that many of them featured blond or auburn hair and light-colored eyes. "Ancient sculptures weren't white, they were pink!" runs a gleeful headline at VDARE, mocking claims that ancient coloration complicates their claims. And too much focus on the original colors of these sculptures risks distracting attention from the very real racist history of those that Identity Evropa chose for their flyers. An influential work of racist pseudoscience called *The Types of Mankind* (1854) argued that African people were anatomically closer to apes, and therefore more primitive, than Europeans. It illustrated this with a diagram in which drawings of the skulls of an African person and an ape were contrasted with a drawing of the head of the Apollo Belvedere, the same portion of the sculpture shown in the Identity Evropa flyer.[13]

The response to debates about the racial identity of ancient people must be to reject the idea that modern racialized identities tell us anything meaningful about ancient people: investigations into the ancestry or appearance of historical figures (or sculptures) only perpetuate the racial categories that are fundamental to white nationalist appropriation of that past. One way that historians have attempted to do this has been to call attention to evidence indicating that skin color in antiquity did not carry the same connotations it does in the modern world. When Athena wants to make Odysseus more beautiful, for example, she makes his skin black. Casting a Black man to play Zeus in *Troy: Fall of a City* can be paralleled in the appearance of an African Zeus onstage in ancient Athens in a play by Sophocles—*Inachos*—that survives only in fragments. Beginning in 1947, the African American classical scholar Frank Snowden dedicated his career to collecting evidence showing that there was no "color prejudice," as he put it, in the ancient Greco-Roman world. This was a timely and provocative claim for a Black scholar to make in the early days of what would become the American civil rights movement. Later scholarship, especially that of Lloyd Thompson and more recently Sarah Derbew, has complicated this picture somewhat, arguing that blackness could carry a wide range of meanings in the ancient world. Derbew, in particular, has demonstrated how modern anti-Blackness has hampered many scholars' ability to understand the meanings of blackness in antiquity.[14] Highlighting differences between ancient and modern attitudes toward blackness significantly undermines white nationalist racial ideology, which requires that concepts of race be stable throughout history. Such differences demonstrate that these concepts change to suit the desire of the politically powerful to divide human beings into categories that justify the unequal distribution of resources. It's a historical truth that strikes at the heart of white nationalist ways of thinking about the ancient world, and about race itself.

But it does not, in itself, make the ancient world unavailable to white nationalist thinking. As open racism became shameful in the final third of the twentieth century, scholars became reluctant to use such terminology to analyze the ancient world. Snowden's work began to be interpreted to mean that the ancient world was innocent of racist thought and even that the very concept of race did not exist. Bernard Knox, the director of Harvard's Center for Hellenic Studies, wrote in 1993 that "racism in our sense was not a problem of the Greeks" because "their homogeneous population afforded no soil on which that weed could easily grow." Peter Jones, one of the most prominent classical scholars in Britain thanks to his weekly column in the *Spectator*, argued in a 2008 book that "the Greeks and Romans were not racist" because "they had no interest in distinguishing 'barbarians' by genes or physiology," that is, by genetics or appearance. But as the historian of race Denise McCoskey has noted, "Snowden's work did not prove that the ancients were not racist, only that if racism existed in antiquity it was not premised on skin color."[15] Knox's idealizing view of the ancient world, one that rescues it from the infesting "weed" of racism, ignores evidence that the ancient Greeks and Romans did categorize and even rank human beings. It ignores the similarities between the modes of thinking that created these categories and those that inform modern concepts of race. And it plays right into the white nationalists' hands. Because if the ancient world is perceived to be innocent of racism, these ancient ways of categorizing humans can be treated as evidence of ancient wisdom about the true nature of human difference.

Even setting aside Knox's embrace of the white nationalist idea that racial hatred is inevitable in diverse societies, his description of Greek homogeneity is patently false. Ancient literary and artistic sources preserve a myriad of descriptions and representations of diverse peoples. Textbooks of Greek art hardly ever do justice to the diversity of representations of humanity found in these materials, leaving generations of students with the same impression that Knox had about the supposed homogeneity of the Greek world. By contrast, white nationalists point to these sources as evidence that the Greeks believed that variation in human beings was significant. One of their favorite passages is a fragment of the philosopher Xenophanes, who poked fun at the way humans imagine their gods as looking like themselves, noting that Ethiopian gods have dark skin and that those of the Thracians have red hair and blue eyes.[16] There is nothing prejudicial about this quip, but for white nationalists it shows that Greeks paid attention to differences in skin color just as they believe modern people should.

Steve Sailer, a columnist for VDARE who was instrumental in creating an online community of people interested in using genetics to prove the biological reality of race, uses evidence like this to argue against the idea that "race" is an anachronism when applied to the ancient world. Writing in *Taki's Magazine*, whose founder called members of Greece's neo-Nazi Golden Dawn Party "good old-fashioned patriotic Greeks," Sailer observes that ancient sources assume that the further one travels from Greece, the more different people appear.[17] From this, Sailer claims, the Greeks developed a theory of something like a sliding scale of human difference. People within Greece looked one way, the people in neighboring regions looked a little different, the next closest regions a little different from them, and so on. If this seems to be nothing like the modern theories of race that Sailer seeks to validate, it is because, he argues, the Greeks were unable to travel as widely as Europeans of the colonial era did. If they had, he claims, they would have encountered differences that can't be explained as incremental differences from region to region. They would have, he concludes, developed a theory of race as full-blown as that of the modern period because, this line of argument implies, such a concept of race is self-evident to anyone with a view of the full scope of global human difference. Sailer has extrapolated a tremendous amount from simple descriptions of human difference, but his analysis begins with the same assumption of homogeneity in ancient Greece made by Knox.

Ancient Racism by Another Name

But Sailer does not need to invent theories of human difference for the Greeks. They had plenty of their own. Both the logic underlying them and in some cases their specific claims resemble those of modern race-thinking. For example, there is a school of ancient thought known as "environmental determinism," which claimed that climate determined not only people's appearance but their character. The oldest surviving statement of this theory is found in a collection of texts called the "Hippocratic Corpus" because they were associated in antiquity with the name Hippocrates, known to modernity as "the father of medicine." In the text known as *Airs, Waters, Places*, the unknown author advises traveling physicians that the warm and temperate climate of "Asia" (by which he meant what we would now call the Near East) produces people who are both larger and more beautiful in appearance but also "gentler" and "less warlike" compared to people who live in the harsher climate of Europe. Versions of this belief appear in the works of a wide range of ancient thinkers, including Aristotle, the Roman architectural writer Vitruvius, and the geographer Strabo.[18]

The description of the peoples of Asia in *Airs, Waters, Places* will not strike modern ears as prejudicial. But the underlying assumptions are the same as those of modern race-thinking. Both ancient thought, using climate as its cause, and modern thought, using genetics, link physical appearance and character to factors outside an individual's control and then assign them to all members of the group to which those individuals belong. And it did not take long for a theory such as that found in *Airs, Waters, Places* to develop into one that resembles modern racism even more concretely. It is only a short leap from the claim that environment determines appearance and innate qualities to the claim that an observer can predict these innate qualities from someone's appearance. For example, a work known as the *Physiognomy*, which has been attributed to Aristotle but probably dates from the third century BCE, puts special emphasis on the usefulness of skin color and hair texture as a means of predicting a person's character. It argues that people with black skin and curly hair, such as Egyptians and Ethiopians, are cowardly and deceitful.[19]

It is true that this text also claims that pale skin is a sign of effeminacy and that other ancient sources treat black skin as admirable and beautiful, in contrast to the ugliness modern anti-Blackness ascribes to Africans. But this does not mean that anti-Blackness did not exist in antiquity, and we must beware of how denying its existence in antiquity risks minimizing how these ancient theories legitimated those of later theorists of race. Ancient claims about inherent differences between groups were easily translated into pseudoscientific racial hierarchies. Intellectuals in the European Middle Ages used ancient physiognomic thought to produce a dichotomy between a spiritually pure whiteness and sinful Blackness. The French naturalist Georges Cuvier (died 1832), who first divided humanity into "White," "Yellow," and "Black" races, invoked climate as the factor that produced beauty in white skulls and ugliness in those of others. Early theorists of the supposed inferiority of Africans to Europeans, such as David Hume, Voltaire, and Immanuel Kant, all took as their starting point the environmental theories of antiquity, even as genetic claims began to supplant environmental ones.[20]

None of these architects of modern scientific racism felt the need to minimize ancient race-thinking. They positively embraced it. So do contemporary white nationalists, particularly the environmental theories of the Hippocratic corpus and those influenced by it. Richard Lynn, a former professor of psychology in Northern Ireland who served for many years as the editor in chief of *Mankind Quarterly*, an academic journal devoted to publishing racist science, used the pseudonym Hippocrates when writing a regular column on the genetic reality of race for *American Renaissance*. That magazine's editor, writing an obituary for its longtime columnist and conference speaker Samuel T. Francis, who held a PhD in political science and advised Patrick Buchanan's presidential campaigns on his way to becoming one of the leading intellectuals of late twentieth-century white nationalism in America, chose to demonstrate the breadth of Francis's learning by writing, "When I first became acquainted with the Greek historian and geographer Strabo, Sam, of course, knew all about him and why he was important." Strabo, as I noted above, was an exponent of ancient environmental theories of human difference. Writing at a time when the Roman emperors ruled regions stretching from modern Spain to modern Turkey, Strabo wrote that savagery among non-Romans was inevitable because of the effects of their climate. But, he added, Roman conquest could lessen this savagery.[21] It's a way of thinking that simultaneously paints foreigners as inherently and inevitably uncivilized, and justifies violence against them as beneficial. One can hardly imagine a formulation better suited for neofascist politics.

Defending White Racial Consciousness

So white nationalists have some basis for claiming, as a contributor to the *Occidental Observer* did, that the Greeks had "a primitive and unsystematic racial theory." By this they mean not only the theories of human difference described above but the simple fact that ancient writers seem to have developed a basic understanding of the heritability of traits. The same essayist for *American Renaissance* who collected descriptions of white skin in antiquity noted that the Roman historian Tacitus, in a work describing the Germanic tribes who lived beyond the northern boundaries of the Roman Empire, guessed that the people of Caledonia (modern Scotland) must be related to the Germans because they both had red hair. Kevin MacDonald finds evidence that ancient thinkers understood inheritance to encompass more than physical features in the *Odyssey*, when Menelaus praises Odysseus's son Telemachus for speaking in a way that shows he is "of good blood."[22]

Homer, then, understood that children sometimes possess skills and proclivities similar to those of their parents, and Tacitus understood that parents and children usually share physical traits. And a few ancient thinkers, such as Theognis and Plato, translated this understanding into a primitive form of eugenics, citing the example of dog- and horse-breeding as a model for how "better" human beings might be produced. According to Plutarch's biography, the Spartan lawgiver Lycurgus mocked other cities for concerning themselves with the "fine breeding" of animals and not with that of human offspring.[23] White nationalist intellectuals, however, take this limited understanding of heredity to indicate that the ancient Greeks and Romans accepted the reality of race as it is understood in modern race-thinking, trusting that the American public's persistent confusion of ancestry with race will make this interpretation seem plausible. With the fraudulent science and historical arbitrariness of genetic concepts of race increasingly being exposed, white nationalists use evidence like this to claim that their views have long and distinguished intellectual pedigrees.

And if, they argue further, modern historians and scientists have attempted to dismiss this venerable tradition, it is because they are in thrall to the anti-white hostility that white nationalists believe defines the particular degeneracy of modernity. A contributor to AltRight.com wrote that "identity throughout history has much more closely resembled the ancient conception of identity than the postmodern." Ancient thought, on this view, not only recognized the biological reality of race but positively affirmed that the maintenance of racial identity is crucial to civilizational strength. That is, the ancient Greeks understood what the modern white people to whom Richard Spencer addressed his *Who Are We?* video did not: that they are racially distinct from other people in the world and that such racial distinctiveness should be preserved.

A passage from Herodotus's *Histories* is of primary importance to white nationalists who seek to find such "racial consciousness" in the ancient world. Writing about the latter days of the second Persian invasion of Greece at the beginning of the fifth century BCE, Herodotus records that when a Persian envoy attempted to entice the Athenians to submit to Persian rule in exchange for gifts of land and other wealth, the Athenians reassured the Spartans that they would never join forces with the Persians against the Spartans. According to Herodotus, they gave two reasons. First of all, they said, the Persians had recently destroyed the city of Athens. White nationalists have little interest in that aspect of the Athenians' reasoning for refusing to ally with them. They focus instead on the Athenians' second reason for siding with the Spartans. The Greeks, the Athenians replied, constitute "one race speaking one language, with temples to the gods and religious rites in common, and with a common way of life. It would not be good," the Athenians told the Spartans, "for Athens to betray all this shared heritage."[24] According to an essayist at Counter-Currents, in this passage Herodotus has diagnosed the key requirements of a prosperous civilization: in any nation in history "these four elements of identity"—ties of kinship, language, religion, and customs—"are either present or absent, to varying degrees, and a people are correspondingly either strong or weak." The Greeks were strong, this reasoning goes, because they understood that homogeneity, including that of "race," made them so; the modern world, by contrast, with its denial of the reality of race, is weak.

It is unlikely that Herodotus intended this passage to present anything like what the Counter-Currents essayist calls a "comprehensive working definition of national identity." Interpreted in the context of the period in which Herodotus was writing, it seems more likely that he is either contributing to the anti-Persian ideology of Greek unity that developed during and following the Persian Wars or, writing in the run-up to the Peloponnesian War, attempting to mute or mend hostilities between the major Greek states. Yet the white nationalist publications I've cited are hardly the first, or most influential, interpreters to understand this passage as they do. John Quincy Adams clearly had Herodotus's passage in mind when he wrote in a letter to his father, former president John Adams, "The whole continent of North America appears to be destined by Divine Providence to be peopled by one nation, speaking one language, professing one general system of religious and political principles and accustomed to one general tenor of social usage and customs." John Jay cited Herodotus too in the *Federalist*, no. 2, to celebrate the nascent nation's uniformity. More recently, Harvard University's Samuel Huntington wrote that Herodotus gave "classic form" to "the key cultural elements which define a civilization" before claiming a "significant correspondence" between groups of people differentiated by these "cultural characteristics" and groups of people differentiated by race.[25] The traditional understanding of this passage is very much in line with white nationalist thought.

Nor was Herodotus the only ancient writer to differentiate the Greeks and Persians in this way. A contributor to the *Occidental Observer* finds further evidence for Greek racial consciousness in another set of passages about the Persian Wars, this time in Plato's dialogues. In the *Republic*, Socrates argues that war between Greeks should be conducted differently than war between Greeks and "barbarians." Because "Greeks are bonded to one another by internal ties of blood and kinship," Socrates says, they will not do things against other Greeks that they do to "barbarians," such as enslaving them or destroying their fields and homes. And, perhaps most productively of all for the white nationalist search for racial consciousness among the Greeks, in Plato's last dialogue, the *Laws*, a character known as "the Athenian stranger" expresses relief at Greek victory in the Persian Wars in apparently racial terms. "If it hadn't been for the joint determination of the Athenians and the Spartans to resist the slavery that threatened them," Plato has his character say, "we should have by now virtually a complete mixture of the races: Greek with Greek, Greek with barbarian, and barbarian with Greek."[26]

The references in the passages above—all taken from white nationalist publications—appear to suit very well claims that the ancient Greeks recognized and valued their shared racial identity. The language strikes all the right notes: the Greeks are "one race" with "ties of blood" that require them to treat each other more humanely in war, while the Persian Wars threaten a "complete mixture of races." However, a look at the original language that Herodotus and Plato use in these passages shows that these translations retroject the modern confusion of genetics and racial identity onto these passages. The Greek word that Herodotus uses to describe the shared identity of the Greeks is *homaimon*, which means "shared (*hom-*) blood (*aimon*)"; this can only refer to "race" under the modern logic that collapses the concepts of ancestry and race. There is, by contrast, no reference to "blood" in Plato's treatment of warfare between Greeks and barbarians; the Greek words that Plato uses indicate that the Greeks share ancestry (*suggenes*) as members of the same family (*oikos*). The passage from Plato's *Laws* might better be translated as describing the "complete mixture of ancestries" (*gene*). These passages do indicate that shared ancestry was one component of Greek identity in this period, but it is only modern race-thinking that makes shared ancestry the determiner of an entire population's intelligence or morality.

It would be wrong, however, to hold up these passages as evidence of white nationalist distortion of history. They have not produced their own translations with an eye toward importing race-thinking into ancient texts. The translations they quote are from widely available modern versions published by mainstream presses such as Oxford and Penguin. Long before white nationalists quoted them, these translations had already injected modern race-thinking into ancient Greek articulations of identity. Nor can we call this an idiosyncratic quirk (or campaign) on the part of these specific translators: all the major dictionaries for translating ancient Greek into English use the terminology of "race" in defining these and other terms related to birth and ancestry. One might expect this in older works such as Liddell and Scott's *Greek-English Lexicon*, which was first published in 1843 and so unsurprisingly reflects the confusion of race and ancestry prevalent at that time. But scholars compiled and published new dictionaries of ancient Greek in 1995 (in Italian; the English edition was published in 2015) and 2021.[27] Both retain and even extend the language of race for all these terms: whereas Liddell and Scott only use "race" for one specific example of the word that Plato employed to describe the kinship of the Greeks (*suggenes*), the 2015 lexicon defines the word to mean "of the same race, family, or kin." The implication that being a member of a kinship group is equivalent to being the member of a race is precisely the one that white nationalist interpretations of these passages depend on. It's a belief so widespread that it can be found in the fundamental reference works for understanding ancient literature.

Pride in the Past

Classical scholars aren't the only professional researchers who find it hard to think outside the paradigms of modern race pseudoscience. In 2017, *Nature* published an essay on the "genetic origins of the Minoans and Mycenaeans."[28] The authors analyzed DNA recovered from nineteen individuals who died in antiquity and found, they wrote, that the ancient people known to archaeologists as "Minoans" were "genetically similar" to the people known to archaeologists as "Mycenaeans." The relationship of these two groups of people—the first associated with the island of Crete and the enigmatically frescoed palace complexes that have been found there, the latter with the Greek mainland and the historical period that informed the Homeric epics—remains a much debated topic in Bronze Age archaeology and history. The study's findings seemed to link them to each other despite the many differences archaeological research has uncovered. But if it was the study's groundbreaking laboratory techniques that earned it a place in one of the most prestigious scientific journals in the world, it was its second conclusion that earned it widespread media attention. "Modern Greeks resemble the Mycenaeans," wrote the authors, a finding that "support[s] the idea of continuity but not isolation in the history of the populations of the Aegean."

An old prejudice made this new finding provocative. Beginning in the nineteenth century, when western European countries began supporting uprisings against the Ottoman Empire in the territory that is now the modern nation-state of Greece, intellectuals within those same countries began to assert that they had a more direct ancestral link to ancient Greece than the revolutionaries did. Those people, symbolically tainted by the centuries-long domination by the Muslim Ottomans and regarded as culturally and technologically backward in comparison to the rest of Europe, were derided as being more Slavic or Turkish than Greek. Lamenting that "physical beauty, intellectual brilliance, [and] innate harmony and simplicity" could not be found in modern Greece, one critic of the Greek revolution wrote that "not the slightest drop of undiluted Hellenic blood flows in the veins of the Christian population of present-day Greece." Making "dilution" of genetics an explanation for supposed ugliness or stupidity is transparently a racist argument. But the pride reflected in the Greek press at the *Nature* study's apparent refutation of this prejudice—"Greeks are descendants of Mycenaeans" was the headline in the *Greek Reporter*—should be understood as a product of race-thinking as well. This is also why white nationalists embraced the study so enthusiastically. "Ancient Minoans were Europeans," reported the newsletter of the organization that William Pierce founded. Greece's neo-Nazi Golden Dawn political party made explicit the race-thinking that was implicit in other expressions of pride that the article inspired. Their headline trumpeted that "the racial continuity of Greeks for over four thousand years" had been "confirmed."[29]

As with so many of the examples we have considered in this chapter, this is not, or not merely, an example of white nationalists twisting a legitimate finding to suit their political agenda. They rely on the public's belief in the reality of race to assign meanings to findings like this that are congenial to white nationalist politics. And as several archaeologists have pointed out, the study itself, despite the sophistication of its scientific techniques, reproduced outdated and unscientific models of racial identity that made it easier for white nationalists to embrace it as confirmation of the racial distinctiveness of the ancient Greeks and, by extension, the civilization they supposedly created. The *Nature* article assumes, for example, that "Minoan" and "Mycenaean" are a genetically meaningful way of categorizing ancient people, when in fact these terms were invented by eighteenth- and nineteenth-century archaeologists to describe remains found in Crete and the Greek mainland with no ancient evidence that anyone referred to themselves or anyone else by these terms. If DNA evidence suggests genetic similarities between people who were buried in sites designated "Minoan" or "Mycenaean," this points not to the relatedness of two distinct ancient groups but to the unreality of archaeologists' model of categorizing people. More seriously, the authors of the *Nature* study substantiate their findings of genetic continuity with reference to "colorful frescos and pottery" that "depict people with mostly dark hair and eyes." These are the same types of representations of appearance that white nationalists invoke to claim that the ancient Greeks were blond and blue eyed, as if there is anything surprising, as Yannis Hamilakis wrote, "about a few modern individuals living in the Eastern Mediterranean . . . shar[ing] genetic material with a few individuals who lived in the same region in the Bronze Age."[30] Because that's all the study really shows. It doesn't show anything meaningful about the people who lived then, or now, except that those in a very small sample size share genetics that can produce hair and eye color. It is only if we, with white nationalists, regard genetics as a source of shame, or pride, that it can mean anything else.

The commercial application of advances in genetic testing has provided new fuel to the white nationalist belief in the significance of racial identity. The "genetic ancestry testing" industry promotes the belief that genetics are a source of meaningful information, and even pride, about ourselves, because they profit from it. It is now so easy and affordable to submit DNA to be analyzed that tens of millions of people have done so. The marketing of these tests varies from company to company: 23andMe, probably the most well known of them, promotes its testing primarily as a source of information that consumers can use, for example, to evaluate their risk for developing certain forms of cancer or neurological conditions, or that adoptees can use to learn about their birth parents and grandparents. Their largest competitor, AncestryDNA, emphasizes instead how their tests will help users "connect with your people in new ways," referring both to unknown relatives in the present and to those of past generations. Unsurprisingly, white nationalist message boards include lively discussions of how to interpret results that show less-than-desired genetic purity. But even though none of the major testing providers uses the terminology of "race" in their marketing, the widespread assumption among consumers that invented racial categories have a genetic basis means that even if most users do not fetishize "purity," they will nevertheless understand their results in terms of modern racial identities. As the anthropologist Katharine Tyler has documented in a study of mainstream attitudes toward genetic testing, the increasing popularity of such tests "unintentionally supports everyday discourses of race and racism," including, among some people whose attitudes Tyler studied, those that "reproduce racial hierarchies and distinctions that support white power and privilege."[31]

Perhaps the most insidious "everyday discourse" that DNA testing might reinforce among consumers is a belief in the genetic reality of racial identities. A related question, however, is how the promotional materials of services that feature ancestral pride might influence public attitudes toward history. Genomelink, for example, offers an "ancient bloodline DNA report" that promises to reveal "the connection between you and famous ancestors"; MyTrueAncestry offers a "Royalty DNA" test by which "you can determine if you share common male or female ancestors with nobility and some other famous people." Both of these services mention global identities on their websites, but the majority of the imagery they use centers on Europe, and in particular on Greco-Roman antiquity. Genomelink lists "Ancient Greeks" as one type of "famous ancestor" their clients may discover and the button to its "database of hundreds of archaeological DNA samples" is decorated with a classical column and a Spartan military helmet. MyTrueAncestry's logo incorporates the same type of helmet, and it shows on its landing page reenactments of Greek warriors fighting or a toga-clad Roman man pouring wine surrounded by legionary soldiers. On both sites, the possibility of a genetic link to Greco-Roman antiquity is held out as a desirable result. Even MyTrueAncestry's pricing puts a premium on classical origins: whereas the lower-cost tiers have names derived from medieval courts (commoner, footman, knight, and king), the higher tiers in the pricing structure all have classical names: above king are Caesar, Zeus, Olympus, and, at the top of the list, Odyssey. To have a genetic link to the classical world, these tests suggest, is to place oneself in an elite and prestigious group. Like the popular confusion between genetics and race, such admiration for the ancient world is so widespread that most people embrace it without realizing that it is foundational to white nationalist politics. It is not hard to imagine that someone who saw Richard Spencer's video urging white people to feel pride in their classical ancestry might find the promise of scientific proof of it attractive.

The belief in the biological reality of race has profoundly shaped the modern world. To cite only the example of the United States, the White House Council of Economic Advisors reported in 2024 that racial discrimination explains inequalities in employment, access to capital, and the economic well-being of neighborhoods better than any other explanatory factor.[32] Those who accept the biological reality of race, whether they identify as white nationalists or not, are often skeptical that changes in law or policy will rectify this inequality because it derives, on this view, from inalterable human differences and not from discrimination. And for avowed white nationalists, this conviction forms a fundamental part of the interlocking system of beliefs that define their worldview. Such a belief system holds that white heroism is distinct from that which other people might possess. And it holds that a loss of racial purity can only be understood as decline because such a loss entails the disappearance of a unique set of qualities and traits that only white people possess. From these conclusions it is only a short step to the idea that the white race is not only unique but superior.

CHAPTER FIVE

The Prometheans

HEADLINE-GRABBING EXECUTIVE ORDERS were one of the hallmarks of Donald Trump's first presidency: the notorious "Muslim Ban"; his order to construct the wall along the U.S.-Mexico border that he promised during his campaign; an order—later declared unconstitutional—barring federal funding to cities that refused to enforce his administration's immigration policies; a ban on certain kinds of antidiscrimination trainings; and the establishment of the 1776 Commission to promote "patriotic education" via a report that historians described as "a hack job" promulgating "outright lies." The thinly veiled racial politics of these orders goes some way to explaining how much attention they received. But one of the orders that received the most press seems incongruous with the others on this list. This was Executive Order 13967, entitled "Promoting Beautiful Federal Civic Architecture," stipulating that "classical architecture should be the preferred and default architecture for Federal public buildings."[1]

This order was so provocative that it was in the news long before the president signed it in the final days of his presidency. A preliminary version, entitled "Make Federal Buildings Beautiful Again," was leaked to *Architectural Record* in February 2020, prompting a flurry of public statements of condemnation. Most of these objected to the limits this order would place on architecture, arguing that diverse contexts demand diverse architectural styles. A statement from the American Institute of Architects, the profession's largest and oldest organization, noted, too, that Greco-Roman antiquity itself featured a much wider range of architectural styles than the order envisioned. The appeal to historical reality in this latter objection may appear to constitute a definitive critique of the executive order, but it actually confuses the matter because, as an architectural term, "classical" refers less to the way ancient buildings actually looked than to the grand, often columnated, facades that European architects began building in the eighteenth century. More perceptive, historically speaking, were the observers who detected something more sinister in the executive order than a misunderstanding of ancient history or an overly restrictive theory of architecture. Contributors to *Forbes*, *Slate*, and the *Guardian* pointed out that architecture such as that which the executive order promoted was also the preferred style of dictators such as Adolf Hitler and Benito Mussolini.[2] The executive order seemed to confirm what Trump's political opponents had long claimed: that he wanted to establish himself as a dictator. Joe Biden repealed this and several other executive orders on the first day of his presidency, but Trump continued to speak about the subject during his successful campaign for his second term, telling the Conservative Political Action Conference in 2023 that, if reelected, "we will get rid of bad and ugly buildings and return to the magnificent classical style of western civilization." On the first day of his second term as president, Trump issued a new executive order that included "classical architectural heritage" as one way to "uplift and beautify public spaces and ennoble the United States."

One has to wonder, however, whether these orders would have been so provocative if they hadn't come from the desk of a president as controversial as Trump. The objectives the first order sets for federal architecture—that it should be "sturdy," that it should "inspire," and that, above all, it should be "beautiful"—are hard to argue with. Not only that, but most people would probably agree that those terms describe the best-known architectural symbols of the United States, many of which do indeed evoke the classical in their design. Glenn Brown's *History of the United States Capitol*, which influenced the commission that set the planning priorities for Washington, DC, in the twentieth century (including, for example, the placement of the Lincoln Memorial), certainly saw the Capitol Building that way. Noting its imitation of "that most perfect of all buildings, the Parthenon at Athens," Brown praised it for "the charm of simplicity, the beauty of line, the harmony of the parts," which he said were "all subject to established and recognized laws" that constituted what he described as "the common language of architecture the world over."[3] What's not to like?

Trump's apparent admiration for classical architecture is not a peculiarly American phenomenon. The logo of the United Nations Educational, Scientific, and Cultural Organization (UNESCO), which determines what should be designated a "World Heritage Site," is similarly modeled on the Parthenon, with elongated versions of the letters UNESCO standing in for the building's iconic columns. At the unveiling of this logo in 1982, UNESCO general director Amadou-Mahtar M'Bow described the Parthenon as "a fine symbol of the quest for balance and harmony which sums up one of the primary missions of our Organization in regard to relations with nations." This choice of logo thus makes classical architecture representative of anything that is, as the founding convention of UNESCO's World Heritage Program says, of "outstanding universal value" to humanity.[4]

As art historian Lyra Monteiro has shown, classical architecture is every bit as significant a source of inspiration for white nationalists as it was for Glenn Brown or the UNESCO officials who chose the Parthenon for their organization's logo. Take, for example, one of the oldest white nationalist websites in the world, Stormfront.org, which has been online since 1994 and whose "new members introduce yourself" forum has more than eighty thousand posts.[5] Each time you visit the site, it presents you with a new logo. One shows the Wright Brothers' airplane. Another shows the Royal Observatory in Greenwich, England. Two in the rotation feature classical monuments: one shows the Pont du Gard aqueduct, built by the Romans in what is now France, and the other the Parthenon as it appears in a nineteenth-century painting of an idealized classical Athens. Both of these, it so happens, are UNESCO World Heritage Sites.

The placement and annotations of these logos make clear the meaning these symbols carry for white nationalists. These rotating logos always appear alongside another that reads, "White Pride World Wide," and each bears the caption "Every Month Is White History Month." It's a thinly veiled jab at the observance of Black History Month, which, according to Gerald Ford's speech establishing it, "honor[s] the too-often neglected accomplishments of black Americans in every area of endeavor throughout our history." The accomplishments of white people, the administrators of Stormfront all but state, are more extensive than those of any other people. This argument was made more fully in an article published in the *Occidental Observer* dismissing the concept of Black History Month. It listed "the wisdom of ancient Greece" as one of the supposedly innumerable "accomplishments" of white people. Both there and at Stormfront, it is clear, Greco-Roman antiquity stands for the superiority of white people. The prevalence of these attitudes among white nationalists makes it unlikely that they find much to disagree with in UNESCO's ascription of "outstanding universal value" to these monuments. In fact, UNESCO's World Heritage listings read like a declaration of European superiority. Only one hundred sites—about 8 percent—of the listed sites are located in Africa. Italy, France, Spain, and Germany boast more than fifty each.[6]

Making Violence Beautiful

Recognizing that a United Nations agency and a neo-Nazi Web forum invoke the same monument in their logos should prompt a consideration of which political interests the symbol serves. Wikipedia, which, as one of the most visited websites in the world, provides a reasonable indication of mainstream perceptions of its topics, introduces the Parthenon as "an enduring symbol of ancient Greece, democracy, and Western Civilization." As a symbol of democracy, it would not seem to lend itself very well to neofascist politics, but the history of the monument itself tells a more complex story than its popular symbolic meaning suggests. The Parthenon was built to celebrate Athens's role in defeating the Persian Empire's army when it invaded Greece in the early fifth century

BCE. During that invasion the Persians burned Athens and destroyed nearly every building on the Acropolis, as the rocky outcropping at the center of the city is known, including a temple to Athena that was still being built. After the end of the Persian War, the Athenians began building a bigger and more elaborate temple to Athena on the Acropolis, the Parthenon as we know it. The Athenians themselves undoubtedly saw this building as a symbol of their city's resilience and postwar rebirth. It is this symbolism that informs the admiration of architectural historians, UNESCO, and the tourists who travel to Athens from all over the world to see it.

This inspiring narrative leaves out the material and political conditions that enabled the Athenians to undertake such a massive building project in the first place. Despite the destruction of the city, Athens established itself as a dominant power among the Greek city-states after the Persian War, using its naval power to coerce many of them into agreements under which they paid annual tribute to Athens, nominally in exchange for protection from further Persian aggression. But these were no benevolent alliances: when the city of Mytilene revolted, Athens executed a thousand citizens and replaced them with loyal Athenians. The people of Melos fared even worse when they refused to submit to Athenian control: Athens executed or sold everyone in the city into slavery. Historians now recognize this as an "Athenian Empire," the establishment of which was orchestrated by the Athenian general Pericles, the same man who oversaw the financing and construction of the Parthenon. Enslaved prisoners of war provided much of the labor to build the temple, and the materials and paid labor were funded with money raised from the tributes from vassal states, which were eventually even stored within the temple itself. Thus, in addition to its symbolism of rebirth, the Parthenon symbolized imperial power. It symbolized, that is, values we associate with Stormfront—domination and violence—at least as much as it symbolized those we associate with the United Nations.[7]

The classical architecture that graces the capital city of the United States contains both symbolic meanings as well. Conventionally understood, it ennobles the democratic ideals of our nation. But, as the archaeologist Elizabeth Thill wrote following the leak of Trump's executive order, the men who promoted classical architecture in the capital city of the fledgling United States did so not (only) because of its beauty but because of the affinity they felt for the way that the Roman Empire used such architecture. Whenever the Romans erected a temple with columns in a newly conquered region, Thill argued, they were symbolically declaring "This is ours now."[8] It was a message that the government of the newly founded United States found necessary to convey, both in its capital city and throughout all the territory that its colonists would spread across, marking their expansion with classically inspired buildings as they displaced or exterminated those who were living there. Trump's executive order is disturbing not only because it resembles the architectural politics of fascist regimes but because it papers over the imperial dimension already present in our own nation's architectural traditions.

Scholars such as the archaeologist Yannis Hamilakis and the historian Lylaah Bhalerao have called attention to how the Parthenon epitomizes this aspect of nationalist propaganda. By suppressing the imperial values the Parthenon originally symbolized, the elevation of that monument in Greece as a national symbol attempts to purify the history of the Athenian acropolis of any foreign elements that would complicate the story of national continuity with admirable ancient values. Visitors to the Acropolis today will find little reference to the Parthenon's function as a Christian church in late antiquity, still less to its transformation into a mosque when Greece was under Ottoman control. Scores of buildings built by post-classical Greeks and the Ottomans were demolished to "restore" the Acropolis to its classical form. The markers for the burial plots of innumerable Muslims who were buried on the Acropolis, including those killed in the Greek War of Independence, have been cleared away, the graves covered with cement in some cases. The racial politics of such purification are clear: whatever can be designated white and European has been kept, whatever is Asian, Eastern, Islamic, and foreign has been removed, all in the service of creating a symbol of the supposedly "universal values" of democracy.[9]

Seen in this light, UNESCO's use of the Parthenon as a logo begins to look like a similar act of historical amnesia. The "World Heritage Site" citation for the Acropolis makes no reference, for example, to the Islamic history of the site. Meanwhile, the logo at Stormfront, a community that has no objection to the expulsion of Muslims from history or the modern nation-state, looks like the more historically complete appropriation. The classical architecture of our own nation has its own history, of course, but a similar dynamic is at work, both in the way it declares a right to ownership of land that was already inhabited by others and in the contradiction, recognized by African American observers at the time of the construction of the Capitol, between the ideals the architecture is supposed to represent and the state violence from which those ideals distract attention.[10]

If we find classical architecture beautiful, sturdy, inspirational, or reflective of any of the terms found in the executive order, it is because we have been taught to find it so. Taught, that is, by the nationalist propaganda that seeks to replace consciousness of imperial violence with ideals that can be cast as universal, uncontroversial, and apolitical. In this case, the supposed beauty of the architecture—in the ancient world as today—provides a justification for that violence, which is presented as worthwhile if it resulted in the establishment of such lofty and impressive structures. The (supposedly) valuable replaces the valueless. The (allegedly) superior replaces the inferior. Claims of beauty, then, disguise not only violence but declarations of superiority. And when Greco-Roman antiquity provides the symbolic material for such declarations, as it so often does, it disguises a claim of white racial superiority, especially when such claims are being made in mainstream contexts where open racism is taboo. But white nationalist intellectuals see no need to disguise a declaration of white racial superiority. It's one of their core beliefs. Their overt arguments for the superiority of white people so often reveal what is implicit, disguised, or suppressed in mainstream culture. Nowhere is this clearer than in their embrace of Greco-Roman antiquity in support of this belief.

Freedom and Despotism

White nationalists are well aware that numerous ancient Greek sources articulate a sense of Greek superiority over foreigners. This was particularly true in the years after the Greek victory over the invading Persian army. No less a figure than Socrates himself, according to the ancient biographer Diogenes Laertius, declared that he "thanked fortune for three things: 'first that I am a human and not a beast; second that I am a man and not a woman; third that I am a Greek and not a barbarian.'" White nationalists at *Arktos Journal*, the *Occidental Observer*, and AltRight.com quote this passage, which is not an aspect of Socrates that most introductions to Greek philosophy emphasize. But perhaps they should, because it fits well with what we know of ancient Athenian attitudes toward both women and foreigners. The "barbarian" was not simply a non-Greek foreigner but an inferior type of person, marked by cowardice and slavishness. Aristotle provides the fullest statement of this ideology in his *Politics*, writing that "the peoples of Asia are intelligent and skilled but cowardly" and so "are in a perpetual state of subjection and enslavement," while the Greeks "are intelligent and courageous," with the result that they "possess the best political system" and "the ability to rule over others."[11] When paired with the racialization of the Greeks as white, these and other passages concerning the supposed differences between Greeks and "barbarian" Persians provide white nationalists with examples of respected intellectuals who shared their belief in white superiority.

The most extensive ancient description of the Persian Wars is to be found in Herodotus's *Histories*, written around 430 BCE, several decades after the war in a time marked by increasing tensions between city-states that would ultimately metastasize into the Peloponnesian War. Looking back on and possibly seeking to rekindle the sense of pan-Hellenic unity against an external enemy that had prevailed during the Persian Wars, Herodotus attempts at various points in his narrative of those wars to define the nature of Greekness, often (but not always) contrasting this with those qualities he attributes to the Persians. Herodotus's emphasis on these contrasts has made his *Histories* a favorite text for white nationalists.

An illustration of the use to which they put this text is a review in the *Occidental Quarterly* of a new edition of Herodotus published in 2007 and aimed at general readers, *The Landmark Herodotus*. The reviewer was Christopher Moore, who holds a PhD in political science and has been described as "the leading voice of far-right gender politics" for his writings under the pseudonym F. Roger Devlin.[12] Moore praised the edition for the same reasons that reviewers in mainstream venues did: the clarity of its translation and the editor's inclusion on almost every page of maps, timelines, and other annotations to help the reader make sense of what is otherwise a bewilderingly complex work. But Moore also used his review to argue for the importance of Herodotus to the *Occidental Quarterly*'s readers. This importance resides, he suggested, in Herodotus's extensive analysis of the same civilizational dichotomy that Socrates and Aristotle articulated. "Herodotus' great theme," Moore wrote, is "the contrast between Greek and Barbarian, and more particularly the struggle of Greek freedom with Asiatic despotism."

Moore cites several passages from Herodotus to support this interpretation, all of which trade on the supposedly servile nature of Eastern peoples. In one, Herodotus argues that democratic institutions made the Athenians more militarily successful: "The Athenians, while ruled by tyrants, were no better in war than any of the peoples living around them, but once they were rid of tyrants, they became by far the best of all." In another, Herodotus reports that a Persian official expressed surprise to some Spartan envoys that Greek leaders did not choose the stability and prosperity that accepting Persian rule would offer them. The envoys replied to the official that he could think this only because "you know very well how to be a slave but have not yet experienced freedom."[13] For Moore, such passages are why "generations of schoolboys" in Britain, Germany, and the United States "once read the *Histories*:" "to learn who they were—in other words, what it meant to be men of the West." But, Moore worries, the "heritage of freedom" that he believes defines "what Western man has been" is being forgotten under what he describes as a "traitorous leadership [that] consciously abandons our heritage of freedom to a barbarism worse than Persian." With this phrase, the politics that had been implicit in Moore's review become explicit. I understand Moore's reference to the threat of "traitorous leadership" as an allusion to the Great Replacement conspiracy theory based on that theory's similar preoccupation with alleged governmental hostility to the white race. Moore's gesture toward it suggests that he finds in Herodotus's meditations on how "the Greek way was different" an ancient analogue to contemporary white nationalist thinking that not only distinguishes white civilization from those of other peoples but categorizes them hierarchically.

Historians have questioned various aspects of this interpretation of Herodotus and, more generally, of the nature of Greek attitudes toward barbarians. Alongside overt statements of superiority such as Aristotle's, one finds in ancient sources, including within Herodotus's *Histories*, expressions of curiosity and respect as well as extensive evidence for material and cultural exchange between Greece and Persia. This has prompted some scholars to question whether xenophobia was fundamental to Greek attitudes toward Asia. It must be admitted, however, that, whatever these ancient attitudes actually were, Moore's understanding of Herodotus has been the dominant one. J. B. Bury, the Regius professor of modern history at Cambridge for twenty-five years, wrote, like Moore, that "the keynote of the History of Herodotus" was a "contest between the slavery of the barbarian and the liberty of the Greek, between Oriental autocracy and Hellenic constitutionalism." An introductory work on Herodotus published in 1870 translated this "keynote" into white nationalist terms, declaring that the Greek victories in the Persian Wars "indicated for ever the superiority of Europeans over Asiatics." Such readings of Herodotus's *Histories* provided evidence for European superiority that proved useful in justifying various aspects of European colonialism. E. B. Tylor, the first professor of anthropology, cited Herodotus to support his claim that "primitive" cultures should be considered "childlike" in comparison to those of modern Europe: "The modern barbarian represents the ancient." And the "schoolboys" to which Moore refers were not just any children but, in Britain at least, the majority of entrants to the Indian Civil Service, who had studied classical languages and literatures, including Herodotus, at Oxford on their way to careers as agents of imperial domination.[14]

You don't have to go back to the nineteenth century, however, to find Herodotus being read in this way. The Cornell historian Barry Strauss, like Moore, reviewed *The Landmark Herodotus* and highlighted the same themes. The first line of his review was "Herodotus is the historian of freedom." Another ancient historian, Donald Kagan of Yale University, in a series of lectures available on

YouTube, cites Herodotus's explanation for Athens' military success as evidence of the value of this freedom, just as Moore did. The same passage is of central importance in the analysis of classical scholar and Hoover Institution fellow Victor Davis Hanson in his 2001 book *Carnage and Culture*, which surveys "landmark battles in the rise of Western Power." So too is the other passage Moore used, in which the Spartans differentiate themselves from the Persians, who, the Spartans claim, know only how to be slaves. And UCLA political scientist Anthony Pagden, who uses Herodotus in his 2008 book *Worlds at War* to argue that conflict between Europe and Asia is eternal and inevitable, seems to be thinking of this passage when he writes that the difference between the Greeks' and Persians' "understanding of what it means to be human and to live like a human being" was that the Greeks "could all distinguish freedom from slavery." Whether or not these analyses reflect Herodotus's view of the Persian Wars—Pagden's quotation of Herodotus's description of "perpetual enmity" between East and West comes from a published translation whose interpretation of the original Greek few other translators have shared—it is plain that the Aristotelian distinction between Greek freedom and Asiatic servility continues to shape perceptions of this period. Kagan's lectures have been viewed three quarters of a million times. Hanson was awarded the National Humanities Medal by President George W. Bush in 2007. Both Hanson and Pagden have written political commentaries for many major newspapers.[15]

Part of the reason this way of interpreting Herodotus and the Persian Wars has proven so durable is its stark dichotomy, inherited from Aristotle, between Greek freedom and Asiatic slavery. Who would seriously take the side of tyranny against freedom? But just as the terminology of architectural "beauty" sanitizes the imperial violence that classicizing architecture represents, celebrations of Greek freedom overlook a more complex, and less appealing, history. Many people are aware, of course, that freedom, even in the city-state of Athens that is so often cited as democracy's birthplace, was partial and exclusive. If we are to consider it the defining characteristic of the Greek worldview, then that worldview must also be said to sanction the exclusion from its supposed benefits of women, anyone who lived in Athens but was born elsewhere, and the enslaved. But more fundamentally, Greek thinkers articulated the notion of freedom itself primarily in relation to oppressive hierarchies. Orlando Patterson has argued that "freedom" emerged as a political concept only to serve the desire of the citizenry to mark itself as different from, and superior to, those they enslaved. And Kurt Raaflaub has shown that discourses of freedom gained currency in Greece only in the aftermath of the Persian Wars, when Greeks felt a parallel desire to differentiate themselves from the defeated Persians.[16] That is, freedom had no meaning without slavery and xenophobia, and its prominence in Greek thought is an index of the pervasiveness of both. Seen in this light, the ancient Greek conceptualization of freedom does not work very well for those who wish to celebrate the supposedly universal value of the political traditions of the modern "West" by giving it an ancient pedigree. But for white nationalists, who believe that hierarchy and xenophobia are essential elements of a successful state, it's precisely the tradition they need.

Kagan, Hanson, and Pagden studiously avoid the language of race or overt statements of European supremacy. In fact, Moore, in a review essay for the *Occidental Quarterly*, has condemned Hanson in particular for this avoidance. Even so, the belief in the superiority of those who enjoy freedom over those who do not, a belief fundamental to Greek conceptions of freedom, finds its way into scholarship of this type. The philosopher Hegel's remark that "never in history has the superiority of spiritual power over material bulk . . . been made so gloriously manifest" as at the battle of Salamis, where the Athenian navy defeated the Persians, is not just an artifact of the nineteenth century but the epigraph to Hanson's chapter on the battle in *Carnage and Culture*. And even if Hanson does not overtly claim superiority for anything European except the "superior discipline" that freedom is supposed to have afforded the Greeks, one can sense in his conclusion his conviction of the superiority of the Greek worldview over that of Persia. "Without a free Greek mainland," he writes, "the unique culture of the polis would have been lost, and with that ruin the values of a nascent Western civilization itself."[17]

Such assumptions of superiority are one of the primary ways that celebrations of Western civilization, as Charles Weller has argued, "coincide historically with and have much in common" with white nationalist politics. Both, Weller asserts, make an "implicit, even if unintended connection between white civilization and Western civilization." This link is anything but "implicit" in white nationalist publications: "Western civilization is white civilization" ran a headline in *American Renaissance* when Iowa congressman Steve King was in the news for wondering: "White nationalist, white supremacist, Western civilization—how did that language become offensive?" But even professional scholars can sometimes blur the line between the phenomena Weller describes. Bruce Thornton, whose book *Greek Ways: How the Greeks Created Western Civilization* illustrates his investment in the concept, wrote an essay entitled "Free Citizens Do Not Kneel" for the journal of the David Horowitz Freedom Center, where he was a fellow in 2020 and whose founder has been described as "a driving force of the anti-Muslim, anti-immigrant and anti-black movements" by the Southern Poverty Law Center. Thornton criticizes those who knelt in protest of the murder of George Floyd, quoting the same passage from Herodotus that Moore cited, in which the Spartan envoys who praised liberty to the Persian official refused to kneel before the Persian king Xerxes "since it was not their custom to prostrate themselves before any human being."[18] Describing demonstrations by the overwhelmingly peaceful Black Lives Matter movement as "violent coercion," Thornton calls the "ritual of public kneeling" in acknowledgment of police violence and systemic racism "a surrender to tyranny," just as, he argues, "Herodotus showed 2,500 years ago." The racial politics of this formulation are barely concealed; indeed, they are clear enough that *American Renaissance* reprinted the essay on its own site, likely finding attractive its implication that any recognition of human rights for Black Americans constitutes an example of the kind of threat to "the very foundation of citizen self-rule and political freedom" that concerns Thornton. On this interpretation, however, Thornton's essay not only acknowledges but endorses what many celebrations of these alleged values of Western civilization leave out, that in most places conventionally described as "the West," state-sanctioned violence against some members of our communities has been, and continues to be, permissible. And if this exclusive version of freedom falls short of the idealized version that proponents of Western civilization celebrate, it can at least be said to reproduce the exclusions and violence of the ancient world that they argue gave birth to it.

Dynamism and Stagnation

The terminology of Western civilization that Thornton and many others have used to assign special value to the Greco-Roman world performs a rhetorical function similar to the language of beauty in the executive order with which this chapter began. The term is used to celebrate a set of ideas that are supposed to be characteristic of "the West," and that are supposed to have originated in ancient Greece. Thornton's enumeration of these in *Greek Ways* includes "science and technology," of which his examples are "antibiotics and advanced weaponry," as well as "the powerful ideas of individual autonomy and human rights." These are the gifts, the argument goes, of the ancient Greeks, via the people who have lived in the regions that are now designated "the West" and who have developed the intellectual traditions whose central components were pioneered by the ancient Greeks, to all of humanity. On the surface, Thornton's account of the benefits Greece has conferred upon the modern world is convincing. Few people would willingly choose to live in a world without antibiotics, for example. But this narrative grossly simplifies the history of human progress, ignoring, for example, that the German scientist Paul Ehrlich developed antibiotics in collaboration with the Japanese bacteriologist Sahachiro Hata. And the suppression of such connections outside Europe in favor of a Eurocentric view of history is only the tip of the iceberg when it comes to the more complex and less flattering history that this terminology suppresses.[19]

The historical narrative outlined above explains global European economic, military, and cultural dominance as the result of cultural factors (primarily derived from that other purificatory value, freedom) that are allegedly inherent to the "Western" identity. It's a story that has been complicated in various ways. Most of the achievements attributed to Western civilization are better understood as incorporating philosophical and technological elements from a diverse range of cultures and regions. Emphasizing the benefits to humanity of the work of European intellectuals minimizes both the colonial violence for which those same intellectuals often developed sophisticated justifications and the degree to which the wealth—both material and intellectual—of Europe is derived from resources acquired through that violence. It has even been suggested that the modern preeminence of Europe, the United States, and the rest of "the West" has nothing to do with the culture of the people living there but is the result primarily of a lucky coincidence of geographical and environmental factors. These critiques of the category of Western civilization as it is usually meant reveal both how much it leaves out, and how that distortion of historical complexity supports a claim of European superiority that very often is indistinguishable from a claim of white racial superiority.[20]

The entanglement between this white nationalist idea and mainstream celebrations of Western civilization finds explicit expression in the work of Ricardo Duchesne, a former professor of sociology at the University of New Brunswick. In 2011, one of the oldest academic presses in the world, Brill, published a 527-page book by Duchesne entitled *The Uniqueness of Western Civilization*. The publisher made no effort to conceal the politics of the book's argument, promoting it on their webpage as a study of "the roots of the West's superior intellectual and artistic creativity." Following its publication, Duchesne became a regular fixture in white nationalist venues, attracting the attention of journalists and prompting more than one hundred of his colleagues at the University of New Brunswick to sign an open letter in 2019 condemning his "views about multiculturalism and immigration as racist and without academic merit." Duchesne took early retirement and published his next book at Arktos, began speaking regularly at the *American Renaissance* annual conference, and contributed book reviews to the *Occidental Quarterly*, while the *Occidental Observer* and Counter-Currents reprinted essays written for his personal website. His recent work includes the introduction to a reprint of a nineteenth-century translation of Homer's *Iliad* for a publisher that specializes in works by historical figures associated with the development of fascism, such as the French political theorist Georges Sorel, and more recent neofascist activists such as Jonathan Bowden.[21]

Duchesne sounds very much like a mainstream proponent of Western civilization when he praises the Greeks in an essay at

Counter-Currents for the "discovery of logos . . . [and] dialectical reason, the invention of prose, tragedy, citizen politics, and face-to-face infantry battle." But it is not the superficial similarities like these that make Duchesne's work an illustration of how such discourses frequently overlap with the white nationalist belief in white superiority. Rather, the intellectual tradition he documents illustrates this entanglement, of which his own views are nothing more than a symptom.

For example, Duchesne's explanation of European superiority repackages nineteenth-century racist science that is now discredited but that played a central role in European colonialism. "I trace the uniqueness of the West," he writes for Counter-Currents, "back to the aristocratic warlike culture of Indo-European speakers as early as the fourth millennium." Duchesne is referring to a group of prehistoric, horse-riding nomads known as the "Proto-Indo-Europeans." Similarities in vocabulary and structure among most of the languages spoken in modern Europe, from Iceland to Russia, indicate that those languages are all derived from the language that these people spoke.[22] Almost as soon as these similarities were recognized and systematically studied in the eighteenth century, these Proto-Indo-Europeans were celebrated as the ancestors of white Europeans and claimed, because their language spread across so much of the world, to represent the origin of the supposedly unique dynamism of Europeans.

This claim of racial ancestry is easily refuted. Most egregiously, it requires that the language a person uses be an indicator of their racial identity, which is an invented category anyway. Furthermore, many of the ancient languages of peoples that European colonialism rarely found convenient to racialize as white, particularly in Persia and India, are also related to Proto-Indo-European. But as Léon Poliakov has shown, this racialization of the Proto-Indo-Europeans as white provided justification for the formation of the European nation-states along ethnic lines, served to justify colonial projects outside of Europe, and, most notoriously, formed the basis of Nazi race science. Duchesne simply represents the latest iteration of this influential way of thinking about European prehistory. Nor is he alone: the academic *Journal of Indo-European Studies* was published, until his death in 2023, by Roger Pearson, a white nationalist anthropologist who received funding from the Pioneer Fund and collaborated with notorious racists such as Willis Carto, best known as the founder of the Holocaust-denying Institute for Historical Review.[23]

The importance Duchesne assigns to the Greeks in the development of the supposed dynamism of the Proto-Indo-Europeans draws on a similarly popular and influential way of viewing ancient history. This holds that so many people speak languages descended from Proto-Indo-European because their ancestors were forced to adopt this language when the Proto-Indo-Europeans conquered them. There are other, less violent, ways that languages can spread: intermarriage and cultural exchange are no less "dynamic" than conquest. But white nationalists remain committed to the image of the Indo-Europeans as violent raiders because it casts colonial domination as a desirable racial trait. "There is a beautiful creativity in European expansionism," said Duchesne in an interview with the *Occidental Observer*.[24]

Nevertheless, Duchesne sees white European superiority as encompassing much more than martial valor, and this is where he turns from the Proto-Indo-Europeans to the Greeks. Duchesne writes in *The Uniqueness of Western Civilization* that it was the Greeks who "sublimate[d]" the "excessive, disorganized, and 'barbaric' impulses" that Duchesne believes characterized the Proto-Indo-Europeans into what he calls, in an essay for Counter-Currents, the "civilized creativity" of the Greeks. "The restlessness of barbarian individuals was the primordial source of all that has been noble and great in Western civilization," he writes in a later section of his book, arguing that the Greek achievement of "self-mastery over their willful nature . . . created the 'Greek Miracle.'" Here Duchesne invokes a term for celebrating the supposedly unprecedented philosophical, scientific, and aesthetic accomplishments of the Greeks that was first employed by the French intellectual Ernst Renan (1823–92). Renan is remembered not only as an influential theorist of national identity but also as a major figure in the history of European antisemitism, whose confidence in the superiority of the "Aryan race" informed much of his scholarship.[25] Knowingly or not, all invocations of this "Greek Miracle," including, for example, the 1992 exhibition using that name that collected "Classical Sculpture from the Dawn of Democracy" in the National Gallery of Art in Washington, DC, participate in the same narrative of European exceptionalism.

Duchesne can cite numerous classical scholars who have contributed to this narrative. These include, for example, Werner Jaeger and Bruno Snell, who were both prominent intellectuals in the middle of the twentieth century. Jaeger, who began his career in Germany but moved to Harvard amid the rise of Nazism, wrote that "the cultural development of Greece ennobled the whole human race by offering it a program for a higher form of life." Snell's *Discovery of the Mind: The Greek Origins of European Thought* argued that no other segment of humanity had experienced consciousness before the ancient Greeks "discovered" it; as a foundational text for psychologist Julian Jaynes's *Origins of Consciousness in the Breakdown of the Bicameral Mind*, published in 1976 and nominated for a National Book Award, Snell's book became one of the twentieth century's most influential works of classical scholarship.[26] Few scholars nowadays read or cite Jaeger or Snell, but this way of characterizing the Greeks as uniquely innovative, creative, or foundational persists. Duchesne published a review on Counter-Currents of several recent books with titles that reflect this orientation: *The Beginnings of Philosophy in Greece; Speech and the Coming of Wisdom in Ancient Greece; The Founders of Western Thought: The Presocratics.* None of these books make white supremacist claims, but the rhetoric of their titles serves to remind us just how persistent this way of valuing the ancient world is, at least in the marketing of the significance of the ancient past.

To read Duchesne is to glimpse the breadth of the tradition of using the ancient Greeks to demonstrate the supposedly superior creativity of white Europeans. But even Duchesne's survey understates this pervasiveness, because classical symbolism has been used to promote this idea far beyond academic circles. Tomislav Sunić, who holds a PhD in political science and sits on the board of the American Freedom Party with Kevin MacDonald and James Edwards, the host of a white nationalist radio show and podcast, wrote in the *Occidental Observer* that Prometheus, the mythological figure who gave humans control of fire after stealing it from Zeus, is "the prime symbol of the White man's irresistible drive toward the unknown, toward the truth." Goethe, Shelley, and Bacon all made Prometheus a symbol of human potential during the European Enlightenment, a period marked, to use Sylvia Wynter's term, by a "Janus-faced contradiction" between the articulation of ideals such as equality and human rights within Europe and the ruthless colonization and enslavement of the rest of the world.[27]

Seen in that light, Prometheus might himself be recognized as a sanitizing symbol of European violence and alleged superiority. So too might the sculpture of Prometheus in New York City's Rockefeller Plaza, located as it is in an architectural complex that features a mural by Lee Lawrie (*The Story of Mankind*) that "chronicles mankind's progress." This is no politically neutral space: a mural by the Mexican artist Diego Rivera was removed from the center in 1934 because it presented a less idealized view of modern capitalism (as well as an unflattering portrayal of the Rockefeller family). But identifying the racial implications of the popularity of the Prometheus myth does not require subtle investigation: Henry Luce, the editor of *Time Magazine*, told the Commonwealth Club of San Francisco in 1965 that "the myth of Prometheus" is "the one story which perhaps better than any other illustrates the profound difference in the soul of the East and of the West."[28] It's the same Orientalist trope of Greek dynamism over Eastern stagnation that we found in Aristotle, as fundamental to the editor of a major news periodical as it is to Sunić or Duchesne.

Ranking the Past

The popularity of Duchesne's work on the "uniqueness" of the Greeks in white nationalist circles is symptomatic of the way admiration for the Greeks has long been entangled with claims of white superiority. Well outside the boundaries of organized white nationalism, praise for the supposedly unique qualities of the Greeks—the beauty of their art, the freedom of their culture, the rationality of their worldview—has, historically speaking, encoded praise for the supposedly unique qualities of white people. The public perception that ancient Greece produced the best of human thought is so deeply entrenched that it rears its head, as a series of reviews by Katherine Blouin shows, even in textbooks published with the express purpose of providing an introduction to the ancient world that goes beyond the traditional focus on Greece and Rome.[29] So it is only to be expected that white nationalists would harness this perception to claim that white superiority is a fact of nature. Central to this argument is the use of lofty ideals like beauty, freedom, or creativity to erase the violence and hierarchy of the ancient world. If ancient Athens is idealized as a vital and creative society of free citizens producing art and philosophy, then its apparent dynamism confers innocence on the modern hegemony of Europe. If the art and political ideals are understood to be embedded in violent systems of oppression, then we have a clearer picture of the human and moral price of that hegemony.

Belief in ancient Greek exceptionalism is remarkably durable, making the racial politics it often implies equally so. In 2016, several data scientists at MIT announced a new database that would "help you explore the geography and dynamics of the most memorable people in our planet's history." This database would rank these "memorable people" by analyzing the prominence of more than eleven thousand historical figures on Wikipedia. The more often a name appeared, the higher that figure would rise in the rankings. They gave the project a classical name: Pantheon.[30]

Even though the project's architects attempted to control for bias, such as by giving extra weight to biographies written in languages other than English, this classically named database produced an overwhelmingly classical list. The most memorable person on Pantheon's initial list was Aristotle, whose articulation of Greek superiority lies at the root of so much of the material discussed in this chapter. He was followed by Plato, with Socrates, Alexander of Macedon, Homer, and Pythagoras all within the top ten. The Roman general Julius Caesar was eighth. The Italian scientist Leonardo da Vinci was the only figure born within the last two thousand years, and Jesus (number 3) and the Chinese philosopher Confucius (number 7) were the only non-Europeans in the top ten.

This initial publication attracted the attention of the Council of Conservative Citizens (CCC), the white nationalist organization whose newsletter Samuel T. Francis edited until his death and whose publications were among those that were cited as inspirations by the terrorist who murdered nine Black people during a

Bible study at a church in Charleston, South Carolina, in 2015.[31] The brief report that the CCC published left it to its readers to reach their own conclusions about the significance of the list, but the Daily Stormer reprinted the report with the headline "White Males Dominate List of Culturally Significant Figures Determined by MIT Study." "This proves," Andrew Anglin wrote in his commentary, "that races of other people should really be more appreciative of what White men have contributed to the world."

Pantheon illustrates the pervasiveness of Greek and, by extension, European exceptionalism outside of overtly white nationalist circles. Classical figures are more prominent in Wikipedia pages in twenty-five languages, so they rise to the top of the list. And since Pantheon considers how often a page is viewed in establishing its rankings, we can infer that classical figures receive more attention from visitors to Wikipedia as well. Why should this be? The lopsidedness of this list is a product of Wikipedia's well-documented biases in coverage, emphasis, and representation, which are nearly inevitable in a source in which the vast majority of articles are written and edited by white people and only a tiny minority of articles—in any language—are devoted to subjects unconnected to European history. Pantheon's lists merely reproduce these biases. As Pantheon has incorporated more data and refined its algorithms, its rankings have diversified somewhat: Muhammad has taken the top place in the rankings from Aristotle, who is now sixth. But they remain overwhelmingly Eurocentric because the data upon which the database is built are overwhelmingly Eurocentric.[32]

Pantheon's innovation is in the scale of its analysis, not in its methodology. Ranking historical figures by reference to their prominence in historical writing has a long and sordid history, going back to the beginnings of modern eugenic thought. In the original publication of Pantheon's methods and findings in the *Nature* journal *Scientific Data*, the authors validate Pantheon's initial findings by noting the high correlation between their findings and those of an earlier analog study that used print encyclopedias and other historical surveys to measure the "significance" of artists and scientists. This was the 2003 book *Human Accomplishment*. Its author, Charles Murray, achieved notoriety for his earlier book *The Bell Curve*, which argued that public policy should take into account racially based differences in intelligence, citing research on the topic published by contributors to the white supremacist journal *Mankind Quarterly*. Both books are, unsurprisingly, favorites in white nationalist circles. Murray himself, when asked by an interviewer who is a staff writer at VDARE to name the single most significant figure in human history, chose Aristotle, the same ancient thinker who topped the original Pantheon list.[33]

But Murray himself, and by extension Pantheon, have simply continued a line of argumentation developed by Francis Galton, who coined the term *eugenics* and who is recognized as a major figure in the development of scientific racism. In 1869, Galton published his book *Hereditary Genius*, which argued, among other things, that the ancient Greeks constituted "the ablest race of whom history bears record" and that "of the various Greek subraces, that of Attica"—that is, of the area in which Athens is located—"was the ablest." Galton's praise for Athens was, however, inseparable from his contempt for Black people: the "average ability of the Athenian race," Galton wrote, was "very nearly two grades higher than our own—that is, about as much as our race is above that of the African Negro."[34]

Galton reached this conclusion following much the same method as that employed by Murray or Pantheon's engineers: consultation of biased sources. The supposed genius of the Athenians, he wrote, can be "easily gauged by a glance at the contents of a railway book-stall," while his evidence of the supposed inferiority of Africans includes the claim that "it is seldom that we hear of a white traveler meeting with a black chief whom he feels to be the better man." One wonders what conclusions Galton would have reached had he weighed equally the assessment of these travelers by those "chiefs," whose perspectives he had not, however, taken the time to collect on any of his several trips to Africa. At any rate Galton's book appeared at a time when arguments for European superiority found ready audiences: diamonds had recently been discovered in South Africa, and only the year before its publication hundreds of African Americans were murdered without legal consequences in three separate massacres.[35]

When most people hear the term *white supremacist* they imagine a skinhead, someone dressed up in a Nazi uniform or, possibly, a young white man plotting one of the many mass shootings that the United States has experienced in recent years.[36] These are, to be sure, the most visible exponents of the idea that white people are superior to all others. The promotion of this belief by biographies in encyclopedias, a data science project at MIT, and UNESCO's World Heritage Site listings is much less obvious, and therefore much more insidious. And even these represent only the tip of the iceberg of how this belief is continually rearticulated and promoted in mainstream media.

An example of how popular treatments of ancient history bring theories of white superiority to mass audiences is the 2022 Netflix series *Ancient Apocalypse*. In this show, the journalist Graham Hancock repeats a theory that he has been promoting for thirty years: that there was a sophisticated human civilization on Earth that was forgotten after it was destroyed by a cataclysmic flood in prehistoric times. This idea is not, of course, new to Hancock, but can be traced back to Greek antiquity and Plato's description of a powerful island civilization that disappeared beneath the sea: Atlantis. Plato almost certainly invented this lost island, but Hancock treats Plato's story, along with other flood myths from around the world, as evidence for his own theory. This and most of the other arguments Hancock has made about human prehistory throughout his thirty-year career have been extensively and repeatedly debunked by archaeologists, but this has done little to diminish their appeal. Hancock is, after all, only the latest author who has attempted to capitalize on the popularity of the story of Atlantis, which already in 1978 was estimated to be the subject of more than twenty thousand books.[37]

This idea may seem to be nothing more than harmless quackery, but the assumption of white superiority lurks at its core. For at least the past 150 years, the civilization that Atlantis is supposed to have represented has been racialized as white, making the sophisticated technologies that Hancock claims this civilization developed—among them agriculture and monumental architecture—the invention of white people and not, as overwhelming evidence indicates, the inventions and discoveries of non-Europeans from around the world. This, at any rate, is how Atlantis figured into the work of the American congressman Ignatius Donnelly, who first popularized the Atlantis myth in his 1882 book *Atlantis: The Antediluvian World.* And this is why Nazi occultists made Atlantis into what the historian of Nazism Eric Kurlander has described as a "prehistoric source of divine, possibly extra-terrestrial, racial and spiritual perfection." As the archaeologist Flint Dibble has documented, Hancock's most popular book contains several references to the whiteness of the lost civilization he is attempting to recover.[38]

No such language appears in *Ancient Apocalypse*, and when Hancock learned that an American neo-Nazi had described his work as "a good way of introducing people to white superiority," he issued a statement condemning "any kind of racial supremacism." But whether or not Hancock intends to advance white supremacist understandings of history, indigenous leaders and archaeologists argue that shows like *Ancient Apocalypse* nevertheless do. When *Ancient Apocalypse*'s production company announced plans to film an episode in the Grand Canyon, tribal groups who have lived in that region for two millennia protested the way "[Hancock] presents his theories as being superior to what the first inhabitants of the area say about their own history" (the episode was not filmed). And following the show's release in 2022, the Society for American Archaeology issued a statement requesting that Netflix categorize Hancock's show as "science fiction," arguing that "Hancock's narrative emboldens extreme voices that misrepresent archaeological knowledge in order to spread false historical narratives that are overtly misogynistic, chauvinistic, racist, and anti-Semitic."[39]

The popularity of Hancock's work—his book has sold millions of copies and has been translated into twenty-seven languages—illustrates that you don't have to read white nationalist publications to encounter narratives that align with white supremacist understandings of history. They're right there on our streaming services. *Ancient Apocalypse* was among the most popular shows on Netflix when it aired. A second season ratchets up the star power of the show, featuring the Hollywood star Keanu Reeves in conversation with Hancock. The History Channel's *Ancient Aliens* is a similarly pseudoscientific show—produced, incidentally, by Prometheus Entertainment—that has been so popular it has been renewed for twenty seasons; in 2023 it released an episode entitled "The Gods of Greece." Crackpot theories that extraterrestrial beings built the pyramids or taught the Maya astronomy amount to the same thing as fantasies about Atlantis: an attempt to minimize or deny the architectural, scientific, and cultural achievements of non-Europeans.[40]

White nationalist intellectuals recognize that the seeds of belief in the superiority of white people continue to be planted in American culture, in both serious analyses of world history and kooky fantasies of alien influence. So they do not need to create new theories of white superiority; they only need to reassure their audiences that such a belief is natural and respectable. For this, they turn to ancient Greece, which is nothing if not respectable. Large numbers of people have learned to assign a white racial identity to the ancient Greeks. Even more have learned to associate attractive qualities like freedom, beauty, and creativity with Greek culture. As long as those two perceptions of ancient Greece are widespread, they can be combined to suggest not only that white people are superior but that they always have been.

CHAPTER SIX

The (Un)Natural Order

A YOUNG MAN STANDS holding a shield. Emblazoned on its front is an image of rods bundled around an ax. It's an enduring symbol of ancient Rome known as the *fasces.* He is not alone. Around him are other young men wearing the same uniform, carrying the same shields. They are in formation. They begin to march.

This may sound like a maneuver of a Roman legion, but this is not a scene from ancient history. The shields are handmade of cardboard. No ancient shields bore such insignia. The "uniform" these men wear is a white polo shirt. The year is 2017, and they are marching in the Unite the Right rally in Charlottesville, Virginia. Many Americans first learned about the movement calling itself the Alt-Right from media coverage of this rally, where demonstrators chanted slogans such as "Jews will not replace us." One of the men carrying a shield decorated with the *fasces* later drove his car into a group of counterprotestors, injuring many of them and killing Heather Heyer.[1]

These Roman-inspired shields were only one of several elements of classical symbolism at the rally. The promotional poster for the event featured the abbreviation S.P.Q.R., which stands for "The Senate and People of Rome" in Latin (*Senatus Populusque Romanus*) and is commonly understood as a symbol of the Roman

Empire. One of the headline speakers had legally changed his name to Augustus Sol Invictus, taking inspiration from the first Roman emperor and the deity of a religious cult ("the unconquered sun") associated with Roman imperial power.[2] Mr. Invictus, as he was called in the press, was arrested in 2020 on charges of kidnapping and domestic violence, but in 2017 he represented a new breed of American politician whose Roman name conveyed his inclination to neofascism.

The term *fascism* is derived from the symbolism of the *fasces* that appeared on the demonstrators' shields. At a rally that aimed to "unite" anti-government, neo-Nazi, and nationalist groups, such symbolism may seem apt, given that it is commonly understood to represent unity: the rods are stronger together than individually. In fact, the *fasces* only acquired this meaning in the Renaissance. In Roman times, the *fasces* were carried by the attendants of certain magistrates and symbolized the power of that magistrate to inflict violence upon his subjects. It's thus an ideal symbol for a political movement that claims to advocate unity but that actually seeks to formalize a racial hierarchy in which white men dominate all others. No surprise, then, that the Anti-Defamation League has documented at least five white nationalist groups that have incorporated the *fasces* into their logos.[3]

With the symbolism of the *fasces* comes admiration for the Roman Empire as a neofascist model. Richard Spencer, one of the organizers of the Charlottesville rally, had called for a "White Ethno-state on the North American continent" at the 2013 *American Renaissance* conference. He described his vision as "a reconstitution of the Roman Empire," striking a similar note to that of Benito Mussolini, who had made the Roman Empire the model for the autocratic and militarily powerful fascist state he envisioned for Italy. Such comparisons suggest that the scale, longevity, and antiquity of Rome demonstrate the naturalness and desirability of the principles that fascists and neofascists find in it. These include the notion that violent masculinity should be nurtured and encouraged, or the alleged right of the "civilized" to dominate or exterminate the "barbarian." Here, however, I consider the white nationalist insistence on the desirability of a related idea: hierarchy, in which the few enjoy greater wealth and power than the many.[4]

Charlottesville was well chosen as a venue to affirm this white nationalist belief. The city council there had recently proposed removing a statue of the Confederate general Robert E. Lee from a public park, and the Unite the Right rally was as much about protesting that proposal as it was about the political future of white nationalism in America. The commemoration of the past is intertwined, of course, with that vision for the future, because many white nationalists look back nostalgically on the Confederate States of America as a model for the hierarchical, white supremacist social order they would like to see renewed in the United States at large.

Nostalgia for the Confederacy has always required idealizing, minimizing, or ignoring the centrality of mass enslavement to its economy, politics, and identity. Defenses of Confederate memorials, for example, often appeal to "heritage" and "tradition" to mask what is being commemorated and celebrated.[5] White nationalist nostalgia for the Confederacy employs such idealizing language as well, often in connection with the symbolism of Greco-Roman antiquity. A contributor to Counter-Currents wrote that the Jackson and Lee monument in Baltimore, Maryland, evoked a "Hellenic" feeling of "the time of kings and heroes, before the rise of democratic communities like Athens, when monumental architecture is of single heroes, who will be incorporated in later collective monuments, like the Parthenon." That monument was removed just days following the Charlottesville rally. The link that such elegiac rhetoric creates between memorials to Confederate leaders and soldiers and ancient monuments to "kings and heroes" is little more than vague nostalgia for both: the essayist may have in mind archaic Greek sculptures of muscular naked youths (known in Greek as *kouroi*), some of which celebrated victories in athletic competitions. Other commentators, however, make more explicit claims concerning the desirability of the politics that the Confederacy represented: "The South," wrote another contributor to Counter-Currents, "was a North American manifestation of ancient Greece and Rome" and "represented a continuation of the Classical worldview that was based upon tradition, hierarchy, and ordered inequality." The removal of Confederate monuments, this essayist warns, amounts to the destruction of this putatively valuable inheritance, including its insistence on the naturalness of hierarchy.

The presence of classical symbolism at the Charlottesville rally illustrates how the work of white nationalist intellectuals such as that published by Counter-Currents informs the actions of violent white nationalist activists in the real world. So too do the activities of the terrorist who murdered nine African Americans in their church in Charleston, South Carolina, in 2015, an act that, more than any other, spurred many city councils and state legislatures to begin considering the removal of the very Confederate monuments the Charlottesville demonstrators sought to preserve. His act of mass murder had this effect because his admiration for the Confederacy was so clear from the photographs he posted with his online manifesto. One he took of himself with the Confederate flag garnered the most media attention. But as Lyra Monteiro has noted, classical symbolism recurred in his documentation of his tour of sites relating to Confederate history. The neoclassical columns and facades of the plantation houses he visited were, she argues, every bit as legible to him as symbols of white supremacy as the Confederate flag itself. So too, Monteiro argues, was the celebrated neoclassical architecture of the University of Virginia selected by Richard Spencer and his co-organizers as the backdrop for the Unite the Right rally.[6]

Contemporary white nationalists did not invent the link between Greco-Roman antiquity and the Confederacy, which encompasses much more than the preferred architectural style of wealthy enslavers. John C. Calhoun and numerous other Southern politicians who rallied around states' rights as a defense of their slave economies looked to the city-states of ancient Greece as proof that a civilization could prosper without a centralized government. Basil Gildersleeve, the most influential American classical scholar of the nineteenth century, wrote voluminously—first in pro-Confederate publications like the *Richmond Examiner* but later in venues such as the *Atlantic Monthly*—about his experiences growing up in the South and fighting in the Confederate army. He used analogies to Greco-Roman antiquity to idealize the South and to minimize the importance of slavery in the Civil War. He cast that conflict as "our Peloponnesian War," likening the Confederacy to Athens in its noble struggle, as he understood it, against the Spartans to preserve their freedom.[7] In this analogy, a kind of classical version of the "lost cause" rhetoric so common in celebrations of the Confederacy, it was the Union that sought to impose political slavery on the white people of the South.

Classical symbolism similarly attended many of the monuments that were erected in the decades following the Confederate defeat. The speech given at the 1913 dedication of the North Carolina monument portraying a Confederate soldier who is popularly known as Silent Sam (now in storage after being toppled by protestors in 2018) began with a reference to the Trojan War and compared the mothers of Confederate soldiers to the mythological figure Niobe; the Confederate memorial in Arlington National Cemetery (removed in 2023) featured a quote—consonant again with Confederate "lost cause" narratives—from the Latin epic poet Lucan describing the suicide of Cato the Younger when he realized he could not win his war against the avengers of Julius Caesar's assassination. The full-scale replica of the Parthenon in Nashville, Tennessee, may seem simply to illustrate America's fascination with the Greco-Roman world, but in fact stands as a monument to the Confederacy's self-identification with ancient Athens. It was this link that prompted Identity Evropa, the white nationalist organization that terrorized college campuses with posters featuring classical sculpture, to announce its 2018 Leading Our People Forward conference on its steps.[8]

There is, in fact, an entire subculture of white nationalists, known to observers as the "neo-Confederate" movement, that has made idealization of the Confederacy central to its politics. Greco-Roman antiquity has played a key role in its growth: one of this movement's premier organizations, the League of the South, was founded in 1994 by a group of intellectuals including Thomas Fleming, who holds a PhD in classics. Fleming left the League of the South board sometime before 2002, but over his long career devoted his energies both to opposing the integration of schools and to promoting, as editor of the paleoconservative magazine *Chronicles*, educational programs involving "Greek and Latin classics" that could produce the kind of "aggressively virile" citizens that he believes have characterized "all healthy and successful cultures." Shortly after the formation of the League of the South, Fleming and several other founding members published the "New

Dixie Manifesto" in the *Washington Post.* Their president, Michael Hill, was found guilty of civil conspiracy for his involvement in the Charlottesville rally, but at the time of the publication of the "New Dixie Manifesto" in 1995 he was respectable enough to be interviewed on National Public Radio. In that interview, he said the same thing about the culture of the Confederacy as the contributor to Counter-Currents would more than twenty years later: "The South has always preferred a natural hierarchy."[9]

Hierarchy in Ancient Political Practice and Thought

Hierarchy defined the social and political order in ancient Greece at least as much as it did in the antebellum American South. Slavery is the most obvious evidence for this similarity, even after allowing for significant differences between the two, the most important being that white Americans almost exclusively enslaved black Africans and African Americans, whereas any prisoner of war in ancient Greece, no matter where they were from or what they looked like, could be enslaved. But there is a fundamental similarity in the degree to which mass enslavement of foreign-born people (and then their children) was integral to the economic and political lives of both the early United States and the Greek (and Roman) world, particularly in the famous and most admired city-states of Athens and Sparta. Nor should the considerable variation between the modes of enslavement practiced in different cities in antiquity—in Sparta, for example, a class of people called Helots, who performed agricultural labor for the ruling Spartiate citizen class, have been described by some scholars as serfs rather than slaves—disguise the pervasiveness of the institution. The legal status and living conditions endured by the Helots show that they were slaves, even if their relatively unsupervised lives in the countryside appear different, on the surface, from those of the laborers enslaved in the Athenian silver mines.[10] The hierarchy of free and enslaved defined ancient societies, making them a powerful touchstone for those who wished to maintain such hierarchies in the modern era.

Unlike in the United States, where abolitionist activism predates the foundation of the nation itself, we know of no meaningful opposition to slavery in antiquity. Aristotle notoriously argued in his *Politics* that "it is manifest that there are cases of people of whom some are free and the others slaves by nature, and for these slavery is an institution both expedient and just." And the distinction between free and enslaved people was just the most obvious marker of status in this highly hierarchical world. In Athens, for example—the supposed "birthplace of democracy"—Deborah Kamen has identified no fewer than ten gradations of social and political status that Athenian legal practice demarcated. Among the people these structures sorted into more and less politically powerful groups were the *metics*, or resident noncitizens, who were subject to laws not dissimilar from those that white nationalists envision for their racially pure ethnostates. The *metics* were subject to special taxes and legal restrictions in order to reside in Athens and had no means of ever becoming citizens.[11] If one wishes to find distinguished historical parallels for the slave economy of the American Confederacy, ancient Greece is an excellent place to look.

White nationalists who admire the Confederacy do not generally spell this out explicitly. This is partly because they recognize that calls for the restoration of slavery will alienate rather than entice potential adherents to their belief system. A contributor to the *Occidental Observer* notes that "in the age of automation the enslavement of foreigners is particularly unnecessary," but argues that ancient slavery still illustrates "the important point of principle" that "better people" should rule. White nationalists also regard any importation of foreign-born people as a threat to the racial purity of their society. Slavery in both antiquity and American history, they argue, drove race-mixing and racial degeneration.[12] So they do not put much energy into sanitizing ancient slavery in order to legitimize their hierarchical politics.

Nor do they need to. There are so many other passages in ancient political thought that are almost ready-made to be used in support of a hierarchical view of humanity. Aristotle's theory of natural slavery is only one facet of his preoccupation with the naturalness of hierarchy. His *Politics* also makes the claim that "the relation of the male to female is naturally that of the superior to the inferior" alongside other less provocative but equally hierarchical declarations. These include an argument that "it is natural and beneficial to the affective [that is, emotional] part of the soul that it should be ruled by the reason and the rational part" and a comparison between the relationship of a ruler to his subjects and "paternal rule over children."[13] These latter passages are quoted in the *Occidental Observer* to argue that hierarchical states are "grounded in human biology."

The work of Aristotle's teacher, Plato, also abounds in declarations of the desirability and naturalness of hierarchy. The centrality of hierarchy to Platonic thought has been noted by the philosopher's detractors and admirers alike. In the aftermath of the Second World War, Karl Popper's *The Open Society and Its Enemies* (1945) identified Platonic philosophy as a precursor to twentieth-century fascism. In the early days of the American "culture wars" of the 1980s and '90s, Allan Bloom turned to Plato in his *Closing of the American Mind* (1987) as a remedy for what he saw as the creeping relativism of American culture, writing that "no one thinks a man like Socrates should be ruled by inferiors or have to adjust what he thinks of them."[14] Plato is thus a crucial thinker for white nationalists who seek to promote the naturalness of hierarchy and inequality.

The list of passages in Plato that lend themselves to this interpretation is long even if we confine ourselves to those quoted explicitly by white nationalist intellectuals. Plato's famous dialogue *The Republic* is of primary importance, as is a less well-known work, his *Laws*, in which a character known as "the Athenian stranger" lists the different justifications for one group to rule over another. These include parents over children, those of "high birth" over those of "low birth," elders over the young, enslavers over the enslaved, the strong over the weak, and—what the character describes as "the most important claim"—the "wise" over the "ignorant." Plato's character quotes the lyric poet Pindar describing the rule of the strong over the weak as a "decree of nature," thereby hammering home the argument that the political categories included in this list are every bit as natural as those implied by parenthood, age, and physical strength. True justice, the same character argues later in the dialogue, "consists of granting the 'equality' that unequals deserve to get."[15]

These ancient philosophical texts do not just promote hierarchy, they criticize democracy, and in particular the democratic belief in the equality of all human beings. In a passage from Plato's

Republic that receives extensive quotation in an essay at the *Occidental Observer*, Socrates derides such a political system as "giv[ing] equality to equals and unequals alike." Among the political principles that democracy "tramples," according to Socrates, are that subjects should obey rulers, sons should respect fathers, students should fear teachers, and the young should respect elders. These hierarchical arrangements may strike some readers as reasonable, perhaps even desirable, but Socrates ranks their erosion as a threat to social order comparable to what he calls "the high-water mark of mass-freedom," "when those who have been bought as slaves . . . are every bit as free as those who bought them." Almost as an afterthought Socrates adds that democracy also disregards the natural hierarchy of men over women, likening the freedom that he claims women enjoy under democracy to that of livestock and dogs that are allowed to wander outside their pens.[16] Socrates, in the *Republic*, hits all the points a neofascist social theorist might emphasize.

And if anyone is surprised to find this critique of democratic equality articulated by Socrates, a figure conventionally associated with such admirable qualities as truth-seeking, truth-telling, and rigorous self-examination, this is because that is the image of Socrates that Plato created in his dialogues, which is anything but an accurate portrayal of the historical figure himself. Evidence for the life of Socrates from outside of Plato's works suggests, by contrast, that the Athenians executed Socrates in 399 BCE not, as Plato has it, as an act of tyrannical censorship, but because of Socrates' personal and ideological connection to the recently ousted junta that had ruled Athens as an oligarchy following the Peloponnesian War. Led by Socrates' student (and Plato's relative) Critias, these oligarchs confiscated prominent citizens' property and oversaw the executions of many more. This history shows that when the preface to David Duke's autobiography compares Duke to Socrates as a "seeker of truth" and a "shifter of paradigms," the comparison is not quite as outrageous as the author—a Florida State University professor of genetics—likely intended it to be.[17]

Aristotle is not as strident a critic of democracy as Plato. The regime he endorses in the *Politics* incorporates a mixture of aristocratic and popular elements. But even this recommendation assumes a hierarchical structure because Aristotle accepts without question the narrow definitions of citizenship that prevailed in most Greek city-states, limiting civic rights to property-owning men and excluding women and foreigners. Indeed, Aristotle's political theory holds that the ideal political regime is one that best serves the interests of the entire citizen body—but then defines the citizen body so narrowly that hardly anyone qualifies. This presents a difficulty for scholars seeking to understand how Aristotle's political theory might inform modern liberal democracies, but it presents no difficulty to white nationalists. Greg Johnson, who holds a PhD in philosophy and is editor in chief at Counter-Currents, for example, has written that Aristotle "would probably take a dim view" of American democracy as a result of "the extension of the vote to women, non-property owners, and cultural aliens" and "would predict that multiculturalism and non-white immigration will destroy the cultural preconditions of popular government." This sounds just like the kind of thing one would find in a white nationalist journal like Johnson's, except that Johnson didn't originally publish it at Counter-Currents. It's from an essay he contributed to a book on libertarian philosophy that was edited by Tibor Machan, a professor at Auburn University, and published by Stanford's Hoover Institution.[18]

It is, of course, possible to complicate the white nationalist interpretations of Aristotle and Plato in various ways. When white nationalists quote Aristotle saying that justice "does mean equality—but equality for those who are equal, and not for all," they ignore the fact that Aristotle is not endorsing this view but summarizing someone else's theory of equality.[19] In the case of Plato, the philosopher's choice of dramatic dialogues as his medium means that we cannot always distinguish which arguments Plato's characters make from those he himself accepts. However, these interpretive interventions do not change the fact that ideas highly congenial to the white nationalist belief in the naturalness of hierarchy have obtained respect and legitimacy by appearing in the works of two of the most respected and influential philosophers in history.

Legitimizing Hierarchy

Aristotle's respectability made his theory of natural slavery a favorite source of justification for those who sought to defend the enslavement of Africans in the United States. The popular perception of ancient Greece and Rome as admirable civilizations provided further legitimacy for slavery, as its defenders could look to the slaveholding societies of the ancient world to argue, for example, that "this high civilization and domestic slavery did not merely coexist, they were cause and effect." This perspective justifies slavery for the leisure it provided to enslavers to pursue philosophy and literature, including, perversely, the development of philosophical doctrines to justify that very enslavement. Such arguments are not common today, although in 2020 the U.S. senator from Arkansas Tom Cotton appeared to accept the idea that slavery, as he put it, was "the necessary evil upon which the [United States] was built." Cotton's remark came as part of a rejection of the idea that slavery and its legacy are of central importance in understanding American history. Something parallel can be observed in the desire of some classical scholars to discount the centrality of slavery to ancient societies, claiming that particular focus on Greco-Roman slavery is unwarranted because slavery existed in nearly all premodern societies.[20] *American Renaissance*'s editor Jared Taylor has made the same argument, which ignores that it was Greco-Roman slavery, not those systems found in other places and times, that provided the most potent justifications for its modern form. The violence of Greco-Roman slavery must be exposed and condemned with particular force because the idealization of it has extended that violence into the modern era.

The history of eugenics provides a parallel case of ancient material legitimizing violent hierarchical thought. Practices that seek to control what kinds of people are allowed to live and who is allowed to reproduce are the inevitable product of a belief in human hierarchy. In Plato's *Republic*, Socrates recommends that "sex should preferably take place between men and women who are outstandingly good, and should occur as little as possible between men and women of a vastly inferior stamp." He further suggests that "the children of inferior parents, or any deformed specimen born to [better parents], will be removed from sight into some secret and hidden place, as is right." Aristotle, too, wrote that "there should certainly be a law to prevent the rearing of deformed children," and Plutarch reports that in Sparta, "ill-born and deformed" babies were thrown into a chasm "in the conviction that the life of that which nature had not well equipped at the very beginning for health and strength, was of no advantage either to itself or the state." A character in Plato's *Laws* even extends eugenic violence beyond infanticide, arguing that "to purge the state drastically" is "the best way." His example is that "when there is a shortage of food," the "underprivileged . . . are to be regarded as a disease that has developed in the body politic."[21]

Debby Sneed has shown that infanticide was nowhere near as common in Sparta or anywhere in the ancient world as these sources imply, but this has not prevented these sources from being cited to give the murder of infants and other eugenic practices a distinguished intellectual pedigree. Already in 1813, Thomas Jefferson wrote to John Adams to say that a certain passage from the Greek lyric poet Theognis describing the breeding of horses would, if applied to humans, "produce a race of veritable *aristoi*" (the ancient Greek word for "the best people" and the root of English "aristocracy"). But it was in the early twentieth century that eugenics enjoyed widespread popularity and scientific legitimacy, especially in Britain and the United States, and the approval of persons as notable as President Theodore Roosevelt and the feminist Margaret Sanger.[22]

Influential eugenicists who looked to Greco-Roman antiquity for inspiration, such as Francis Galton and Madison Grant, have already appeared in this book. To these we may add the Cambridge University professor Ronald Fisher, who has been described as "a genius who almost single-handedly created the foundations for modern statistical science." Fisher devoted the latter portion of his *Genetical Theory of Natural Selection* (1930) to "The Decay of Civilizations," which attempted to explain the "decadence" of ancient Greece and Rome in eugenic terms. This includes a section in which Fisher uses Greco-Roman antiquity to negate any moral objections to infanticide. Fisher claims that if ancient thinkers after Plato and Aristotle became more hostile to the idea of infanticide, this was the result not of any moral objections but simply because infanticide itself removes from the gene pool those whose heredity makes them most inclined to practice infanticide, creating, over time, a population less likely to endorse it. Fisher himself does not openly promote infanticide in this section of his work, but his attempt to diminish the authority of moral objections tends in that direction. Fisher was active in American circles as well. When Charles Darwin's son Leonard was too infirm to travel to New York City to deliver an address to the Third International Congress of Eugenics held at the American Museum of Natural History in 1932, Fisher delivered it for him. Darwin's "message" warned that without "wide-spread Eugenic measures," "Western civilization" would succumb to the same "slow and gradual decay" as "every great ancient civilization."[23]

Fisher cites Gibbon's *Decline and Fall of the Roman Empire* as his source for ancient history in *Genetical Theory of Natural Selection*, but eugenicists in general were aided in linking their theories with celebrated classical thinkers by a book by an Oxford University fellow entitled *Ancient Eugenics*. Ancient theorists of eugenics such as Plato and Aristotle, the author argued, "realized many of the problems which, 2,000 years later, are still confronting Eugenists [*sic*], and they realized in part the remedies." The book won a literary prize in 1913, and has been reprinted on many white nationalist websites. Meanwhile, it was not only within the academy that eugenic principles and Greco-Roman antiquity were linked: the Panama-Pacific International Exposition held in San Francisco in 1915 to celebrate the completion of the Panama Canal featured a booth hosted by the Race Betterment Foundation that used images of classical and classicizing sculptures "to advertise," according to the official history of the exposition, "the human race at its best, and get that race interested in its glorious past and possible future." More than 18 million people visited the exposition.[24]

Hierarchy Today

It may be tempting to assume that the hierarchical systems Greco-Roman antiquity has been used to justify are things of the past: slavery was abolished in the United States in 1862 and the Eugenics Records Office in Cold Spring Harbor, New York, the most active eugenics research institute in the United States, was closed in 1939. This assumption is wrong.

There are still millions of people whose labor is unfree, including victims of sex and organ trafficking, a subset of agricultural laborers (including in the United States), and those in debt bondage in various industries around the world. Whether or not we describe these people as "slaves," they exist at the bottom of a brutal and dehumanizing economic hierarchy. As an organ trafficker in Bangladesh told one researcher, "Some people are worth less. That is the reality of our world." Many people believe this violence is the work of a limited number of evil cartels, but as the sociologist Julia O'Connell Davidson has argued in her critique of the rhetoric of "modern slavery," exploitation of human labor is in fact an integral component of neoliberal capitalism and an inevitable byproduct of restrictive immigration and border-control policies. When such violence is embedded in the central ideologies of modernity there is little need to turn to history, ancient or otherwise, to justify it. Nevertheless, Greco-Roman antiquity has continued to play a role in minimizing the dehumanizing violence of slavery. "Happy Slave" narratives are common in introductory Latin textbooks. Conventions for high school students studying Latin featured mock slave auctions as fundraisers as recently as 2018.[25]

Eugenic practices, too, have persisted, most notably the forced sterilization of women by governmental organizations, primarily poor women and women of color. A 2015 survey of examples published by the *Annual Review of Genomics and Human Genetics* documented examples of forced sterilization not only in the heyday of eugenics before the Second World War but throughout the twentieth century and even into the twenty-first. In the United States a chapter of the Human Betterment League fostered sterilizations in Iowa in the 1940s and '50s, and the Indian Health Service sterilized Native American women throughout the 1960s and '70s. California has a particularly grim history, having allowed involuntary sterilization of Latinx women in California prisons between 2006 and 2010. But eugenic thought persists out in the open as well. Disability rights activists argue, for example, that "Quality Adjusted Life Years," a common metric used to set healthcare policy and expenditure priorities, places a lower value on the lives of people with disabilities than on those of people without. And prominent technology moguls such as Elon Musk and Peter Thiel have invested heavily in "human enhancement." This multibillion-dollar industry began as a speculative exercise at the intersection of philosophy, science fiction, and computer science known as "transhumanism." Many of the principles of this movement are hardly distinguishable from those advocated by eugenicists of past ages, and some of its leading thinkers have quoted Plato and Aristotle in support of their theories.[26]

One reason why the assumption that some people are superior or worth more than others continues to inform our social, economic, and political systems is that so many well-known and respected political thinkers embraced ideas about the naturalness and desirability of hierarchy. White nationalist intellectuals have only to point to this tradition to claim a distinguished pedigree for their promotion of hierarchy. One of their favorite accounts of this intellectual tradition is the book *Nobilitas: A Study of European Aristocratic Philosophy from Ancient Greece to the Early Twentieth Century* (2001), published by a respected academic press, the University Press of America (now Rowman and Littlefield) and written by Alexander Jacob, who earned a PhD from Penn State University with a dissertation directed by three philosophers, a classical scholar, and a professor of energy science. Many of the political thinkers Jacob identifies as advocates of hierarchy—Jean Bodin, Joseph de Maistre, Johann Gottlieb Fichte, Arthur Schopenhauer, Thomas Carlyle, and Heinrich von Treitschke—either cited Platonic or Aristotelian thought as an inspiration for their views, or promoted views that Jacob likens to those of Plato. Jacob's political investments are evident in his introduction, where he complains that "the democratic system of America . . . has dulled the national psyche to such an extent that it has lost almost all of its racial character and the spiritual power that that represents," and from the prominence he gives to any and all elements of antisemitism in the work of the thinkers he profiles. Jacob went on to contribute book reviews to several white nationalist publications and to translate works of influential European antisemites into English for Arktos and other white nationalist presses.[27]

Jacob's focus is European "aristocratic thought," but the framers of the U.S. Constitution drew on the same Platonic and Aristotelian political theories to ensure that, despite the Declaration of Independence's insistence that "all men are created equal," hierarchy would prevail as the dominant political structure in their new nation. Attractive slogans such as "with liberty and justice for all" tend to obscure the hierarchical elitism that informed the so-called "founding fathers" of the United States, but white nationalist historians see this current in American political thought, and its grounding in classical texts, very clearly. They are fond of quoting, for example, the pamphlets that have been collected as *The Federalist*, written by Alexander Hamilton, James Madison, and John Jay to advocate for ratification of the Constitution of the United States. Several of these argue against the sharing of political power too broadly, including the claim that "had every Athenian citizen been a Socrates, every Athenian assembly would still have been a mob."[28]

White nationalists can find much to admire in the framers' desire to distribute political power unevenly. The original Constitution institutionalized political hierarchy by establishing property qualifications for voting and by giving state legislatures, not the people, the power to elect senators. This was done to protect the wealth of landowners against what James Madison called a "leveling spirit" among the general population that might otherwise lead to land redistribution. And although the framers declared that hereditary aristocracies would have no place in their new nation, Jefferson argued that such hierarchies should be replaced not with true equality but with what he called a "natural aristocracy," an idea he may have derived from Plato's enthusiasm for the rule of the wise. That a man who insisted on the innate and inescapable inferiority of Africans would harbor such a theory should not surprise us; what is perhaps less well known is that Jefferson founded the University of Virginia as the final stage of an educational system that would produce this aristocracy by distinguishing the people he described as "the best geniuses" from "the rubbish"—yet another way that the classical architecture of that university provided an ideal backdrop to the Charlottesville rally.[29]

Such symbolism is not confined to the University of Virginia campus. The same image of the *fasces* that appeared on the shields at Charlottesville graces many prominent American civic monuments and buildings. I have already noted that the common interpretation of the *fasces* as a symbol of unity exists alongside its original, more hierarchical, meaning of the magistrate's power to inflict violence on those he governs. Perhaps the artists who first deployed the *fasces* in commemorating George Washington, or the architects who adopted it for projects such as the U.S. Capitol, had the first meaning in mind. But the adoption of this symbol by nativist political parties shows that the original meaning always lurked just below the surface. *Fasces* appeared in the campaign materials of the xenophobic Know Nothing Party in 1856, for example, and those of the Constitutional Union Party of 1860, which was complicit in the defense of slavery by remaining neutral on the issue. Party leaders may have claimed that the symbol represented "unity," but there is evidence that its association with violence was legible to observers as well: when a sculpture that incorporated both the *fasces* and a "freedman's cap" was proposed for the recently expanded U.S. Capitol in 1854, then secretary of war Jefferson Davis, the cabinet member overseeing the project, rejected the proposal. Certainly the freedman's cap, which in antiquity was worn by emancipated slaves, would have struck the man who would later become the president of the Confederacy as an unacceptable endorsement of the cause of abolition, but his stated objection to the design was that the *fasces*, with their endorsement of state violence against citizens, was unacceptable for the nation's capitol. Claiming that *fasces* represent "unity" has always been a sanitization of its true meaning.[30]

Nor did Mussolini's adoption of the symbol diminish American enthusiasm for it. *Fasces* were incorporated into the designs of eight federal structures that were built during the period of Mussolini's fascist dictatorship in Italy, including the U.S. Supreme Court building and the National Archives. Martin Luther King delivered the "I Have a Dream" speech flanked by three-meter-high *fasces* on the faces of the stones framing the steps of the Lincoln Memorial.[31] That stark juxtaposition foretold just how resistant our society would prove to be to the egalitarian message of that day.

Fifty years after King's movement won federal protection for voting rights, the U.S. Supreme Court removed key provisions of those protections amid the development and deployment of voter suppression tactics analogous to those that were employed against Black people in the Jim Crow South. Many decry this as an erosion of democratic institutions, but white nationalists likely see this as a reversion to the founding principles of the nation. Writing for *Arktos Journal*, someone using the classical pseudonym John Q. Publius contrasted the "founding fathers'" vision for America—one informed, he writes, by Plato's critique of democracy and the later historian Polybius's application of that critique to Rome—and its modern form. "The degradation of the Republic," he writes, "has coincided with the extension of the franchise." As the anti-fascist journalist Shane Burley has written, fascism and American democracy are not as antithetical as our national myths would lead most people to believe. Rather, "Fascism grows out of and reinforces authoritarian tendencies and systems of oppression that are deeply rooted in our society."[32] Hierarchical, inegalitarian political principles from ancient sources were central influences on the founding of our nation. The fact that ancient authors are not cited by the current architects of the restoration of those principles does not mean the nation is not returning to them.

It may be more accurate to say we never abandoned them. Many Americans don't want equality. They want hierarchy. They just don't say it as openly as white nationalists do. Overwhelming evidence indicates that success in America depends on inherited wealth and elite social connections, but survey after survey shows that Americans—especially white Americans and, perhaps surprisingly, especially white American women, believe that success depends more on hard work and intelligence. This "myth of meritocracy," as economists and sociologists have labeled it, is promoted in American schools, in American workplaces, and in American media, especially reality TV competitions that mythologize the "best" rising to the top. Faith in meritocracy—a word that first entered the English language as a satire of eugenics—carries with it an inverse belief that lack of success is an indicator of a lack of work ethic or intelligence. As the Marxist critic Raymond Williams put it, meritocracy "sweetens the poison of hierarchy," thereby justifying the many inequalities that plague American society: inequalities in wealth, in income, in employment, in access to housing, in access to healthcare, in access to food. And because these inequalities disproportionately affect people of color, the myth of meritocracy makes not just class hierarchies but racist ones seem natural and inevitable. Isabel Wilkerson has argued that racism in the

United States is best understood not as a matter of difference but of hierarchy.[33]

When these hierarchies are so deeply engrained in the social and political life of a nation, the authority of antiquity is hardly needed to legitimize them. And yet, search online for the phrase "the worst form of inequality is to make unequal things equal" and you will find hundreds of memes, discussions on message boards, lists of famous quotations, and even custom T-shirt designs that attribute that line to Aristotle. It doesn't, in fact, appear anywhere in his work, but as we have seen, it's an idea that Aristotle certainly could have expressed.[34] But that's how popular the belief in the naturalness of hierarchy is. We'll even make up ancient quotes to justify it.

There is no need, of course, to resort to spurious quotations if you want to link Greek antiquity to the idea that hierarchy is natural. Plenty of the authors surveyed here imply—or even say—as much. That's why it's hard to find examples of white nationalist intellectuals quoting this made-up quotation (although Ricardo Duchesne included it for a time on the front page of his personal website). They don't need to quote made-up material when they have so much authentic material to work with, much of it in the work of some of the most influential and admired thinkers in history. All they need to do to build their movement is to remind Americans who are already resistant to any policy that might decrease hierarchy and inequality that such resistance has an ancient pedigree.

CHAPTER SEVEN

The Dream of a White Homeland

IMAGINE A POLITICIAN WHO has made opposition to immigration central to his brand. He becomes famous—some would say notorious—for saying things about immigrants that (his supporters claim) many people think but are too afraid to say. His provocative forthrightness on this topic makes him an outsider in his own political party but, paired with his arguments that his nation should reduce its dependence on foreign economies, wins him support from the working class. His opponents worry that his proclamations give xenophobia mainstream respectability and embolden violent extremists.

Is the politician you're picturing also a prodigy of a classical scholar who was compared to Demosthenes for the rhetorical power and sophistication of his political speeches? I didn't think so. But the paragraph above describes Enoch Powell, who at age twenty-five became the youngest professor of ancient Greek in the British Empire before beginning a career in government as a member of Parliament and minister for health that would last for almost forty years. He is best known for a speech he delivered in 1968 to Conservative Party supporters in Birmingham, England, in which he criticized an act that had recently been proposed in Parliament to outlaw racial discrimination in housing, employment, and public services. Powell called the protections of the proposed act "the very pabulum" that "dangerous and divisive elements . . . need to flourish." The "elements" he had in mind were immigrants who, he argued, bring with them violence to Britain. To illustrate this, he recounted a story he claimed an anonymous elderly constituent had told him about being "abused" by Black people in neighborhoods that had, according to Powell, become "place[s] of noise and confusion" as a result of immigration. He concluded the speech by citing a line from Virgil's epic poem *The Aeneid* to describe the violence that he claimed immigration would bring to Britain: "As I look ahead, I am filled with foreboding: like the Roman, I seem to see 'the River Tiber foaming with much blood.'" This incendiary speech, which prompted the Conservative Party's leader to dismiss Powell from his cabinet, quickly became known by this vivid quotation as the "Rivers of Blood" speech.[1]

Except for a flurry of comparisons with Donald Trump during the run-up to the 2016 presidential election, Enoch Powell is not a familiar figure to most Americans. But he remains a hero to white nationalists. Counter-Currents commemorates his birthday every year. Richard Spencer's *Radix* ran an occasional series entitled "Like the Roman" (after Powell's introduction of his quotation from Virgil) reporting on what Spencer considers "positive events," such as a large white nationalist rally in Austria where demonstrators flew flags emblazoned with a symbol meant to represent the shields Spartan warriors carried into battle. The "Classics Corner" in the inaugural issue of the *Occidental Quarterly* featured a transcript of the "Rivers of Blood" speech. White nationalist intellectuals recognize in Powell evidence that one of their core beliefs deserves a place in mainstream politics: that diversity and difference inevitably produce violence.[2]

The resemblance between Powell's "prophetic" warning "of the dangers of massive non-white immigration," as Counter-Currents describes it, and similar articulations by contemporary white nationalist thought leaders is striking. In an essay that became one of the foundational documents for the Alt-Right, the author and video-game designer who uses the pseudonym Vox Day (in imitation of the Latin phrase *Vox Dei*, "voice of God") wrote, "Proximity

+ diversity = war."[3] And the French white nationalist Guillaume Faye, in the last book he completed before his death in 2019, predicted an "Ethnic Apocalypse" in Europe that immigration by Muslims to Europe had made, he argued, all but inevitable. This "civil war with a racial dimension," Faye says, between groups "who should never have been made to live together," will present "a deadly conflict between populations that remain at odds with one another on all levels, whether ethnically, culturally, or religiously."

Classical Greece and the Ideal of Sameness

Powell's quotation of Virgil is undoubtedly memorable, but it does not support his point very well. The line he quoted does come from a prophecy that links human migration and violence. But the immigrants in question are not objects of fear and hatred. They are the heroes of the poem: Aeneas and his men, who have fled the destruction of Troy and come to Italy. Their arrival does indeed lead to violence, as they wage war with the indigenous inhabitants, paving the way for their descendants to found the Roman Empire in accordance with the dictates of Jupiter and fate, at least as these are represented in the poem. Aeneas and his men look more like violent colonizers than the people vilified in Powell's speech, most of whom were themselves descendants of people colonized by the British Empire over the previous century.

Faye, too, turns to Greco-Roman antiquity to support his claim that diversity produces violence. But the sources Faye cites support his case more unambiguously than Powell's did. For example, Faye points to Aristotle for the idea that "the peaceful and economically viable coexistence of ethnically different populations in a single territory is generally impossible." Faye is referring to a passage in the *Politics* in which the philosopher gives many historical examples to illustrate that "difference of race is a cause of faction"—that is, civic discord. These include instances in which, Aristotle claims, a "native" population admitted but then later expelled outsiders (in the cases of Sybaris, Byzantium, and Antissa) and instances in which outsiders joined and then expelled or exterminated the previous citizenry (Thurii, Zancle, and Amphipolis).[4] The limits of our evidence for the histories of these colonies often make it difficult or impossible to verify or refute Aristotle's version of events. But even if we question the veracity of his claims, Aristotle makes a powerful rhetorical ally for Faye. Both of them simplify complex political situations by turning to xenophobic logic.

The political context in which Aristotle formulated his theories undoubtedly influenced them. He begins the *Politics* with the famous declaration "Man is by nature a political animal," by which he asserts that the most "natural" way for humans to live together is in the type of community known in ancient Greek as the *polis*. This word, from which *political* is derived and which is conventionally translated as "city-state," describes the relatively compact and independent communities governed by enfranchised citizens that characterized the political life of classical Greece. Athens and Sparta are the best known *poleis*, but more than a thousand have been identified across the Greek-speaking world of antiquity. Those who seek to form racially pure "ethnostates" in the modern world turn to the Greek city-state as a model that illustrates the desirability of such communities. In a speech to a conference organized by a member of a German neo-Nazi political party, Faye's editor at Arktos, John Bruce Leonard, located the origin of the idea of the ethnostate in "halcyon Hellas, the central taproot of our heritage."[5] Faye himself agrees. To avert civil war, he argues, Europe must "reconnect with the supreme and ancient principle which the union of Greek city-states abided by," that political prosperity depends on "a homogeneous people united with different yet kindred nations and devoid of ethnic diversity."

This link between the Greek city-states and the white nationalist fantasy of the ethnostate is not as outrageous as it might seem at first glance. As the historian of nationalism Azar Gat has argued, for all the emphasis on classical Greek political institutions—democratic in Athens, oligarchic in Sparta—"the little noticed fact is that city-states, while, of course, not wholly homogeneous, were . . . composed of an ethnically related population."[6] In combination with citizenship requirements that made it all but impossible for those born outside the city-state to obtain civic rights, this feature of the Greek *polis* does seem to present a historical analogue to the racially pure societies white nationalist intellectuals believe would best serve the interests of modern white people.

The specific constitutions of the best-documented city-states, Athens and Sparta, further strengthen the analogy that white nationalists seek to establish. In Sparta, for example, citizenship was strictly limited to property-owning men who were able to complete the prescribed military training, and whose father *and* mother were Spartans. Such strictures limit citizenship rights to the descendants of certain families.[7] Seen through the lens of the white nationalist belief that genetics and ancestry correspond to a meaningful racial identity, classical Sparta does indeed appear to be what a contributor to the *Occidental Observer* called "the first self-conscious ethnostate." There is some scant evidence that those whom the citizens enslaved were occasionally granted citizenship in connection with military service, but the dominant impression given in ancient sources is of a society that systematically excluded foreigners—not only from citizenship but even from residency.

The historian Xenophon, for example, claims that in Sparta, "expulsions of foreigners used to occur and absence abroad was not permitted, so that citizens should not be infected by lax habits caught from foreigners." According to Plutarch, the architect of Sparta's constitution, Lycurgus, even forbade Spartan citizens from living outside of Sparta because they would "assum[e] foreign habits and imitat[e] the lives of people who were without training and lived under different forms of government." The evidence for these xenophobic practices is limited and likely biased: besides these references in Xenophon and Plutarch, most of it comes from hostile Athenian sources.[8] White nationalists know that for most people, the mere fact of an ancient author saying something confers authority upon it.

It may not occasion much surprise that white nationalists take inspiration from Sparta, the city-state that Adolf Hitler himself described as "the purest racial state in history." That they also do so with Athens may be more unexpected. A 2024 exhibition at the Tampa Museum of Art entitled *Ancient Athens: Birthplace of Democracy* that "aims to examine what the original ideals of democracy, liberty and justice for all, equality before the law and the pursuit of happiness still mean today" is only the latest example of the popular understanding of Athens as the model for modern liberal democracies. This perception derives in large part from the

Greek historian Thucydides' report that the Athenian general Pericles expressed pride that, unlike the Spartans, the Athenians "throw open our city to all the world and never by exclusion acts debar anyone," a sentiment that has attracted the admiration of political liberals from the nineteenth century to today. During the First World War, quotations from this speech were printed on buses in London, as a prominent classical scholar noted, "to remind us of the ideals which we had to defend"; the failed treaty that attempted to establish a shared constitution for the European Union in 2004 originally opened with a quotation from it. One of the most prominent classical scholars in the world, Paul Cartledge, has written of Periclean Athens, "Bliss it was, in that dawn, to be alive."[9] It is hard to see what Hitler's Nazi Party or contemporary white nationalists could find to admire in an ancient state that is described in these terms.

But historians have challenged these idealizing understandings of Athenian democracy: John Ma, for example, has detailed how violence, exclusion, and domination were as integral to the Greek city-state as was the ideal of civic virtue, and Susan Lape has shown that Athenian politicians promoted a concept of "racial citizenship" in periods of political instability, corroborating many aspects of Athenian society that white nationalists admire. But the high-minded ideals of Pericles' speech continue to exert a tenacious hold on popular attitudes toward ancient Athens, which, as Johanna Hanink has argued, "ow[e] more to the staying power of the city's ancient propaganda than to any objective reality."[10] This propaganda sanitizes a political system that has much in common with white nationalist ideology.

Readers familiar with the Athenian claim that its citizen population was "autochthonous"—"born of the earth," indigenous, never having lived anywhere else—may expect that it is this that makes Athens attractive to white nationalists.[11] But those we are discussing here generally dismiss Athenian claims of autochthony as obvious (if useful) propaganda. Rather, they invoke Athens as a model because it illustrates, they claim, that exclusionary citizenship requirements and marginalization of foreign-born residents are compatible with democratic ideals.

The well-known exclusion of women from voting rights in Athens, which a contributor to Arktos's blog calls "prudent," is only one feature of Athenian politics that white nationalist intellectuals admire. It is the treatment of foreign-born residents of the city, known in antiquity as *metics*, that they believe should be imitated in modern times. Like modern refugees and economic migrants, these immigrants came to Athens, according to Plutarch's biography of the Athenian lawgiver Solon, "for greater security of living," eventually making up a fifth of the city's population, according to even conservative estimates. On the one hand, this considerable presence undermines analogies white nationalists might like to draw between Athens and their concept of the homogeneous ethnostate. But the systematic exclusion and state-sanctioned oppression of these *metics* in Athens (Aristotle was one of them) provides them with a model for the kind of treatment they argue those who wish to reside in Europe or the United States should have to endure for the privilege (as they see it) of residing in prosperous and safe societies. Besides not being able to vote, *metics* in Athens were not allowed to own property, and had to pay a special tax simply to remain in the city. They were not allowed to reside in Athens without having a citizen "patron," and a foreigner without one could be enslaved. The law permitted these *metics*, like slaves but unlike citizens, to be tortured to obtain evidence needed in court. White nationalists have no trouble seeing through the propagandistic erasure of these realities in Pericles' celebratory declaration of the openness of Athenian society to all.[12]

In fact, Pericles himself promoted policies that make Athens an attractive model for white nationalists. Before the period of his influence, to be a citizen required only that you have a citizen father. But Pericles convinced the democratic assembly to establish a requirement more like Sparta's, under which only those with two citizen parents could be citizens. According to Plutarch, the prosecutions of those who attempted to claim citizenship rights following the passage of this law led to the enslavement of a quarter of the previously enfranchised population. These people, who had lost their citizen rights overnight, joined the ranks of a group of foreign-born residents of Athens that was even larger than that of the *metics*, by some estimates outnumbering citizens by as much as three to one: the people Athenians enslaved. Plato and Aristotle both contrast the homogeneous unity of the citizen population with the diversity of the enslaved, commenting that such diversity among the latter is desirable because, Plato argues, people who lack a common origin or language are more likely "to submit to the condition [of slavery] without giving trouble."[13] So even though the population of Athens can hardly be called "pure," its relegation of outsiders to second-class status and outright slavery presents a potent model for a fascist state, complete with a duly elected but authoritarian leader committed to protecting the rights of the few over all outsiders. For his part, Pericles himself later advocated reversing the law he had passed, once his citizen sons had died in battle, leaving only his noncitizen son alive.

White nationalist intellectuals have even identified an episode from Athenian history that they believe provides historical sanction to mass deportations as a means of maintaining homogeneity in a society. Such is the analysis provided by a contributor to Counter-Currents of an episode recorded by the historian Herodotus concerning the expulsion from Athens of a group of people the ancient historian calls the "Pelasgians." This term is used throughout Greek literature any time a Greek writer wished to refer to someone who lived in the region before the arrival of Greek speakers. That is, "Pelasgian" is not a word for a defined group of people but a catch-all term. Nevertheless, traditional scholarship has identified them as racially "other," making any discussion of them in ancient sources as useful to white nationalists as the theories of "Aryan" supremacy that derive from nothing more than linguistic differences.[14]

The passage in question describes how the Athenians deported the Pelasgians who were living in and around Athens to the island of Lemnos.[15] Herodotus gives two possible reasons that the Athenians did this: either as revenge for their rape of some Athenian girls, or because the Athenians simply wanted to take the land the Pelasgians occupied. Whatever the reason—Herodotus declines to decide—the expelled people settled on the island of Lemnos, where they took their own revenge by abducting some Athenian women from a religious festival. Over time, these women gave birth to children on Lemnos and, in Herodotus's account, maintained what might be called their Athenian cultural identity by teaching their children the Attic dialect of Greek and "Athenian customs." Furthermore, these children segregated themselves, Herodotus says, from the Lemnian children, defended each other against bullying from those children, and "took it upon themselves to wield power over the other children and were easily the dominant group." So, Herodotus concludes, the Lemnians killed the children of the Athenian women, and their mothers as well, out of fear that as adults those children would seize power on Lemnos.

Various features of Herodotus's account cast doubt on the historicity of the expulsion he describes, not least the fact that this story provided a pat justification for Athens seizing political control of Lemnos in 510 BCE. As always, however, white nationalists stake the legitimacy of their interpretations on the assumption that an ancient thinker—in this case a historian widely known as "the Father of History"—is sophisticated and credible. In a sense, it doesn't matter to white nationalists whether the expulsion of the Pelasgians happened or not, because the Athenians (and Herodotus), it seems, believed it happened, thereby providing evidence that they understood what white nationalists wish modern politicians understood: that the Athenians and the Pelasgians were never going to be able to live together in peace, whether in Athens or on Lemnos. The essayist on Counter-Currents argues further that the story demonstrates that however unpalatable expulsion (such as the Athenians enacted) may be, it is preferable to extermination (such as the Lemnians perpetrated) as a means of creating a homogeneous society. The dominant class should not hesitate to deport foreigners, this chilling reasoning goes, because the alternative is so much more brutal. And just because the story was probably made up does not mean that the ancient world is innocent of such xenophobic violence. As Dan-el Padilla Peralta has pointed out, the graffito reading "Death to Islam" that was painted on the wall of the Bosnia and Herzegovina Heritage Association in Spokane, Washington, in 2015 reproduces an ancient Roman graffito reading "Death to the Arabs" that defaced the tombstone of a Roman cavalry officer whose burial inscription noted that he was "Arab by birth."[16]

Linking Diversity and Violence in the Hellenistic World

Both Athens and Sparta suffered from internal conflict and dissension throughout the period that white nationalists look to for evidence that homogeneous societies will be peaceful. But the citizenship policies and attitudes toward immigration that ancient sources attribute to these city-states, and that in some cases seem actually to have been implemented in them, indicate for white nationalists that the citizens of ancient city-states at least accepted the desirability of attempting to maintain a homogeneous ruling class. "Would that this was understood by the contemporary political class," writes a contributor to the *Occidental Observer* in an essay on Aristotle's theories concerning diverse populations. This same essay laments that the wise policies of men like Aristotle, Plato, and Pericles have been abandoned by "the hostile elites which rule many Western nations today" and who desire to replace homogeneous societies with "a mass of mongrels without identity" who will be "easier to rule than a self-conscious people." This may seem, at first glance, to be nothing more than yet another framing of history in terms of the Great Replacement conspiracy theory. But white nationalist intellectuals find a historical analogy for these "hostile elites" and their nefarious plots in a figure from the period of history that followed the most celebrated era of the Greek city-state: Alexander of Macedon. If the Greek *polis* provides white nationalists with evidence that prosperity attends homogeneous populations, Alexander's empire, they claim, provides evidence of the opposite—that diversity produces conflict, violence, and decline.

At first glance, Alexander of Macedon, conventionally known as Alexander the Great, might seem to be an ancient figure whom white nationalists would admire. He was, after all, a spectacularly successful military commander and empire builder of the sort that fascist strongmen have historically aspired to be. The prominent Nazi Albert Speer recorded in his diary that Hitler delivered a monologue at his fifty-fourth birthday party praising Alexander along with Pericles, Julius Caesar, and Augustus as individuals whose will had shaped history.[17] And some white nationalist intellectuals have expressed similar admiration for the way Alexander's campaign made "the vast and incontestable superiority of the world's first rational civilization . . . apparent to all the diverse populations of those lands" that he conquered, as the white supremacist classical scholar Revilo Oliver put it in a booklet published by a British press that also published an English edition of *The Protocols of the Elders of Zion*. This makes him "the living embodiment of Aryan dynamism," as Samuel T. Francis wrote in an essay for *American Renaissance*.

But the predominant attitude among white nationalist intellectuals toward Alexander is one of condemnation, and not because of his erotic relationships with other men (whose representation in Netflix's 2024 series *Alexander: The Making of a God* provoked complaints from Greece's minister of culture). The more common view can be found in an essay in the *Occidental Quarterly* by Derek Turner, the former editor of a British magazine called *Right Now!* that featured interviews with British National Party chairman Nick Griffin and race pseudoscientists Richard Lynn and J. Philippe Rushton. There Turner suggests that Alexander's conquests led to the decay of the white race in Europe by creating communities across the Mediterranean basin in which the Greek soldiers who fought in Alexander's campaigns settled and intermarried with conquered non-Europeans. Alexander "seems to have thought he was above biology," he writes. "Imperialism and ethnic well-being are often antithetical . . . imperialism inevitably means ethnic dilution."[18]

Assigning the Greeks a white racial identity and assuming that such an identity carries with it meaningful qualities that could be lost or "diluted" through intermarriage with outsiders are staple white nationalist ideas, but this does not mean that Turner and other white nationalist intellectuals lack ancient evidence to corroborate their racist interpretation of history. According to Alexander's biographer Plutarch, Alexander ignored the advice of his teacher Aristotle—the same thinker who theorized, as we have seen, a link between diversity and conflict—that he should treat Greeks as subjects but non-Greek "barbarians" as slaves. He discarded, that is, the principles of homogeneity and hierarchy that white nationalists, following Aristotle, believe made the Greek city-states prosperous and strong. Alexander ignored this advice, for example, by marrying Roxana, the daughter of a governor of the Persian Empire, and further blurring any hierarchical distinction between Greeks and Persians by adopting the dress and court protocols of the rulers he conquered. Even more provocatively to white nationalists, he not only condoned but even encouraged intermarriage between Greeks and conquered Persians. Plutarch and the historian Arrian record that Alexander arranged a "mass marriage" with Persian women for himself and ninety-one other officials from his army in ceremonies that adhered to Persian customs. He furthermore is said to have invited all his soldiers who had already married conquered women to that wedding feast and to have paid off all their debts and presented each with a golden cup.[19] The fascist occultist Savitri Devi, noting that both the Greeks and Persians spoke Indo-European languages, admired these mass marriages as evidence of Alexander's embrace of what she called "true racialism," a belief that white identity transcends nation, language, culture, and birthplace. But for most white nationalists these actions and policies brand Alexander as "the first apostle of multiculturalism," as a contributor to the *Occidental Quarterly* called him.

Historians have argued that Alexander's adoption of Persian dress and custom, his promotion of intermarriage, and the like, constituted an imperial strategy to establish and maintain power over vast numbers of conquered Persians rather than any kind of policy of demographic "fusion." The weddings, in particular, came shortly after a period of marked unrest and even revolt among both the Persians and Alexander's own troops. A. B. Bosworth points out, for example, that all of the marriages Alexander oversaw or rewarded were between Greek men and Persian women. No Persian men were allowed to attach themselves to Alexander's regime. This attention to Alexander's political strategy may refute the apostolic metaphor employed in the *Occidental Observer:* instead of seeking to create a "brotherhood of men," as some older scholarship on Alexander claimed, Alexander simply sought to establish and maintain political power. But this more realistic understanding of Alexander's motivation does not in itself do much to complicate the white nationalist condemnation of the impact of Alexander's policies. In fact, the ancient historian Arrian suggests that Alexander's troops themselves shared the perspective of modern white nationalists. He reports that Alexander's adoption of Persian dress and his requirement that the marriages he arranged for his officials be conducted in the Persian mode "aggrieved the Macedonians, as they thought that Alexander was going utterly barbarian at heart, and treating Macedonian customs and Macedonians themselves without respect."[20] Whatever Alexander's motivations, and whatever the impact of his policies, such evidence gives historical precedent to white nationalist disgust at attempts to lend prestige to anything foreign.

It is undeniable that Alexander's conquests ushered in a period of unprecedented mobility and social mixing in the Mediterranean world: Alexander and his successors (Ptolemy, Seleucus, Antigonus, and Cassander) settled Greek speakers throughout the Mediterranean. Meanwhile, changing and expanded political boundaries led others to seek opportunities in newly established or growing urban population centers. Similar blending of populations took place throughout the expansion of the Roman Empire. Cities like Rome, Alexandria, and Constantinople are only the best-known examples of cities in which people from all over the Mediterranean world lived alongside each other.[21] Against those who might look to the diverse and blended empire that Alexander's conquest created as proof of the desirability of modern cosmopolitanism, white nationalists can find ancient evidence that they believe proves that the imposition of this diversity heralded violence and decline.

Whatever harmony the subjects of Alexander's empire enjoyed lasted only as long as the conqueror's life. But although his successors waged relentless territorial wars against each other, white nationalist intellectuals recognize that these conflicts arose from the rulers' desire for political and military control of the remnants of the empire, not from the diversity of the population per se. If they mention this violence at all, it is to note that the people displaced by these conflicts accelerated the diversification of populations throughout the former empire. But they do find evidence that diversity itself causes violence in, for example, a description of Alexandria, Egypt, by Polybius, who wrote a history in Greek about Rome's rise to power. In that passage, he describes the Alexandrians as "mongrels" (in Olson's 2012 revision of the widely available Loeb translation by Patton) and expresses disgust that Egyptians and Greeks were unable to coexist peacefully. And a papyrus fragment also from Alexandria known as the *Oracle of the Potter* seems to provide evidence that the inhabitants of Alexandria would agree with his assessment. This text records an apocalyptic prediction of the destruction of the Greek community in Alexandria, apparently written by an Egyptian.[22] Such a prediction, white nationalists argue, reveals the inveterate hostility that existed between the different populations of that city.

None of this evidence transparently indicates what white nationalists say it does. Polybius can hardly be called a neutral observer, since he cites the supposed chaos of Alexandria as justification for the Roman conquest of Egypt. As for the *Oracle of the Potter*, established interpretations do indeed find in it evidence for conflict between Egyptians and Greeks in Alexandria. But whereas white nationalists explain this conflict as inevitable whenever diverse populations live alongside each other, historians have recognized that whatever resentment the "oracle" expresses is likely a product of what a noted papyrologist called the "unequal relations of a privileged and dominant minority and an autochthonous majority which has a lesser capacity to organize its own future." That is, the "oracle" reflects the resentment of the majority Egyptian community toward its Greek-speaking rulers. This scenario—that an oppressed community will resent its oppressors, perhaps even imagine their destruction, as the author of the "oracle" does—is both much more plausible than, and much less convenient for, the white nationalist claim that diversity in itself produces conflict. But more recent scholarship questions even the fact of pervasive conflict between these groups, rejecting what has been termed an "apartheid model" for Alexandria and pointing instead toward evidence of mutual influence and exchange between Greeks and Egyptians in that city. Even the primary evidence for conflict between these populations reflects their interconnectedness: the hatred of the Egyptians toward Greeks expressed in the *Oracle of the Potter* is preserved not in the Egyptian language but in Greek.[23]

This nuanced understanding of the political and social dynamics specific to this particular city reveals the simplistic generalization that underpins the white nationalist understanding of Alexander's empire as proof that diversity produces violence. Such generalizations play a central role in the sweeping narratives of historical decline for which they make Alexander's empire the prototype, including that of the Roman Empire. So even though Hitler wrote in *Mein Kampf* that "Roman history, if properly understood, is and remains the best teacher not only for today, but for all time," and even though Mussolini frequently invoked the Roman Empire as an admirable model for the fascist state, contemporary white nationalists see Rome as having doomed itself by "adopt[ing] the Alexandrian globalist model," as a contributor to Counter-Currents wrote.[24] A self-published book by the antisemitic evolutionary psychology professor Kevin MacDonald, who is also the editor in chief of the *Occidental Observer*, extends this analysis to the modern history of Europe, arguing that openness to outsiders has already put Europe on the same path of violence and decline that he claims the Greek and Roman worlds experienced. He begins his analysis with the Greek city-states, which, he argues (like the commentators described above) excluded outsiders to the proper extent; the Roman policy of incorporating conquered peoples, he argues, brought short-term imperial success but "carried the seeds of its own destruction." It's a narrative that only a grossly simplified perspective could produce, one that, besides making invented racial identities into driving forces of history, ignores the complex and often productive interactions across difference that have characterized human civilization since antiquity.

Writing Histories of Violence

White nationalists, however, are far from alone in embracing simplistic and racialized understandings of Alexander's empire and its legacy. On the one hand, popular perceptions of Alexander are quite different from those described above. To the mainstream public Alexander is, as one of the commentators in the 2024 Netflix series *Alexander: Making of a God* describes him, "the greatest military mind of all time." The trailer to Oliver Stone's 2004 film about him begins with Anthony Hopkins, playing Alexander's general Ptolemy, saying, "I've known many great men in my life, but only one colossus." Such encomiastic praise is the polar opposite of white nationalists' contempt for him as the archetype of the kind of sinister "globalist" leader whose promotion of diversity for personal gain lies at the heart of their conspiracy theories. On the other hand, however, popular representations of Alexander minimize and justify the violence that his campaigns occasioned as much as white nationalists exaggerate and misrepresent it.

To find evidence of this sanitization of violence, one need look no further than the fact that Alexander is conventionally called "the great." The Zoroastrian historical tradition in Persia, which Alexander conquered, remembers him with a different moniker, "the accursed," and the destruction Alexander wreaked on that region—entire cities destroyed, thousands upon thousands killed, at least one leader tortured and crucified for all to see—should preclude any assumption that such a name reflects only the sour grapes of the losing side. But a sanitized view of Alexander asserting that his conquests spread "civilization" in the form of Greek language and culture throughout the world dominated scholarship beginning with the German historian Droysen's *History of Alexander* (1883). This idea is so widespread in mainstream scholarship and culture that the historian Peter Green felt the need to begin his comprehensive history of the period following Alexander's campaigns by denouncing this "pernicious myth." But even the term by which the period following Alexander's conquest is known—"Hellenistic," which Green employs in the title of his book—assumes that his conquest erased local identities and cultural traditions by "Hellenizing" them (that is, making them Greek), even as many scholars have argued that such a conceptual frame ignores extensive evidence for cultural exchange and mutual influence between conquering, local, and immigrant communities in this period.[25] White nationalists may be misrepresenting this period of history, but dominant popular understandings of it are not much better.

More disturbingly, the same assumption of racial decline that shapes white nationalist understanding of the Hellenistic period has characterized mainstream scholarship and popular perceptions. When an essayist for Counter-Currents writes that "the death of the *polis*" left only "second-rate thinkers and dime-novel writers warming themselves over the embers of Plato and Homer," his assessment is not much different than that held by most professional historians throughout the twentieth century who, according to a 2006 retrospective, "dismissed" this period of history as "derivative, decadent, and quite frankly, inferior." The title of Aubrey Diller's 1937 book, *Race-Mixture among the Greeks before Alexander*, all but assumes that "race mixture" defined later Greek culture. The Nazi historian Fritz Schachermeyr certainly thought so, but so did George Grote, an influential nineteenth-century historian of Greece known also for his radical liberal politics. This radicalism did not, however, temper his belief that "compulsory mingling of the different races promises nothing favourable to the happiness of any of them." Results in the case of Alexander's conquests, Grote suggested, included the "decay of productive genius" among the Greeks, "their intellectual brightness dimmed, their spirit broken." In Grote's Britain, this was no mere historical question but bore directly on the governance of Britain's colonial occupation of India, which Alexander had invaded in 326 BCE. Alexander's promotion of intermarriage, among other failings, made him at best an ambiguous model for the European conquest of Asia among officials of the British Empire. They justified their more liberal governance of their colonies in the Americas, which were populated by Europeans, as compared to that of their colonies in India by reference to Aristotle's advice to Alexander to rule Greeks differently than "barbarians"—the very advice that contemporary white nationalists decry Alexander for ignoring.[26]

Condemnation of what was known as Alexander's "policy of the fusion of races" continued into the twentieth century, with William Woodthorpe Tarn writing in *The Cambridge Ancient History* in 1933 that "the intermarriage of Europe and further Asia" resulted in "the loss of the good qualities of both." And Will and Ariel Durant, who brought xenophobic interpretations of the end of the Roman Empire to a broad public, did the same regarding Hellenistic Greece: "The least expected and most profound effect of Alexander's conquest," they conclude, "was the Orientalization of the European soul." This sounds very much like the claim made by the prolific journalist and Ku Klux Klan member Lothrop Stoddard in his *Rising Tide of Color against White World Supremacy* (1920): "From the time of Alexander, the elimination of European blood, classic culture, and finally, of Christianity, went on relentlessly." After the Second World War, scholars became less likely to propose explicitly racial analyses of history, but the assumption of a decline in Greek culture after Alexander persisted. As recently as 1990, a major treatment of the Hellenistic world substantially reproduced the terminology of earlier scholarship, describing the "collapse of the inner spirit animating the polis" and the rise of cosmopolitan cities like Alexandria that, "with its polyglot immigrants and diverse traditions, had no true ethnic or even religious center." Greeks of this period, on this view, suffered from "spiritual malaise," "social fragmentation," and the "loss of cohesive identity."[27] The correspondence between such terminology and that used by contemporary white nationalists to describe the supposedly baneful influence of multiculturalism on the modern world may be unintentional, but it is there nonetheless.

One can find a similar persistence of white nationalist ideas in the history of how the Greek city-states—the other aspect of antiquity that white nationalists cite to promote their belief that diversity leads to violence and homogeneity to prosperity—have been treated by historians, intellectuals, and the broader public. We do not need to confine ourselves to notorious examples, such as the Austrian scholar Schachermeyr, who, despite his active participation in the Nazi Party before and during the Second World War, remained a respected member of academic circles as a professor in Vienna until his retirement in 1963. His biography of Pericles, published in 1969, implicitly likens Pericles to Hitler, but long before that, professional classical scholars had expressed admiration for what one called his "combination of popular and autocratic rule."[28]

Pericles, of course, is only one symbol of the supposed strength of the Greek city-state, which, long before the rise of twentieth-century fascism, served as a crucial point of reference for Enlightenment-era political theorists who, at least implicitly, built an assumption of racial sameness into the then emerging concept of the nation-state. On the surface, such theories proclaimed that a shared commitment to ideals of human equality and freedom should define such states; believing that these ideals flourished in Athens, political theorists such as Diderot, d'Alembert, and Rousseau looked to the Greek city-states, and Athens in particular, as models of citizen solidarity against tyranny. Historians of nationalism, writing during and after the Second World War, also took Athens as a model of what one influential scholar termed "civic nationalism," in contrast to the "ethnic" nationalism that produced the genocidal violence of Nazi Germany.[29]

But as historians of racism such as David Theo Goldberg have demonstrated, the celebration of attractive ideals has disguised racist principles throughout the history of all European nation-states. Even the word we use for the nation—derived as it is from the Latin word *natio*, meaning "to have been born"—betrays the fact that ancestry (and thereby, given the persistence of biological essentialism, race) has been at least as significant to the formulation of the concept of the nation as the ideals that are more often assumed to define it. The Enlightenment thinkers who made Athens a model of their civic ideals minimized the violent exclusions and obsession with ancestry that defined Athenian political institutions. And following the idealistic revolutions that produced these nations, racial concepts of citizenship, usually framed in terms of ancestry and still sometimes misleadingly described by scholars as "ethnic," gained increasing prominence: as Athena Leoussi has shown for both England and France, the return to such understandings of citizenship was informed by a revival in admiration for Greco-Roman antiquity.[30] Reference to Athens provided a convenient way to proclaim a state's ideals while maintaining a belief that citizenship must be restricted in order to maintain the homogeneity of the citizenry and thereby, this reasoning goes, the stability of the state.

Certainly the "founders" of the United States shared with modern white nationalists an assumption that the ancient world demonstrates a link between homogeneity and national prosperity. John Jay, writing under the classical pseudonym Publius, expressed his "pleasure" in the *Federalist*, no. 2, at the homogeneity of his new nation: "a people descended from the same ancestors," he wrote, "speaking the same language, professing the same religion" and "very similar in their manners and customs." Jay does not indicate his source for these criteria, but they are the same ones that Herodotus named as the definitive characteristics of Greekness in a passage that white nationalists quote to claim that classical Greeks conceived of their identity in racial terms. Even before the ratification process that Jay was promoting in the *Federalist* had been completed, the first Congress of the United States passed the Nationality Act of 1790, limiting citizenship to "free white persons" and thus implicitly making racial homogeneity a national objective.[31]

Modern Myths of Purity

Few historians today would praise Athenian democracy without noting its exclusions or the city's dependence on slavery. Fewer still would dismiss the Hellenistic period as "inferior" as explicitly as previous generations did. But the white nationalist idea that difference produces conflict has as wide a currency as ever. America's portrait of itself as a "melting pot," flattering as it may be to our self-image, disguises a deep-seated suspicion of diversity: the melting pot metaphor assumes that the nation's strength lies in the way it assimilates immigrants to the dominant culture, thereby minimizing difference. This suspicion can be traced back to the earliest days of the Republic, when many influential white leaders, including Thomas Jefferson, James Monroe, and James Madison, advocated the deportation of African Americans "beyond the reach of mixture," as Jefferson put it, not only to prevent intermarriage but because they believed white and Black people could never live harmoniously together. Even some abolitionists, including Abraham Lincoln, accepted this reasoning and supported the aims of the American Colonization Society, which sought to establish colonies for emancipated African Americans elsewhere in the world. As with so many of the racist beliefs profiled in this book, white nationalists seeking legitimacy for their ideas need only point to principles that have long been central to American political life.[32]

As far as I am aware, the advocates of mass deportation of emancipated slaves did not cite Greco-Roman antiquity to support their cause (although Jefferson's notorious defense of American slavery for being more humane than its ancient counterpart appears in a work on the topic). But ancient analogies have nevertheless found their way into xenophobic discourses even into the twentieth century. One example, of course, is Enoch Powell's "Rivers of Blood" speech. Another is one delivered by the Texas congressional representative Ted Poe, who sponsored the bill that authorized the construction of one of the first fences on the border between the United States and Mexico. In 2006, Poe told Congress that there was an "obvious . . . analogy" between the Roman Empire and the United States. Just as immigration, he claimed, led to the collapse of the Roman Empire, so too would it weaken the United States. It seems at least possible that Poe took this analogy from an advance copy of one of Pat Buchanan's books, published one month after Poe delivered his speech and featuring a similar comparison of America and Rome. And Iowa representative Steve King, who cosponsored a 2011 bill with Poe entitled the "Deport

Foreign Convicted Criminals Act," similarly warned that immigrants would "have us retreating" just as "in the beginning of the Dark Ages" that many people assume the collapse of Roman political power ushered in.[33]

Classical references have appeared less frequently in the anti-immigrant rhetoric of mainstream politicians in recent years, but the belief that difference produces conflict and violence remains ever present. The most prominent spokesman of this view has been President Donald Trump, who, in the 2015 announcement of his first presidential campaign described immigrants from Mexico as "rapists" who are "bringing crime" to the United States, and who, campaigning again in 2024, called immigrants "scum" and characterized them as "a bigger enemy than China and Russia." But the prevalence of such thinking is not confined to one inflammatory politician. Editorials declaring that "diversity is not our strength" have proliferated. Florida governor Ron DeSantis supported a number of anti-immigrant laws that he argues are needed to "combat the dangerous effects of illegal immigration" and to "safeguard Floridians." And it is not only figures with national profiles and ambitions who propagate this belief. In 2023, when officials in New York City announced that a few hundred asylum seekers would be temporarily relocated to hotels in the region of New York State where I reside, local elected officials reacted with similar rhetoric, complaining about the "potential for harm" and "potential for mayhem" that they believed such a relocation plan posed.[34]

Reference to such politically polarizing figures as Donald Trump and Steve King risks diverting attention from the prevalence of this idea across wide swaths of American society. The endemic segregation of American society suggests that large majorities of white people share the belief that diversity produces violence. Researchers at the University of California, Berkeley's Othering and Belonging Institute, for example, found that more than 150 of the largest cities in the nation were more segregated in 2019 than they were in 1990. Along with the phenomenon of "school district secessions," in which (usually) predominantly white schools leave a diverse school district in order to form a more homogeneous one, this regression in residential integration has meaningfully reversed the integration of public schools that the *Brown v. Board of Education* Supreme Court ruling mandated in 1954. Anyone who has ever used or accepted the terminology of the "bad school" or "bad neighborhood" to describe segregated landscapes has implicitly accepted the logic of the beliefs that this chapter has considered.[35]

There is no empirical evidence that diversity leads to violence. Research shows that immigrants—no matter where they are from and no matter whether they are documented or undocumented—commit fewer serious crimes than native-born citizens. Violent crime in the United States has fallen as immigration has increased, a phenomenon that admits many different explanations but that in any case undermines any claim that immigration brings with it increased violence.[36] To the extent that we believe that difference produces conflict, it is because we have been conditioned to do so by racist narratives about immigrants. Such egregious lies require maintenance, which is why white nationalist intellectuals turn to the ancient world, to the supposed homogeneity of Athens and Sparta and the alleged racial decline of Alexander's empire. They hope that calling attention to prestigious ancient civilizations that viewed outsiders with suspicion and denied them rights that were jealously reserved for citizens (or that suffered because they relaxed this suspicion), and to influential historians who praised them for doing so, will keep us fearful of our new neighbors and fellow countrymen.

Conclusion

Taking the Classics Forward

Readers familiar with the landscape of white nationalist publications may be surprised if, at the end of a book focused on the disturbing depth and sophistication of a certain kind of white nationalist interpretation of Greco-Roman history, I turn to a final example taken from the Daily Stormer. The notorious neo-Nazi website regularly employs racial slurs and other inflammatory language. Its owner and primary contributor, Andrew Anglin, has been found liable for more than $14 million in damages relating to the coordinated programs of harassment and intimidation he has orchestrated through his site. Anglin lives in hiding outside the United States, most likely to avoid paying these damages. This does not seem like a man who intends to make his ideas respectable by couching them in the polished language of the academy.

And yet, in 2013, the year that he launched the Daily Stormer, Anglin published an essay that would be right at home in the more polished "highbrow" publications I have been examining. Entitled "American Civilization and the Classical Heritage," it begins with a quotation from a book entitled *The Golden Age of the Classics in America* in which the author, the respected intellectual historian Carl J. Richard, summarizes the significance that ancient Greece and Rome had for Americans in the nineteenth century. Richard writes that Americans of that period found in "the classics both models and antimodels of personal behavior, social practice, and government form," "consider[ed] their favorite authors wise old friends," and "derived from the classics a sense of identity and purpose that bound them together with one another and their ancestors in a common struggle." Following this quotation, the Daily Stormer essay goes on to discuss examples from American history that illustrate the prevalence of these attitudes toward Greco-Roman antiquity. These include the popular comparison between George Washington and the Roman leader Cincinnatus, the admiration that the framers of the Constitution expressed for the Athenian lawgiver Solon, and the influence of Plato's and Polybius's theories of the decay of governments on John Adams.[1] The essayist concludes that "our classical heritage" provided "the high culture of America during its greatest period" and therefore should be central to the project of "build[ing] an intellectually vigorous resistance to modernity" and "reviving the West."

The appearance of such an essay in a white nationalist publication, even the Daily Stormer, should be unsurprising. But the citation of Richard's history of American attitudes toward Greco-Roman antiquity invites further consideration. Richard's description of how and why nineteenth-century Americans valued that history corresponds almost exactly to how and why contemporary white nationalists value it. Spartan warriors are, for white nationalists, "models of personal behavior"; Augustus's attempts to promote childbirth constitute a "model of social practice"; and the exclusive citizenship requirements of the Greek city-state provide a "model of government form." The Roman Empire, in turn, provides them with an "antimodel" of all three. Plato's and Aristotle's insistence on the naturalness of hierarchy makes them "wise old friends." When Richard Spencer suggests that white people should take pride in Greco-Roman history, he is inviting his followers "to derive from the classics a sense of identity" that "binds them together with one another and their ancestors in a common struggle" against the alleged threat of white genocide. One aim of this book has been to demonstrate that white nationalist understandings of the significance of Greco-Roman antiquity correspond to those promoted by respected and influential intellectuals of the past. The Daily Stormer recognizes this. Do we?

As we have seen, the men who articulated the founding principles of the United States did indeed turn to Greco-Roman antiquity to justify a social order that contemporary white nationalists would admire, one in which only white men enjoyed citizenship rights, one whose institutions reflected a belief in the naturalness of hierarchy, one haunted by the alleged threat of degeneracy and decline. Greco-Roman antiquity may no longer play the same role in maintaining this social order as it did in the "Golden Age of Classics" that Richard describes—the period before the American Civil War, when slavery was still legal in some states and was only gradually being abolished in many others—but it certainly served as a source of rhetorical power for those who established that social order. White nationalist intellectuals, recognizing the centrality of Greco-Roman antiquity to the history of violence and oppression in the United States, use it to strengthen and revive that dimension of American politics, insisting that all they are doing is promoting a return to the same timeless ancient wisdom and values that inspired the "founding fathers" of the nation.

If this seems to ascribe too much rhetorical power to "the classical," consider the popularity of Zack Snyder's *300*. It indicates how attractive such representations of racialized heroism against outsiders is to mass audiences in America—and indeed worldwide. Scholars such as Bret Devereaux, Owen Rees, Roel Konijnendijk, and Myke Cole have written extensively about how such portrayals of the Spartans distort and simplify historical fact, but admiration for the Spartans as models of white masculine heroism continues unabated.[2] This is not because everyone who enjoys *300*, competes in a "Spartan Race," or cheers for the Spartans at a local high school football game is a white nationalist. It is because the version of Greco-Roman antiquity that such a conception of the Spartans represents is not only familiar but comfortable. And this familiar, comfortable vision of Greco-Roman antiquity corresponds in large part to that held by white nationalist intellectuals.

The same is true of all the attitudes about the value of "the classical" that Richard identified in nineteenth-century American intellectual life. These perspectives remain widespread in the twenty-first century. Publishers and educators rely upon them, for example, to demonstrate the continuing relevance of the ancient past to modern concerns. Take, for example, the idea of "ancient wisdom." Edith Hall, one of the most prominent classical scholars in Britain, wrote a book in 2018 entitled *Aristotle's Way: How Ancient Wisdom Can Change Your Life* that received positive attention in the *New York Times*, the *Los Angeles Times*, and *Time Magazine*, venues not usually keyed in to classical scholarship. Princeton University Press publishes a series entitled Ancient Wisdom for Modern Readers on topics ranging from "How to Tell a Joke" to "How to Die." There are now more than thirty volumes. None of these books promotes white nationalist politics. But they do promote, and depend for their appeal on, the belief that ancient authors are "wise old friends," as Richard put it in his description of nineteenth-century attitudes. That's the same attitude that many white nationalist interpretations of antiquity depend on.

Just how big the market for "classical" wisdom is may be gauged by the growing popularity of the "classical education movement" in the United States, which promotes a curriculum modeled on ancient and medieval educational theories (popularly known as the "quadrivium" and the "trivium"). By some accounts, the number of new private and charter schools that promote this "classical" curriculum increased fivefold in 2022 and 2023. Governors in Florida and Tennessee have publicly endorsed the movement and vowed to increase the number of such schools in their states. The Classic Learning Test has gained popularity as an alternative to other standardized tests used in college admissions, primarily at Christian colleges and universities but also, as of 2023, at public colleges and universities in Florida. Susan Wise Bauer's *Guide to Classical Education at Home*, first published in 1999, has been popular enough in the exponentially growing homeschooling movement to have required a fourth edition. The description "classical," it seems, retains considerable cachet. One of the founders of a network of classical charter schools in New York City told the *New Yorker* that when they first recruited families in the South Bronx, they "billed [classical education] as 'this is what the elite get.'"[3]

Much of the reporting on the "classical education" movement has focused on the extent to which the politics of the broader movement reflect the politics of those who are promoting it most vigorously. Florida governor Ron DeSantis has linked the promotion of such a curriculum to policies banning or limiting "discussion about sexual orientation or gender identity" in elementary and middle schools, and banning diversity, equity, and inclusion initiatives in state universities. Many of the schools that have most enthusiastically adopted "classical" curricula are affiliated with Christian denominations that dehumanize members of the LGBTQ community. The early history of the classical Christian education movement was populated by people who minimized the violence of American slavery and sought to celebrate the American Confederacy as a model to be emulated. These include the classical scholar Thomas Fleming, who was an architect of the neo-Confederate movement, and pastor Douglas Wilson, who has argued that "there has never been a multiracial society which has existed with such mutual intimacy and harmony" as the slave society of the American South.[4]

Here, however, I want to focus not on the politics of individuals within the movement (however influential they may be) but on the rhetorical function of the term *classical* in this context. A look at the curricula promoted by the movement reveals that they can be described as "classical" only in a loose sense. Students at classical academies do not generally learn Latin or Greek, the languages in which the ancient Greek and Roman thinkers wrote and lived. Ancient Greek and Roman authors comprise only a small portion of the material studied in such schools. The Classic Learning Test, for example, bases most of its reading comprehension questions on passages taken from an "author bank" that includes far more medieval and early modern authors (such as Benedict, Aquinas, Rousseau, and Gibbon) and fifty-nine "late moderns." The list of readings that the Classical Academic Press's "Classical Reader" recommends for parents includes Virgil's *Aeneid* alongside Hemingway's *Farewell to Arms*, George Eliot's *Adam Bede*, and Martin Luther's *Bondage of the Will*.[5] Ancient Greece and Rome provide only part of the material for this education. "Classical," then, serves not so much to describe this style of education as to promote it.

The growing popularity of the movement reveals that the assumption that ancient Greek and Roman literature is necessarily and inevitably sophisticated, enlightening, and beneficial continues to enjoy wide acceptance in American culture. Jeremy Wayne Tate, the CEO of the Classic Learning Test, told the *New York Times* that classical education is about "passing down" a "treasury of knowledge," singling out Aristotle in particular as a "timeless" thinker whose work "is going to be relevant in 500 years." "If we live in the West," the author of the influential *Guide to Classical Education at Home* has said, "we can't get away from Plato and Aristotle." The essay "Why Your Child Needs a Classical Education," published by one of the largest networks of classical charter schools in the United States, lists "tremendous insights about our common human condition" as one of the fruits of such study.[6] Such assessments of the value and significance of Greco-Roman antiquity minimize and erase both the violence inherent in that history and the oppression that it has been used to justify. An educational curriculum that cultivates such attitudes toward Greco-Roman antiquity perpetuates the same attitudes that make Greco-Roman antiquity a fertile source of prestige for white nationalist ideas.

This is why those who promote classical education often sound troublingly, even if unintentionally, similar to white nationalist intellectuals. The Daily Stormer, for example, wrote that classical education is "the clear answer ... to the problem of intellectually reviving the West." The president of the recently founded Ralston College, whose curriculum begins with an "intensive language residency in Greece" because, their website claims, "the Greek language and the spirit of Hellenism are the very threads that run through the Humanities," has articulated a similar idea: that such a classical education can counter "the civilizational crisis we now face."[7] Jeremy Tate promotes "an education that's focused on antiquity" because it emphasizes "what our ancestors cared about." Richard Spencer's video linking white identity and Greco-Roman antiquity invited his viewers to "rediscover ... what our ancestors took for granted," and a contributor to Spencer's AltRight.com wrote that "as heirs of Seneca, the ancient Romans, of the Greeks ... we pay homage to our ancestors ... through a vibrant embracing of the qualities that make Europeans great."

Such an "embrace" can be found in the "View of Learning" described on the website of one network of classical charter schools, which suggests that because "beauty is not merely in the eye of the beholder ... the classic forms and works of Western music, drama, and visual art should play the central role in forming aesthetic development." This is the view, for instance, of Ricardo Duchesne, who in an interview at the *Occidental Observer* called "the superlative achievements of Europeans in music" and "Europe's superlative achievements in the arts" evidence of white superiority. David Goodwin, the president of the Association of Classical Christian Schools, told the *New Yorker* that classical education doesn't "buy into the cultural philosophy that all cultures are equally valuable and good," arguing that it is "existentially evident that Western culture is the most influential in the history of man." The professor of philosophy Michael Levin, who has spoken several times at the *American Renaissance* conference, wrote an essay for *American Renaissance* entitled "Is There a Superior Race?" in which he made much the same claim, albeit with more explicit racial politics: "It is a matter of verifiable fact that the influence of whites dominates mankind."[8]

These similarities arise not because advocates of classical education are white nationalist activists but because such similarities are inevitable whenever anyone promotes such an idealized understanding of the value of Greco-Roman antiquity. Indeed, as Richard's history of American attitudes toward the classics (as quoted by the Daily Stormer) demonstrates, nothing is more ordinary than to view Greco-Roman antiquity in this way. To argue that such and such a proponent of classical education is a white nationalist or a racist is a distraction from the crucial point. It doesn't matter whether those who promote such interpretations see themselves as agents of white nationalism or not: white nationalist interpretations of the Greco-Roman world will flourish as long as idealizing interpretations of the Greco-Roman world, such as those integral to the current instantiation of classical education, continue to flourish. As long as sufficient numbers of people admire the ancient world uncritically and remain ignorant of the violence that admiration has authorized, the prestige of the "classical" will continue to be available to white nationalist intellectuals as a way of legitimizing the ideas discussed in this book.

One obvious way to disrupt the availability of Greco-Roman antiquity to white nationalist ideology is to cultivate and promote an attitude toward the past that is critical rather than simply admiring.

Such an attitude involves recognizing when the time-honored ways of conceptualizing the ancient world that the Daily Stormer enumerated are invoked: when ancient Greece and Rome are treated as sources of models to be emulated or avoided, when ancient thinkers are treated as repositories of wisdom, or when a beneficial relationship of ancestry, influence, or inheritance is claimed between ancient and modern people. Such an orientation recognizes that finding models in history is a political act that requires the simplification of historical fact even as it disguises that act of curation. It recognizes that the biases of any theorist (ancient or modern) mean that their "wisdom" will serve particular political agendas. And it recognizes that claims of historical continuity are always only apparent, suppressing periods of rupture and excluding alternative linkages and associations. Whenever the ancient world is claimed to have exerted (or to be exerting) a beneficial, enriching, or elevating influence, we do well to ask who has benefited and who has been harmed, who has grown richer and who has been impoverished, and who has been raised up and who has been degraded.

This is not a call to "cancel classics," as opponents of this perspective—including Jeremy Tate of the Classic Learning Test as well as contributors to Counter-Currents and VDARE—allege. It is a call for a different orientation to the value of the ancient Greco-Roman world. This orientation retains the belief that Greco-Roman antiquity should be studied because of its formative relationship to the modern world. "Classics matters because it has mattered," as historian Neville Morley has argued.[9] But it insists that the study of Greco-Roman antiquity must place equal emphasis (or greater emphasis, given the lopsidedness of traditional approaches) on the ways that Greco-Roman antiquity has been used to create modern systems of oppression and violence that should be condemned, rejected, and overthrown. This reorientation need not diminish our interest in the ancient world, although it does change its tenor. This change can be (and in my experience teaching this material is) invigorating. To go on ratifying the existing order is dull. It is exciting to challenge long-held beliefs that serve violence. Being critical is a form of love.

In recent years, there has been a vigorous discussion about how to institutionalize this change within the discipline of classical studies. Some interventions are symbolic, such as the decision of some academic departments to change their names from "classics" or "classical studies," which assert the positive value and prestige of the subject, as no other academic disciplines' names do, to more descriptive ones like "Greek and Roman studies." Such changes need not be purely cosmetic, as long as the change in name also signals a change in the methodologies employed: the UK-based scholars Mathura Umachandran and Marchella Ward, for example, have not only proposed a new disciplinary name, "critical ancient world studies," but begun detailing and putting into practice a set of what they call "epistemological orientations" that differentiate this new discipline from inherited approaches to the study of Greco-Roman history: disowning and critiquing the field's historical Eurocentrism; rejecting the assumption that ancient cultures are uniquely valuable; denying the possibility of neutral or objective scholarship; and a commitment to resisting and subverting the processes that established "classics" as a discipline in the first place.[10]

This last point dovetails with other proposed interventions that are more structural than symbolic. A primary target of such activism is the lack of racial diversity among instructors in secondary schools, colleges, and universities. A more diverse body of teachers and researchers at all levels has the potential to transform future generations' attitudes toward the ancient world because instructors who have been marginalized by the ideologies that Greco-Roman antiquity has been used to create are less likely to perpetuate those ideologies than those who have benefited from them.[11] The white nationalist intellectual traditions I have analyzed reveal the stakes in such efforts. Diversity should not be viewed as an erosion of meritocracy or a concession to "political correctness" but as an urgent reform that, over time, will dislodge conceptions of Greco-Roman antiquity that white nationalists rely on to authorize their views.

Evidence of this potential can be found in the myriad ways that Greco-Roman antiquity has been used to resist, critique, and reject understandings of the past associated with white nationalist thought. Intellectuals in India used similarities between Homeric and Sanskrit poetry to claim dignity for ancient Indian traditions amid the contempt for them held by British colonial administrators; the first Vietnamese classical scholar, Phạm Duy Khiêm (1908–74), questioned French colonial ideology along similar lines, situating classicism as one of multiple hybridities in Vietnamese culture that made it not just equal to but more sophisticated and intricate than French culture. The African American poet Phillis Wheatley, while still enslaved, composed in classical forms treating classical themes and so attracted the attention of white elites both in colonial Boston and London in the 1770s. As Eric Ashley Hairston has argued, this strategy "inject[ed] a resonant Black presence" into "the white intellectual world," shattering the dominant view that Africans were incapable of intellectual or artistic accomplishment. Following emancipation, too, African Americans began to dismantle centuries of American anti-Blackness by citing the undeniable links between Africa and the Greco-Roman world, while playwrights in Brazil drew on those links to challenge the erasure of African identity in the national mythology of that nation. The Nobel-winning Trinidadian author V. S. Naipaul's portrait of colonial power in his novel *A Bend in the River* slyly calls attention to how a colonial administrator misquoted a Latin motto in order to make it support imperial domination more strongly than it did in its original ancient context, thereby highlighting the fragility and tendentiousness of such appeals to Greco-Roman antiquity. These examples of subversive and revolutionary classicism would be forgotten if not for the work of scholars, most of them from groups historically marginalized in the discipline, to document and explicate them.[12] They deserve to be better known than they are.

Care must be taken, however, that celebrations of these engagements retain their subversive qualities. It is all too easy to blunt these political meanings by claiming that such examples illustrate only the "influence" of a supposedly lofty "classical tradition." Many people are aware, for example, that the novels of another Nobel Prize–winning author, Toni Morrison, contain many references to Greco-Roman antiquity. Traditional orientations to the value of the ancient past assume that such references enrich and elevate Morrison's work. But, as Tessa Roynon has shown, Morrison's incorporation of classical material into *The Bluest Eye*, *Song of Solomon*, and *Beloved* in fact complicates that very idea: Morrison's novels stand not as an application of the classical tradition to African American literature but as a meditation on, and celebration of, the presence of Africa and Africans in a classical tradition that too many people believe is the ancestral heritage of white people. The first interpretation makes Morrison—and by extension Black people—the beneficiary of classical wisdom. The second recognizes in her work an incisive critique of the political and racial assumptions that underpin the very concept of that "wisdom."[13]

The reorientation to the value of the classical that Naipaul, Morrison, and so many others have enacted and called for necessitates (it must be admitted) relinquishing some perspectives on the ancient world that many people find attractive. For professional scholars, it requires abandoning the presumption that the Greco-Roman world is somehow more significant or more influential than other periods of history. For those outside the academy, it necessitates replacing a belief that the ancient world offers solutions to modern problems with an understanding that such a belief contributes to them. And it necessitates the loss of the complacent confidence that knowledge about history can be produced and absorbed without making political commitments. The interpretations of the past that white nationalists argue support their politics are very often mainstream traditional interpretations. Only a vigorously and explicitly political mode of interpretation can expose the politics latent in those interpretations and replace them with better ones.

I have taken white nationalist interpretations of Greco-Roman antiquity seriously throughout this book in the conviction that once they are seen to be symptoms of the historical and ongoing entanglement of scholarship in white supremacy, and of the deep-seated presence of white nationalist ideas in our culture, it will become clear just how urgent it is to develop a new way of thinking about and valuing the Greco-Roman past. The cutting edge of classical scholarship must be devoted to defining what this mode will be. The Daily Stormer, in its discussion of Richard's history of classicism, has helpfully delineated the attitudes we must avoid. I have gestured toward how diversifying the identities of those who study and teach about the ancient world will play a role in this reform, as well as toward a few historical models of encounters with antiquity that challenge rather than perpetuate traditional modes. What is needed is the will, among those with power, to support these disciplinary changes. The present moment does not demand that scholars raise their voices in support of historical accuracy. It demands that we do so in support of moral clarity about the history and present conditions of our discipline, and about how our work can contribute to the formation of a more just and equitable world.

In a real sense, however, the practice of historical interpretation is peripheral to what the prominence of Greco-Roman antiquity in white nationalist thought demands. Professional historians have only a limited ability to shape the dominant culture within which our teaching, our institutions, and our fields of study exist. That culture, by contrast, plays a major role in shaping our institutions and disciplines. The historical and ongoing presence of white nationalist ideas in treatments of and attitudes toward the Greco-Roman world is only a microcosm of the historical and ongoing presence of white nationalist ideas in the broader culture of the United States. These are not classical ideas that can be eradicated just by changing the way we think about ancient authors. They are ideas that have shaped and continue to define the American cultural and political landscape. Narratives of American decline continue to proliferate. Audiences flock to displays of masculine violence. Popular understandings of genetics confuse ancestry and race. Popular understandings of world history imply the superiority of white people. Myths about hard work justify social and economic hierarchies. Endemic residential segregation reveals our fear of difference. As long as these beliefs hold currency, they will define attitudes toward the ancient world, no matter how many counternarratives scholars bring into our classes or (re)discover in our scholarship.

Meeting the challenges that white nationalist appropriations of Greco-Roman antiquity pose involves so much more than a defense of a particular period of history, let alone of an academic discipline. White nationalist intellectuals care so much about Greco-Roman antiquity because it allows them to claim a distinguished pedigree for ideas that many Americans already accept on some level. White nationalist classicism demands, instead, that those of us who have an interest in the ancient world—as teachers, as students, as history buffs and fans of literature—assess our relationship to a culture that nourishes white nationalist thought and violence, and commit ourselves to resisting and dismantling that culture. Within the discipline of classics, yes, but more importantly, in ourselves and in the wider world.

Notes

Introduction

1. Homer, *Iliad* 2.488–492.
2. David Montgomery, "What Americans Think about the Roman Empire," YouGov, September 17, 2024, https://today.yougov.com/entertainment/articles/50546-what-americans-think-about-the-roman-empire.
3. Nicholas Kristof, "It's Easy to Feel Righteous in the Trump Era. Liberals, Beware," *New York Times*, June 17, 2023, https://www.nytimes.com/2023/06/17/opinion/trump-conservatives-liberals.html. Cornel West and Jeremy Tate, "Howard University's Removal of Classics Is a Spiritual Catastrophe," *Washington Post*, April 23, 2021, https://www.washingtonpost.com/opinions/2021/04/19/cornel-west-howard-classics/.
4. Avatars on social media: James Greig, "Inside the Far Right's Growing Obsession with Art," *Dazed*, July 21, 2022, https://www.dazeddigital.com/art-photography/article/56588/1/inside-the-far-rights-growing-obsession-with-art-criticism-twitter-degenerate; and Waitman Wade Beorn, "The 'Classical Culture' Social Media Accounts Which Look Like Dog-Whistles for the Far Right," *Byline Supplement*, January 27, 2023, https://www.bylinesupplement.com/p/the-classical-culture-social-media. Telegram: Curtis Dozier, "Anti-Semites Enlist Cicero against Anti-Racism," *Pharos: Doing Justice to the Classics*, May 27, 2020, https://pharos.vassarspaces.net/2020/05/27/anti-semitism-noticer-cicero-european-man/. Proud Boys: Alexandra Minna Stern, *Proud Boys and the White Ethnostate: How the Alt-Right Is Warping the American Imagination* (Boston: Beacon, 2019), 71–76; and Meadhbh Park, "Fight Club: Gavin McInnes, the Proud Boys, and Male Supremacism," in *Male Supremacism in the United States: From Patriarchal Traditionalism to Misogynist Incels and the Alt-Right*, ed. Emily K. Carian, Alex DiBranco, and Chelsea Ebin (London: Routledge, 2022). "Based Spartan": Stephen Hodkinson,

"Spartans on the Capitol: Recent Far-Right Appropriations of Spartan Militarism in the USA and Their Historical Roots," in *Classical Controversies: Reception of Graeco-Roman Antiquity in the Twenty-First Century*, ed. Kim Beerden and Timo Epping (Leiden: Sidestone, 2022), 65–67; Josh Campbell, "Proud Boys Members Ordered to Pay over $1 Million in 'Hateful and Overtly Racist' Church Destruction Civil Suit," CNN Politics, July 1, 2023, https://www.cnn.com/2023/07/01/politics/proud-boys-fined-ame-church-destruction/index.html.

5. Melanie Phillips, "How Studying the Classics Became Racist: A US Professor's Theory of White Supremacism Threatens to Rip out the Roots of Western Culture," *Times*, February 9, 2021.
6. My approach has been shaped by the analyses of Donna Zuckerberg, "'Learn Some F*cking History,'" *Eidolon*, October 30, 2017, https://eidolon.pub/learn-some-f-cking-history-94f9a02041d3; Rebecca Futo Kennedy, "We Condone It by Our Silence," *Eidolon*, May 11, 2017, https://eidolon.pub/we-condone-it-by-our-silence-bea76fb59b21; Dan-el Padilla Peralta, "Anti-Race and Anti-Racism: Whiteness and the Classical Imagination," in *A Cultural History of Race in Antiquity*, ed. Denise Eileen McCoskey (London: Bloomsbury, 2021); Mathura Umachandran and Marchella Ward, "Towards a Manifesto for Critical Ancient World Studies," in *Critical Ancient World Studies: The Case for Forgetting Classics*, ed. Mathura Umachandran and Marchella Ward (Abingdon: Routledge, 2023).
7. On the phenomenon of the "Alt-Right," its continuities with earlier white nationalism, and its distinctive characteristics, see especially Shane Burley, *Fascism Today: What It Is and How to End It* (Chico, CA: AK, 2017), 59–64; Matthew N. Lyons, *Insurgent Supremacists: The U.S. Far Right's Challenge to State and Empire* (Oakland, CA: PM, 2018), 56–82; and Josh Vandiver, "The Radical Roots of the Alt-Right," Political Extremism and Radicalism in the Twentieth Century, 2018, https://www.gale.com/intl/essays/josh-vandiver-radical-roots-alt-right. See also these more general treatments: George Hawley, *Making Sense of the Alt-Right* (New York: Columbia University Press, 2017); and Thomas J. Main, *The Rise of the Alt-Right* (Washington, DC: Brookings Institution Press, 2018).
8. Kathleen Belew and Ramón A. Gutiérrez, eds., *A Field Guide to White Supremacy* (Berkeley: University of California Press, 2021), xv.
9. Homer, *Odyssey* 16.175. Discussions of ancient attitudes toward skin color include Shelley Haley, "Be Not Afraid of the Dark: Critical Race Theory and Classical Studies," in *Prejudice and Christian Beginnings: Investigating Race, Gender, and Ethnicity in Early Christian Studies*, ed. Laura Nasrallah and Elizabeth Schussler Fiorenza (Minneapolis: Fortress, 2002), 29–34; James H. Dee, "Black Odysseus, White Caesar: When Did 'White People' Become 'White'?" *Classical Journal* 99, no. 2 (2003–4): 157–67; Sarah F. Derbew, *Untangling Blackness in Greek Antiquity* (Cambridge: Cambridge University Press, 2022).

10. An engaging narrative of the "invention" of whiteness beginning in Greco-Roman antiquity is Nell Irvin Painter, *The History of White People* (New York: Norton, 2010).
11. On the applicability of "race" to ancient Greece and Rome, see Denise Eileen McCoskey, *Race: Antiquity and Its Legacy* (London: Bloomsbury, 2012), especially 23–27; and Jackie Murray, "Race and Sexuality," in McCoskey, *A Cultural History of Race in Antiquity*, 142–45.
12. Lack of abolitionism in antiquity: Peter Hunt, *Ancient Greek and Roman Slavery* (Hoboken, NJ: Wiley-Blackwell, 2017), 207–8. Hunt also catalogues examples of prejudices against enslaved people in antiquity (173–90). On the question of whether the concept of race is useful in analyzing ancient slavery, see Christopher S. Parmenter, " 'But They Were a Race of Whites': Race and the Making of Ancient Slavery in the Anglophone World, 1785–1980," *TAPA* 154, no. 1 (2024): 295–330.
13. For slavery as a "sin of humanity," see Bruce S. Thornton, *Greek Ways: How the Greeks Created Western Civilization* (San Francisco: Encounter Books, 2002), 11, with similar formulations in Victor Davis Hanson, *Carnage and Culture: Landmark Battles in the Rise of Western Power* (New York: Anchor, 2001), 50, and Zbigniew Janowski, "A Conversation with Mary Lefkowitz," *Postil Magazine*, May 1, 2020, https://www.thepostil.com/a-conversation-with-mary-lefkowitz/. On citations of antiquity in support of slavery, see Mavis Campbell, "Aristotle and Black Slavery: A Study in Race Prejudice," *Race* 15, no. 3 (1974): 283–301; Sara Monoson, "Recollecting Aristotle: Pro-Slavery Thought in Antebellum Argument and the Argument of *Politics* Book I," in *Ancient Slavery and Abolition: From Hobbes to Hollywood*, ed. Edith Hall, Richard Alston, and Justine McConnell (Oxford: Oxford University Press, 2011), 247–78. On Thomas Jefferson's invocation of antiquity to justify enslavement of Africans, see Margaret Malamud, "The Auctoritas of Antiquity: Debating Slavery through Classical Exempla in the Antebellum USA," in Hall et al., *Ancient Slavery and Abolition*, 279–317; Sarah Teets, "Classical Slavery and Jeffersonian Racism," *Eidolon*, August 10, 2018, https://eidolon.pub/classical-slavery-and-jeffersonian-racism-28cbcdf53364; and Parmenter, " 'But They Were a Race of Whites,' " 298–302.
14. The quotation marks around this phrase are intended to convey that "Western civilization" is, as Naoíse Mac Sweeney, *The West: A New History in Fourteen Lives* (New York: Dutton, 2023), notes, "an invented abstract construct, rather than a neutral descriptive term" (ix). This should be understood whenever the phrase appears in this book.
15. Complicating the narrative of Western civilization: Mac Sweeney, *The West*; Josephine Quinn, *How the World Made the West: A 4,000-Year History* (New York: Random House, 2024). On the geographical incoherence of the idea of "the West," see Kwame Anthony Appiah, *The Lies That Bind: Rethinking Identity, Creed, Country, Color, Class, Culture* (New York: Liveright, 2018), 191.

16. On the controversy surrounding the publication of *Black Athena*, see Eric Adler, *Classics, the Culture Wars, and Beyond* (Ann Arbor: University of Michigan Press, 2016), 113–72. On its legacy within classical studies, see McCoskey, *Race*, 177–85; and Denise Eileen McCoskey, "Black Athena, White Power," *Eidolon*, November 15, 2018. Many of Bernal's Black predecessors are discussed by Maghan Keita, *Race and the Writing of History: Riddling the Sphinx* (Oxford: Oxford University Press, 2000), 41–121. On Chesnutt, see John Levi Barnard, *Empire of Ruin: Black Classicism and American Imperial Culture* (Oxford: Oxford University Press, 2018), 107–67; on Cooper, Shelley Haley, "Black Feminist Thought and Classics: Re-Membering, Re-Claiming, Re-Empowering," in *Feminist Theory and the Classics*, ed. Nancy Sorkin Rabinowitz and Amy Richlin (New York: Routledge, 1993), 25–26; and Eric Ashley Hairston, *The Ebony Column: Classics, Civilization, and the African American Reclamation of the West* (Knoxville: University of Tennessee Press, 2013), 121–58; on Du Bois, Hairston, *Ebony Column*, 159–92; and Harriet Fertik and Mathias Hanses, "Above the Veil: Revisiting the Classicism of W.E.B. Du Bois," *International Journal of the Classical Tradition* 26 (2019): 1–9.
17. A pioneering analysis is Derek Bell, *Faces at the Bottom of a Well: The Permanence of Racism* (New York: Basic Books, 1992). See too Charles Mills, "White Supremacy as a Sociopolitical System: A Philosophical Perspective," in *White Out: The Continuing Significance of Racism*, ed. Ashley W. Doane and Eduardo Bonilla-Silva (New York: Routledge, 2003); Keeanga-Yamahtta Taylor, "A Culture of Racism," 31–60, and Ramón A. Gutiérrez, "A Recent History of White Supremacy," 249–64, both in Belew and Gutiérrez, *Field Guide to White Supremacy*.
18. I have not even experienced the harassment and threats of violence routinely directed at women and people of color who publish similar research. Examples include Colleen Flaherty, "Threats for What She Didn't Say," *Inside Higher Ed*, June 18, 2017, https://www.insidehighered.com/news/2017/06/19/classicist-finds-herself-target-online-threats-after-article-ancient-statues; Donna Zuckerberg, "How to Be the Perfect Victim of Internet Harassment," *Cloelia*, January 29, 2018, https://medium.com/cloelia-wcc/how-to-be-the-perfect-victim-of-internet-harassment-151e437b511e; and Padilla Peralta, "Anti-Race and Anti-Racism."
19. Donald Kagan, "Introduction," YouTube, November 20, 2008, https://youtu.be/9FrHGAd_yto?t=64. The concept of "white privilege" was first defined in an essay originally published in 1989 and reprinted in Peggy McIntosh, "White Privilege and Male Privilege," in *The Feminist Philosophy Reader*, ed. Alison Bailey and Chris J. Cuomo (Boston: McGraw-Hill, 2008). A critique of "declarations of whiteness" (such as mine) when those declaring it "do not stay implicated in what they critique" can be found in Sara Ahmed, "Declarations of Whiteness: The Non-Performativity of Anti-Racism," *Borderlands Journal* 3, no. 2 (2004).

20. Scholarship that inspired me to launch Pharos includes Dan-el Padilla Peralta, “Barbarians Inside the Gate, Parts I and II,” *Eidolon*, November 9, 2015, https://eidolon.pub/barbarians-inside-the-gate-part-i-c175057b340f; Donna Zuckerberg, “How to Be a Good Classicist under a Bad Emperor,” *Eidolon*, November 21, 2016, https://eidolon.pub/how-to-be-a-good-classicist-under-a-bad-emperor-6b848df6e54a; Sarah E. Bond, “Why We Need to Start Seeing the Classical World in Color,” *Hyperallergic*, June 7, 2017, http://hyperallergic.com/383776/why-we-need-to-start-seeing-the-classical-world-in-color/; Rebecca Futo Kennedy, “The Dorian Invasion and ‘White’ Ownership of Classical Greece?” *Classics at the Intersections*, January 11, 2018; and Heidi Morse, “Classics and the Alt-Right: Historicizing Visual Rhetorics of White Supremacy,” *Learn, Speak, Act*, February 15, 2018, https://sites.lsa.umich.edu/learn-speak-act/2018/02/15/classics-and-the-alt-right/. Many more appeared in the online journal *Eidolon*. My initial announcement of Pharos is Curtis Dozier, “Doing Justice to the Classics: Introducing Pharos,” *Eidolon*, November 30, 2017, https://eidolon.pub/doing-justice-to-the-classics-24a228893a054. For “settler moves to innocence,” see Umachandran and Ward, “Towards a Manifesto,” 11, 23–25.
21. Cassius Dio 56.7.5, trans. Foster. Although Dio has sometimes been assumed to have fabricated the speeches in his history, a “surprising proportion” of them can be determined to be based on sources available to him, according to Christopher Burden-Strevens, “Cassius Dio the Orator: Approaching Speeches in the *Roman History*, Books 1–53,” in *Cassius Dio the Historian: Methods and Approaches*, ed. Jesper Majbom Madsen and Carsten Hjort Lange (Leiden: Brill, 2021), 153–63. I have generally quoted from other scholars’ translations throughout this book in order to illustrate the degree to which existing translations unintentionally provide language that is rhetorically useful for white nationalist interpreters of the past.
22. Andrew Garrett, *The Unnaming of Kroeber Hall: Language, Memory, and Indigenous California* (Cambridge, MA: MIT Press, 2023).
23. Ibram X. Kendi, “The Heartbeat of Racism Is Denial,” *New York Times*, January 13, 2018, https://www.nytimes.com/2018/01/13/opinion/sunday/heartbeat-of-racism-denial.html.

Chapter One. The Who and Why of White Nationalist History

1. Charlotte Alter, “Talking with Tucker Carlson, the Most Powerful Conservative in America,” *Time*, July 15, 2021, https://time.com/6080432/tucker-carlson-profile/; Andrew Marantz, “The World According to Tucker Carlson,” *New Yorker*, April 25, 2023, https://www.newyorker.com/news/daily-comment/the-world-according-to-tucker-carlson.

2. On Carlson and the "Great Replacement," see Nick Confessore, Ben Decker, Jacob Silver, and Julie Tate, "Inside the Apocalyptic Worldview of 'Tucker Carlson Tonight,' " *New York Times,* April 30, 2022, https://www.nytimes.com/interactive/2022/04/30/us/tucker-carlson-tonight.html. On the "Great Replacement" conspiracy theory, see Barbara Perry, " 'White Genocide': White Supremacists and the Politics of Reproduction," in *Home-Grown Hate: Gender and Organized Racism,* ed. Abby L. Ferber (New York: Taylor & Francis Group, 2003); Alexandra Minna Stern, "From 'Race Suicide' to 'White Extinction': White Nationalism, Nativism, and Eugenics over the Past Century," *Journal of American History* 109, no. 2 (2022): 348–61; and Mattias Gardell, "Fascism and the Violent Replacement of the People," in *The Politics of Replacement: Demographic Fears, Conspiracy Theories, and Race Wars,* ed. Sarah Bracke and Luis Manuel Hernandez Aguilar (Abingdon: Routledge, 2024), 245–61. Examples of mainstream acceptance and promotion of this conspiracy theory can be found in David Neiwert, *Alt-America: The Rise of the Radical Right in the Age of Trump* (New York: Verso Books, 2017), 278–79; Cassie Miller, "SPLC Poll Finds Substantial Support for 'Great Replacement' Theory and Other Hard-Right Ideas," Southern Poverty Law Center, June 1, 2022, https://www.splcenter.org/news/2022/06/01/poll-finds-support-great-replacement-hard-right-ideas; and Nik Linders, "Mainstreaming the Great Replacement: The Role of Centrist Discourses in the Mainstreaming of a Far-Right Conspiracy Theory," in Bracke and Hernandez Aguilar, *The Politics of Replacement,* 162–79. Reporting on surveys of its acceptance includes Anita Snow, "1 in 3 Fears Immigrants Influence US Elections: AP-NORC Poll," *AP News,* May 10, 2022, https://apnews.com/article/immigration-2022-midterm-elections-covid-health-media-2ebbd3849ca35ec76f0f91120639d9d4; and Jared Sharpe, "New National UMass Amherst Poll on Issues Finds One-Third of Americans Believe 'Great Replacement' Theory," University of Massachusetts, Amherst, https://www.umass.edu/news/article/new-national-umass-amherst-poll-issues-finds-one-third-americans-believe-great, accessed July 11, 2024. Some attribute the appeal of this theory to the deleterious effects of neoliberal economic policies. See John Rapley, "The Ungreat Replacement," *Aeon,* 2022, https://aeon.co/essays/the-great-replacement-is-real-but-its-not-what-the-right-says. On the interpretation of census data, see Richard Alba, *The Great Demographic Illusion: Majority, Minority, and the Expanding American Mainstream* (Princeton, NJ: Princeton University Press, 2020).
3. See Khaleda Rahman, " 'Great Replacement Theory' Has Inspired 4 Mass Shootings in Recent Years," *Newsweek,* May 16, 2022, https://www.newsweek.com/great-replacement-theory-inspired-terror-attacks-recent-years-1706953.

4. On Camus, see Curtis Dozier, "Greco-Roman Antiquity in Camus' 'Great Replacement,' " *Pharos: Doing Justice to the Classics*, October 7, 2019, https://pharos.vassarspaces.net/2019/10/07/greco-roman-antiquity-in-camus-great-replacement/; Sarah Shurts, "Far-Right Intellectuals and the Illiberal Discourses of Identity," in *Contemporary Far-Right Thinkers and the Future of Liberal Democracy*, ed. A. James McAdams and Alejandro Castrillon (London: Routledge, 2021), 31–42; and Max Deltau, "Renaud Camus: Revolte gegen den Großen Austausch," in *Schlüsseltexte der "Neuen Rechten": Kritische Analysen antidemokratischen Denkens*, ed. David Meiering (Wiesbaden: Springer, 2022). Camus told Sarah Wildman that "the white [race], which is by far the least numerous of the old major classical 'races,' . . . [is] under the most menace" and that multiculturalism "generates violence, crime, mistrust, misery, ugliness." (Sarah Wildman, " 'You Will Not Replace Us': A French Philosopher Explains the Charlottesville Chant," *Vox*, August 15, 2017, https://www.vox.com/world/2017/8/15/16141456/renaud-camus-the-great-replacement-you-will-not-replace-us-charlottesville-white.)
5. For the terminology of "highbrow white nationalism" and "the intellectual radical right," see George Hawley, *Making Sense of the Alt-Right* (New York: Columbia University Press, 2017), 27; and Mark J. Sedgwick, introduction to *Key Thinkers of the Radical Right: Behind the New Threat to Liberal Democracy*, ed. Mark J. Sedgwick (New York: Oxford University Press, 2019), xiii, with further discussion in the essays collected in that volume. See, too, Carol M. Swain and Russell Nieli, *Contemporary Voices of White Nationalism in America* (Cambridge: Cambridge University Press, 2003); Matthew N. Lyons, *Insurgent Supremacists: The U.S. Far Right's Challenge to State and Empire* (Oakland, CA: PM, 2018), 61–66; Patrik Hermansson, David Lawrence, Joe Mulhall, and Simon Murdoch, *The International Alt-Right: Fascism for the 21st Century?* (London: Routledge, 2020); and McAdams and Castrillon, *Contemporary Far-Right Thinkers.* On "human biodiversity," see Aaron Panofsky, Kushan Dasgupta, and Nicole Iturriaga, "How White Nationalists Mobilize Genetics: From Genetic Ancestry and Human Biodiversity to Counterscience and Metapolitics," *American Journal of Physical Anthropology* 175, no. 2 (2021): 387–98. On "cultural marxism," Jérôme Jamin, "Cultural Marxism: A Survey," *Religion Compass* 12, nos. 1–2 (2018); Tanner Mirrlees, "The Alt-Right's Discourse on 'Cultural Marxism': A Political Instrument of Intersectional Hate," *Atlantis: Critical Studies in Gender, Culture & Social Justice* 39, no. 1 (2018): 49–69; and Joan Braune, "Who's Afraid of the Frankfurt School? 'Cultural Marxism' as an Antisemitic Conspiracy Theory," *Journal of Social Justice* 9 (2019): 1–25. The concept of "traditionalism" cannot be reduced only to a white nationalist euphemism, but traditionalist thinkers, especially René Guénon and Julius Evola, have been embraced by a range of white nationalist intellectuals. See, for example, the

discussion of Benjamin R. Teitelbaum, *War for Eternity: Inside Bannon's Far-Right Circle of Global Power Brokers* (New York: Harper Collins, 2020): 8–14, 276–82.

6. Alfred North Whitehead, *Process and Reality: An Essay in Cosmology* (New York: Free Press, 1985), 39.
7. For this history, see Tamir Bar-On, *Where Have All the Fascists Gone?* (London: Routledge, 2007), 1–32; and Jean-Yves Camus and Nicolas Lebourg, *Far-Right Politics in Europe* (Cambridge, MA: Harvard University Press, 2017), 53–97. On the challenge this reconfiguration posed to fascist studies, see Roger Griffin, "Fascism's New Faces (and New Facelessness) in the 'Post-Fascist' Epoch," in *A Fascist Century: Essays by Roger Griffin*, ed. Matthew Feldman (London: Palgrave Macmillan, 2008).
8. On de Benoist, see Tamir Bar-On, "Alain de Benoist: Neo-Fascism with a Human Face?" 2015, https://www.bpb.de/system/files/dokument_pdf/Bar-On-DeBenoist-Fascismwithhumanface-2015.pdf; Jean-Yves Camus, "Alain de Benoist and the New Right," in Sedgwick, *Key Thinkers of the Radical Right*, 73–90; and Shurts, "Far-Right Intellectuals," 28–39. On Venner, see Bar-On, *Where Have All the Fascists Gone?* 31; and Camus and Lebourg, *Far-Right Politics in Europe*, 127–34.
9. The cases of Italy, France, Austria, Denmark, Slovenia, Bulgaria, Greece, and Great Britain are discussed in the essays collected in Gabriella Lazaridis, Giovanna Campani, and Annie Benveniste, eds., *The Rise of the Far Right in Europe: Populist Shifts and "Othering"* (London: Palgrave Macmillan, 2016). On GRECE, see Bar-On, *Where Have All the Fascists Gone?* 33–77; Camus and Lebourg, *Far-Right Politics in Europe*, 120–51; and Lou Mousset, " 'Reverse Colonization': Early Narratives of Decline in the French New Right," in Bracke and Hernandez Aguilar, *The Politics of Replacement*, 66–81. On the influence of de Benoist and the French New Right in Germany, see Roger Woods, *Germany's New Right as Culture and Politics* (London: Palgrave Macmillan, 2007), 25–64. On metapolitics, see Bar-On, *Where Have All the Fascists Gone?* 79–98; Shane Burley, *Fascism Today: What It Is and How to End It* (Chico, CA: AK, 2017), 102–5; Thomas J. Main, *The Rise of the Alt-Right* (Washington, DC: Brookings Institution Press, 2018), 12–13; Hermansson et al., *The International Alt-Right*, 14–16; Tamir Bar-On, "The Metapolitics of the Alt-Right: A 'Cultural War' for the United States, European Identity, and the 'White Race,' " in *The Right and Radical Right in the Americas: Ideological Currents from Interwar Canada to Contemporary Chile*, ed. Tamir Bar-On and Bàrbara Molas (Lanham, MD: Lexington Books, 2021). Treatments of Italian and German fascism's use of Greco-Roman antiquity include Volker Losemann, "The Nazi Concept of Rome," in *Roman Presences: Receptions of Rome in European Culture, 1789–1945*, ed. Catharine Edwards (Cambridge: Cambridge University Press, 1999), 221–35; Marla Stone,

"A Flexible Rome: Fascism and the Cult of Romanitá," in Edwards, *Roman Presences*, 205–20; Johann Chapoutot, *Greeks, Romans, Germans: How the Nazis Usurped Europe's Classical Past*, trans. Richard R. Nybakken (Berkeley: University of California Press, 2016); and the essays in Helen Roche and Kyriakos Demetriou, *Brill's Companion to the Classics, Fascist Italy and Nazi Germany* (Leiden: Brill, 2018).

10. On Rockwell, see Frederick J. Simonelli, *American Fuehrer: George Lincoln Rockwell and the American Nazi Party* (Urbana: University of Illinois Press, 1999); and William H. Schmaltz, *Hate: George Lincoln Rockwell and the American Nazi Party* (Washington, DC: Brassey's, 1999).

11. The fullest treatment of Oliver is Damon T. Berry, *Blood & Faith: Christianity in American White Nationalism* (Syracuse, NY: Syracuse University Press, 2017), 19–43. See, too, Leonard Zeskind, *Blood and Politics: The History of the White Nationalist Movement from the Margins to the Mainstream* (New York: Farrar, Straus & Giroux, 2009), 393–95; William H. Tucker, *The Cattell Controversy: Race, Science, and Ideology* (Urbana: University of Illinois Press, 2009), 131–32; George Hawley, *The Alt-Right: What Everyone Needs to Know* (Oxford: Oxford University Press, 2019), 37–38; and Curtis Dozier, "Revilo Oliver: The White Supremacist Within," *Pharos: Doing Justice to the Classics*, September 6, 2019, https://pharos.vassarspaces.net/2019/09/06/revilo-oliver-the-white-supremacist-within/. On the "Roman salute" and contemporary neo-Nazis, see Martin M. Winkler, *The Roman Salute: Cinema, History, Ideology* (Columbus: Ohio State University Press, 2009); and Curtis Dozier, "Nazi Leader 'Re-Brands' the Nazi salute as 'Roman Salute,'" *Pharos: Doing Justice to the Classics*, April 27, 2018, https://pharos.vassarspaces.net/2018/04/27/nazi-leader-re-brands-the-nazi-salute-as-roman-salute/.

12. On *The Turner Diaries*, see Aja Romano, "How a Dystopian Neo-Nazi Novel Helped Fuel Decades of White Supremacist Terrorism," *Vox*, January 28, 2021, https://www.vox.com/22232779/the-turner-diaries-novel-links-to-terrorism-william-luther-pierce. On Pierce, see Swain and Nieli, *Contemporary Voices of White Nationalism*, 260–76; and Zeskind, *Blood and Politics*, 17–34, 530–32. According to a laudatory biography of Pierce, it was Revilo Oliver who advised Pierce to write the novel that would become *The Turner Diaries*. On the growth of white nationalist movements as a reaction to the Obama presidency, see Kathleen M. Blee, Robert Futrell, and Pete Simi, *Out of Hiding: Extremist White Supremacy and How It Can Be Stopped* (New York: Routledge, 2024), 21–76.

13. Southern Poverty Law Center, "Extremist Files: Kevin MacDonald," https://www.splcenter.org/fighting-hate/extremist-files/individual/kevin-macdonald, accessed December 22, 2022. See further: Alexandar Mihailovic, "Hijacking Authority: Academic Neo-Aryanism and Internet Expertise," in *Digital Media Strategies of the Far Right in Europe and the*

United States, ed. Patricia Anne Simpson and Helga Druxes (Lanham, MD: Lexington Books, 2015), 84–91; Main, *Rise of the Alt-Right*, 68–79; Jeffrey C. Blutinger, "A New Protocols: Kevin MacDonald's Reconceptualization of Antisemitic Conspiracy Theory," *Antisemitism Studies* 5, no. 1 (Spring 2021): 4–43.

14. On Johnson and Counter-Currents, see Main, *Rise of the Alt-Right*, 108–11; Graham Macklin, "Greg Johnson and Counter-Currents," in Sedgwick, *Key Thinkers of the Radical Right*, 204–23; Liam Stack, "American White Nationalist Is Arrested in Norway," *New York Times*, November 4, 2019, https://www.nytimes.com/2019/11/04/world/europe/greg-johnson-arrested-white-nationalist.html. On Taylor and *American Renaissance*, see William H. Tucker, *The Funding of Scientific Racism: Wickliffe Draper and the Pioneer Fund* (Urbana: University of Illinois Press, 2002), 182–88; Swain and Nieli, *Contemporary Voices of White Nationalism*, 87–113; Zeskind, *Blood and Politics*, 367–80; Russell Nieli, "Jared Taylor and White Identity," in Sedgwick, *Key Thinkers of the Radical Right*, 137–54; Hermansson et al., *The International Alt-Right*, 37–38. On Arktos, see Tess Owen, "How a Small Budapest Publishing House Is Quietly Fueling Far-Right Extremism," *Vice*, May 30, 2019, https://www.vice.com/en/article/3k3558/how-a-small-budapest-publishing-house-is-quietly-fueling-far-right-extremism; Benjamin Teitelbaum, "Daniel Friberg and Metapolitics in Action," in Sedgwick, *Key Thinkers of the Radical Right*, 269–70; and Louie Dean Valencia-García, "The Rise and Fall of the Far Right in the Digital Age," in *Far-Right Revisionism and the End of History: Alt/Histories*, ed. Louie Dean Valencia-García (New York: Routledge, 2020), 305–45, with 313–15 on Jorjani, and 329–30 on Leonard. Jorjani's remarks about Hitler were reported in Jesse Singal, "Undercover with the Alt-Right," *New York Times*, September 19, 2017, https://www.nytimes.com/2017/09/19/opinion/alt-right-white-supremacy-undercover.html.

15. Michael Edison Hayden, "Stephen Miller's Affinity for White Nationalism Revealed in Leaked Emails," Southern Poverty Law Center, November 12, 2019, https://www.splcenter.org/hatewatch/2019/11/12/stephen-millers-affinity-white-nationalism-revealed-leaked-emails. On the Pioneer Fund, see Tucker, *The Funding of Scientific Racism*. On Regnery, see Aram Roston and Joel Anderson, "The Moneyman behind the Alt-Right," *BuzzFeed News*, July 23, 2017, https://www.buzzfeednews.com/article/aramroston/hes-spent-almost-20-years-funding-the-racist-right-it. On the VDARE foundation, see Alex Kotch and Michael Edison Hayden, "Donors Pumped Millions into White Nationalist Group," Southern Poverty Law Center, June 17, 2021, https://www.splcenter.org/hatewatch/2021/06/17/donors-pumped-millions-white-nationalist-group. On the anti-immigration website VDARE, see "Extremist Files: VDARE," Southern Poverty Law Center, https://www.splcenter.org/fighting-hate/extremist-files/group/vdare, accessed November

19, 2024; Rebecca Nelson Jacobs, "VDARE," in *Anti-Immigration in the United States: A Historical Encyclopedia*, ed. Kathleen R. Arnold (Santa Barbara, CA: ABC-Clio, 2012), 481–82; Main, *Rise of the Alt-Right*, 199–203; Neiwert, *Alt-America*, 267–73.

16. Donna Zuckerberg, *Not All Dead White Men: Classics and Misogyny in the Digital Age* (Cambridge, MA: Harvard University Press, 2018), 45–88.
17. Stephanie Quinn Katz, "Keynote Address to the Conference on Teaching the Ancient World," in *Classics: A Discipline and Profession in Crisis?* ed. Phyllis Culham and Lowell Edmunds (Lanham, MD: University Press of America, 1989); Caroline Winterer, *The Culture of Classicism: Ancient Greece and Rome in American Intellectual Life, 1780–1910* (Baltimore: Johns Hopkins University Press, 2002), especially 179; Lee T. Pearcy, *The Grammar of Our Civility: Classical Education in America* (Waco, TX: Baylor University Press, 2005), 22–25; Seth L. Schein, " 'Our Debt to Greece and Rome': Canon, Class, and Ideology," in *A Companion to Classical Receptions*, ed. Christopher Stray and Lorna Hardwick (Chichester: Wiley-Blackwell, 2008).
18. This perspective is foundational to the subfield of classical studies known as reception studies, on which see Charles Martindale, "Thinking through Reception," in *Classics and the Uses of Reception*, ed. Charles Martindale and Richard F. Thomas (Malden, MA: Blackwell, 2006), 1–13.
19. Hecataeus on Jewish people is summarized by Diodorus 40.3.4. Tacitus: *Histories* 5.5. Cicero: *Pro Flacco* 66, trans. Yonge. Seneca is quoted by Augustine, *Civitate Dei* 6.11, trans. McCracken. Strabo is quoted by Josephus, *Jewish Antiquities* 14.115–116. The translation given is that of Ralph Marcus, the editor of the Loeb translation of Josephus. In a note, he admits that the Greek verb he has translated as "made its power felt" has a more "usual meaning" of "gained mastery." It is tempting to infer that Marcus, as a Jewish scholar publishing his translation in the same year that Adolf Hitler was named chancellor of Germany, felt the weight of the political implications of his choice.
20. Raphael Cohen-Almagor, *Confronting the Internet's Dark Side: Moral and Social Responsibility on the Free Highway* (Cambridge: Cambridge University Press, 2015), 211.
21. Deborah E. Lipstadt, *Antisemitism: Here and Now* (New York: Knopf, 2019). On Nazi historians: Chapoutot, *Greeks, Romans, Germans*, 298–305. On Tacitus's *Germania*, see Christopher B. Krebs, *A Most Dangerous Book: Tacitus's Germania from the Roman Empire to the Third Reich* (New York; London: Norton, 2012). On Enlightenment antisemitism: Arthur Hertzberg, *The French Enlightenment and the Jews* (New York: Columbia University Press, 1968), 299–313. Mommsen: Benjamin H. Isaac, *The Invention of Racism in Classical Antiquity* (Princeton, NJ: Princeton University Press, 2004), 440, 445. Isaac notes that a similar idea appears in the work of the eminent historian A. N. Sherwin-White. On Mommsen's influence on

Hitler and other prominent Nazis, see Christhard Hoffmann, "Ancient Jewry—Modern Questions: German Historians of Antiquity on the Jewish Diaspora," *Illinois Classical Studies* 20 (1995): 191–207, especially 191, 195–201.

22. These sources are discussed by Erich S. Gruen, *Rethinking the Other in Antiquity* (Princeton, NJ: Princeton University Press, 2011), 304–6, 311–12, 324–25.
23. Michael Hill, "Synagogue Shooter Was Obsessed with Jewish Refugee Agency," *AP News*, October 30, 2018, https://apnews.com/article/33d4571da68d4b5cbcef8685c5e27f09. Juvenal's description of Jewish children is in *Satires* 14.96–108. On the question of the applicability of "antisemitism" to antiquity, see, for example, Isaac, *The Invention of Racism*, 499–500; and Benjamin H. Isaac, "The Ancient Mediterranean and the Pre-Christian Era," in *Antisemitism: A History*, ed. Albert S. Lindemann and Richard S. Levy (New York: Oxford University Press, 2010), 45–46. However, it is argued by Nicholas De Lange, "The Origins of Anti-Semitism: Ancient Evidence and Modern Interpretations," in *Anti-Semitism in Times of Crisis*, ed. Sander L. Gilman and Steven T. Katz (New York: New York University Press, 1991), that in antiquity one can "discern a certain progression . . . in the emergence of specific elements of later anti-Semitism" (35). Meanwhile, René Bloch, *Ancient Jewish Diaspora: Essays on Hellenism* (Leiden: Brill, 2022), admits: "In my earlier research, I had avoided using the term 'antisemitism' for those centuries before the term itself was coined in the late nineteenth century. Today, I hesitate less" (233).

Chapter Two. The Last Stand against Modernity

1. Lyra Monteiro, "How a Trump Executive Order Aims to Set White Supremacy in Stone," *Hyperallergic*, 2021, http://hyperallergic.com/614175/how-a-trump-executive-order-aims-to-set-white-supremacy-in-stone/. A transcript of the president's January 6 speech is provided by Brian Naylor, "Read Trump's Jan. 6th Speech, a Key Part of Impeachment Trial," NPR.org, February 10, 2021, https://www.npr.org/2021/02/10/966396848/read-trumps-jan-6-speech-a-key-part-of-impeachment-trial. On the insurrection, see Lane Crothers and Grace Burgener, "Insurrectionary Populism? Assessing the January 6 Attack on the U.S. Capitol," *Populism* 4, no. 2 (2021): 129–45, especially 139–42.
2. On the Proud Boys and white nationalism, see Alexandra Minna Stern, *Proud Boys and the White Ethnostate: How the Alt-Right Is Warping the American Imagination* (Boston: Beacon, 2019), 71–76; and Meadhbh Park, "Fight Club: Gavin McInnes, the Proud Boys, and Male Supremacism," in *Male Supremacism in the United States: From Patriarchal Traditionalism to Misogynist Incels and the Alt-Right*, ed. Emily K. Carian, Alex DiBranco, and Chelsea Ebin (London: Routledge, 2022). On the Oath Keepers, see

Matthew N. Lyons, *Insurgent Supremacists: The U.S. Far Right's Challenge to State and Empire* (Oakland, CA: PM, 2018), 41–55; and Sam Jackson, *Oath Keepers: Patriotism and the Edge of Violence in a Right-Wing Antigovernment Group* (New York: Columbia University Press, 2020).

3. For a journalistic treatment of false claims about the 2020 election results, see Glenn Kessler and Salvador Rizzo, "President Trump's False Claims of Vote Fraud: A Chronology," *Washington Post*, November 6, 2020, https://www.washingtonpost.com/politics/2020/11/05/president-trumps-false-claims-vote-fraud-chronology/. For a technical analysis of results, see Bernard Grofman and Jonathan Cervas, "Statistical Fallacies in Claims about 'Massive and Widespread Fraud' in the 2020 Presidential Election: Examining Claims Based on Aggregate Election Results," *Statistics and Public Policy* 11, no. 1 (January 5, 2024).
4. Robert A. Pape, "Deep, Divisive, Disturbing and Continuing: New Survey Shows Mainstream Community Support for Violence to Restore Trump Remains Strong," Chicago Project on Security and Threats, January 2, 2022, https://d3qioqp55mx5f5.cloudfront.net/cpost/i/docs/Pape_AmericanInsurrectionistMovement_2022-01-02.pdf?mtime=1641247264.
5. On 1980s skinhead movements, see Kyle Burke, " 'It's a White Fight and We've Got to Win It': Culture, Violence, and the Transatlantic Far Right since the 1970s," in *Global White Nationalism: From Apartheid to Trump*, ed. Daniel Geary, Camilla Schofield, and Jennifer Sutton (Manchester: Manchester University Press, 2020), especially 264–68, 283–84. Southern Poverty Law Center, "Terror from the Right: Archives," July 23, 2018, https://www.splcenter.org/terror-from-the-right-archives catalogues incidents of racist violence.
6. On the fascist politics of *300*, see Thomas E. Jenkins, *Antiquity Now: The Classical World in the Contemporary American Imagination* (Cambridge: Cambridge University Press, 2015), 112–20; and Carl Plantinga, "Fascist Affect in *300*," *Projections* 13, no. 2 (2019): 20–37. On *300*'s aesthetic and philosophical affinities with Nazi propaganda films, see Martin M. Winkler, *Classical Literature on Screen: Affinities of Imagination* (Cambridge: Cambridge University Press, 2017), 249–96, especially 250–67. The xenophobic politics of Frank Miller, the author of the graphic novel on which the film is based, are documented in George A. Kovacs, "Truth, Justice, and the Spartan Way: Freedom and Democracy in Frank Miller's *300*," in *Classics in the Modern World: A "Democratic Turn"?* ed. Lorna Hardwick and Stephen Harrison (Oxford: Oxford University Press, 2013), 385–88, 391–92. The racism of the film was transparently legible to audiences in Iran; see Lloyd Llewellyn-Jones, "Trouble in the Tehran Multiplex: Xerxes, *300*, and *300: Rise of an Empire* in Iran," in *Epic Heroes on Screen*, ed. Antony Augoustakis and Stacie Raucci (Edinburgh: Edinburgh University Press, 2018), 191–205.

7. Quoted by Helen Roche, " 'In Sparta Fühlte Ich Mich Wie in Einer Deutschen Stadt' (Goebbels): The Leaders of the Third Reich and the Spartan Nationalist Paradigm," in *English and German Nationalist and Anti-Semitic Discourse, 1871–1945*, ed. Geraldine Horan, Felicity Rash, and Daniel Wildmann (Oxford: Peter Lang, 2013), 92, 97. On the Nazi fascination with Sparta, see further Johann Chapoutot, *Greeks, Romans, Germans: How the Nazis Usurped Europe's Classical Past*, trans. Richard R. Nybakken (Berkeley: University of California Press, 2016), 214–25, 373–76; and the essays in Helen Roche and Kyriakos Demetriou, *Brill's Companion to the Classics, Fascist Italy and Nazi Germany* (Leiden: Brill, 2018). On earlier German attitudes toward Sparta, see Elizabeth Rawson, *The Spartan Tradition in European Thought* (Oxford: Oxford University Press, 1969), 306–43. On contemporary ones in Germany and Austria, see Julia Müller, "Pop Culture against Modernity: New Right-Wing Movements and the Reception of Sparta," in *Classical Controversies: Reception of Graeco-Roman Antiquity in the Twenty-First Century*, ed. Kim Beerden and Timo Epping (Leiden: Sidestone, 2022), 103–23.
8. On David Lane: Mattias Gardell, *Gods of the Blood: The Pagan Revival and White Separatism* (Durham, NC: Duke University Press, 2003), 191–207; and George Michael, "David Lane and the Fourteen Words," *Totalitarian Movements and Political Religions* 10, no. 1 (March 1, 2009): 43–61. On Bronze Age Pervert: Josh Vandiver, "Metapolitics, Masculinity, and Technology in the Rise of 'Bronze Age Pervert,' " in *Contemporary Far-Right Thinkers and the Future of Liberal Democracy*, ed. A. James McAdams and Alejandro Castrillon (London: Routledge, 2022), 242–63; on his identification, see Graeme Wood, "How Bronze Age Pervert Charmed the Far Right," *Atlantic*, August 3, 2023, https://www.theatlantic.com/magazine/archive/2023/09/bronze-age-pervert-costin-alamariu/674762/.
9. Herodotus 9.122, trans. Waterfield. Specialists may dispute the white nationalist understanding of the Greek word *arete*, but the most widely used ancient Greek lexicon, that of Liddell-Scott-Jones, begins its definition of this word by specifying "in Homer, esp. of manly qualities."
10. On the Golden Dawn and related political organizations in Greece, see Antonis A. Ellinas, "The Rise of Golden Dawn: The New Face of the Far Right in Greece," *South European Society and Politics* 18, no. 4 (2013), 453–565; Gabriella Lazaridis and Vasiliki Tsagkroni, "Posting for Legitimacy: Identity and Praxis of Far-Right Populism in Greece," in *The Rise of the Far Right in Europe: Populist Shifts and "Othering,"* ed. Gabriella Lazaridis, Giovanna Campani, and Annie Benveniste (London: Palgrave Macmillan, 2016), 208–234; and Christina Verousi and Chris Allen, "From Obscurity to National Limelight: The Dramatic Rise, Fall and Future Legacy of Golden Dawn," *Political Insight* 12, no. 1 (March 1, 2021): 22–25. On the short-lived "Spartans" party, see Niki Kitsantonis, "Far-Right Greek Party Is Banned from E.U. Parliament Elections," *New York Times*, April 25, 2024,

https://www.nytimes.com/2024/04/25/world/europe/greece-far-right-european-parliament.html. On Anglin and the Daily Stormer, see Luke O'Brien, "The Making of an American Nazi," *Atlantic*, November 14, 2017, https://www.theatlantic.com/magazine/archive/2017/12/the-making-of-an-american-nazi/544119/; David Neiwert, *Alt-America: The Rise of the Radical Right in the Age of Trump* (New York: Verso Books, 2017), 248–61; and "Extremist Files: Andrew Anglin," Southern Poverty Law Center, https://www.splcenter.org/fighting-hate/extremist-files/individual/andrew-anglin, accessed February 28, 2025. James C. Russell, author of *The Germanization of Early Medieval Christianity: A Sociohistorical Approach to Religious Transformation* (New York: Oxford University Press, 1994), touted his work founding and running an anti-immigration organization in materials for his (failed) 2008 campaign to represent New York in the U.S. Congress: "Jim Russell for Congress," archived August 2, 1998, https://web.archive.org/web/20080802012757/http://russellforcongress.com:80/.

11. As reported in Just Jared, "Gerard Butler: *300* Movie Photocall," February 15, 2007, https://www.justjared.com/2007/02/15/gerard-butler-rodrigo-santoro/. On the murder of Pavlos Fyssas and the subsequent convictions of Golden Dawn members, see "Greek Court Rules Golden Dawn Leaders Ran a Crime Group," eKathimerini.com, October 7, 2020, https://www.ekathimerini.com/news/257787/greek-court-rules-golden-dawn-leaders-ran-a-crime-group/.
12. The foundational analysis of what has come to be called "hegemonic masculinity" is Raewyn Connell, *Gender and Power: Society, the Person and Sexual Politics* (Redwood City, CA: Stanford University Press, 1987), especially 85, 184–85. On the promotion of violent masculinity in contemporary media, see Jackson Katz, "Advertising and the Construction of Violent White Masculinity," in *Gender, Race, and Class in Media: A Critical Reader*, ed. Gail Dines and Jean McMahon Humez (Thousand Oaks, CA: SAGE, 2011), 261–69; and Michael S. Kimmel, *Manhood in America: A Cultural History*, 3rd ed. (Oxford: Oxford University Press, 2012), 269–75, with 211–37 on the history of this form of masculinity as a reaction against feminism and neoliberal economic policy.
13. Cynthia Miller-Idriss, *Hate in the Homeland: The New Global Far Right* (Princeton, NJ: Princeton University Press, 2020), 93–94, 101.
14. Gavin Weedon, "On the Entangled Origins of Mud Running: 'Overcivilization,' Physical Culture, and Overcoming Obstacles in the Spartan Race," in *Endurance Running: A Socio-Cultural Examination*, ed. William Bridel, Pirkko Markula, and Jim Denison (London: Routledge, 2015), 39–41. On historical novels about the Persian Wars, see Emma Bridges, "The Guts and the Glory: Pressfield's Spartans at the Gates of Fire," in *Cultural Responses to the Persian Wars: Antiquity to the Third Millennium*, ed. Emma Bridges, Edith Hall, and Peter J. Rhodes (Oxford: Oxford University Press, 2007), 407–10.

On Pressfield, see Lynn S. Fotheringham, "The Positive Portrayal of Sparta in Late-Twentieth-Century Fiction," in *Sparta in Modern Thought: Politics, History and Culture*, ed. Stephen Hodkinson and Ian Macgregor Morris (Swansea: Classical Press of Wales, 2012), 420. *Gates of Fire* appeared on the 2013 "Commandant's Professional Reading List" (https://www.marines.mil/News/Messages/Messages-Display/Article/895256/revision-of-the-commandants-professional-reading-list/, accessed October 29, 2024) and is still included on the "Foundational" professional reading list of the Marine Corps' Commandant (https://www.mca-marines.org/resource/commandants-professional-reading-list/, accessed October 29, 2024). It also appeared on the U.S. Army Chief of Staff's "Professional Reading List" for 2011 (https://history.army.mil/html/books/105/105-1-1/CMH_Pub_105-1-1_2011.pdf, accessed October 29, 2024).

15. "We will fight in the shade": Herodotus 7.226.2; prohibition against living abroad: Plutarch, *Lycurgus* 27.3; infanticide: Plutarch, *Lycurgus* 16; murder of slaves: Plutarch, *Lycurgus* 28. The epitaph at Thermopylae is recorded by Herodotus 7.228. The translation given here is that used in Miller's graphic novel and the film *300*. It is not as unambiguously honorific as is usually assumed: see Ioannis Ziogas, "Sparse Spartan Verse: Filling Gaps in the Thermopylae Epigram," *Ramus* 43, no. 2 (2014): 1–19; and Matthew A. Sears, *Sparta and the Commemoration of War* (Cambridge: Cambridge University Press, 2024), 64–99.
16. Stephen Hodkinson, "Was Sparta an Exceptional Polis?" in *Sparta: New Perspectives*, ed. Stephen Hodkinson and Anton Powell (Swansea: Classical Press of Wales, 2009), 417–72. On Sparta's "mediocre" military, see Myke Cole, *The Bronze Lie: Shattering the Myth of Spartan Warrior Supremacy* (Oxford: Osprey, 2021); and Bret Devereaux, "Spartans Were Losers," *Foreign Policy*, June 5, 2024, https://foreignpolicy.com/2023/07/22/sparta-popular-culture-united-states-military-bad-history/. On the biases of sources for Sparta, see Nigel M. Kennell, *Spartans: A New History* (London: Wiley-Blackwell, 2011), 9–16; Paul Christensen, "Xenophon's Views on Sparta," in *The Cambridge Companion to Xenophon*, ed. Michael Flower (Cambridge: Cambridge University Press, 2016); Noreen Humble, "Silencing Sparta," in *Plutarch's Unexpected Silences: Suppression and Selection in the "Lives" and "Moralia,"* ed. Jeffrey Beneker, Craig Cooper, Noreen Humble, and Francis Titchener (Leiden: Brill, 2022), 223–31; and Ália Rodrigues, "Plutarch's 'Life of Lycurgus': Greek Lawgivers and the Construction of Spartan Exceptionalism," in *Sparta in Plutarch's Lives*, ed. Philip Davies and Judith Mossman (Swansea: Classical Press of Wales, 2023).
17. Cole, *The Bronze Lie*, 19. For an accounting of Laconophilic names for American municipalities and athletic teams, see Andrew J. Bayliss, *The Spartans* (Oxford: Oxford University Press, 2020), 144; and Sean R. Jensen, "The Reception of Sparta in North America: Eighteenth to

Twenty-First Centuries," in *A Companion to Sparta*, ed. Anton Powell (Hoboken, NJ: Wiley, 2018), 712. On the Alamo and Thermopylae, see David S. Levene, "Xerxes Goes to Hollywood," in Bridges, Hall, and Rhodes, *Cultural Responses to the Persian Wars*, 394–98. On the racial politics of the "Heroic Anglo Narrative" of Texas history, see Bryan Burrough, Chris Tomlinson, and Jason Stanford, *Forget the Alamo: The Rise and Fall of an American Myth* (New York: Penguin, 2022), 217–33. On the Spartans in eighteenth-century French political thought, see Rawson, *The Spartan Tradition*, 231–54; Humble, "Silencing Sparta," 236–37; and Sears, *Sparta and the Commemoration of War*, 198–202.

18. The title of Paul Cartledge, *Thermopylae: The Battle That Changed the World* (New York: Macmillan, 2006), obscures the book's real focus, which is the effect of the battle on discourses of freedom, not the heroism of the Spartans against an invader; Rebecca Futo Kennedy, " 'Western Civilization,' White Supremacism, and the Myth of a Greco-Roman Past," in *Polarized Pasts: Heritage and Belonging in Times of Political Polarization*, ed. Elisabeth Niklasson (New York: Berghahn Books, 2023), 94, describes the title as "fluff." On the history of scholars promoting Spartan exceptionalism, see Stephen Hodkinson, "Spartans on the Capitol: Recent Far-Right Appropriations of Spartan Militarism in the USA and Their Historical Roots," in Beerden and Epping, *Classical Controversies*, 59–84. See Debby Sneed, "Disability and Infanticide in Ancient Greece," *Hesperia* 90, no. 4 (2021): 747–72, on the scanty evidence for infanticide. A recent example of scholarship that takes ancient sources at face value is Paul Anthony Rahe, *The Spartan Regime: Its Character, Origins, and Grand Strategy* (New Haven, CT: Yale University Press, 2016), especially 4–6, 66–67. On Rahe's use of "jihad," "crusade," and "holy war" to characterize the Persian invasion of Greece, see Bernard J. Dobski, "Classical Regimes at War: Spartan Republicanism vs. Athenian Democracy," *Society* 53, no. 6 (2016): 659.

19. On the gender politics of white nationalist movements, see Jessie Daniels, *White Lies: Race, Class, Gender and Sexuality in White Supremacist Discourse* (New York: Routledge, 1997), 33–69; Abby L. Ferber, *White Man Falling: Race, Gender, and White Supremacy* (Lanham, MD: Rowman & Littlefield, 1998), 85–143; with twenty-first-century movements addressed in Patrik Hermansson, David Lawrence, Joe Mulhall, and Simon Murdoch, *The International Alt-Right: Fascism for the 21st Century?* (London: Routledge, 2020), 181–93. On the role of women within white nationalism, see Kathleen M. Blee, *Inside Organized Racism: Women in the Hate Movement* (Berkeley: University of California Press, 2002); and Eviane Leidig, *The Women of the Far Right: Social Media Influencers and Online Radicalization* (New York: Columbia University Press, 2023). Ancient treatments of Spartan women include Xenophon, *Constitution of the Lacedaemonians* 1.3–10, and Plutarch, *Lycurgus* 14. Humble, "Silencing

Sparta," 240, notes that feminist scholars have been, at times, uncritical of the apparently progressive aspects of ancient descriptions of Spartan women. Sarah E. Bond called for highlighting the "flaws" of Sparta: "This Is Not Sparta," *Eidolon*, May 7, 2018, https://eidolon.pub/this-is-not-sparta-392a9ccddf26.

20. John M. Finnis, "Law, Morality, and 'Sexual Orientation,' " *Notre Dame Law Review* 69, no. 5 (1994): 1055, referring among other sources to Plato, *Laws* 1.636c, and Xenophon, *Constitution of the Lacedaemonians* 2.13. Jeffrey Carnes, "Plato in the Courtroom: The Surprising Influence of the 'Symposium' on Legal Theory," in *Plato's Symposium: Issues in Interpretation and Reception*, ed. Debra Nails, Frisbee Sheffield, and James Lesher (Washington, DC: Center for Hellenic Studies, 2006), summarizes the case, as well as philosopher Martha Nussbaum's argument against Finnis, presented at trial. On homophobia in white nationalism, see Daniels, *White Lies*, 39–41, 49–51; and Hermansson, Lawrence, Mulhall, and Murdoch, *The International Alt-Right*, 194–204. Against the idea of antiquity as a "gay utopia," see Alastair Blanshard, "The Myth of the Ancient Greek 'Gay Utopia,' " *Conversation*, December 14, 2017, http://theconversation.com/friday-essay-the-myth-of-the-ancient-greek-gay-utopia-88397.

21. The fullest ancient source on this regiment is Plutarch, *Life of Pelopidas* 18. Ancient sources as early as Aeschylus (fragments 135–37) describe a sexual relationship between Achilles and Patroclus. On the difficult problem of Alexander's relationship with his general and confidant Hephaestion, see Marilyn B. Skinner, " 'Alexander' and Ancient Greek Sexuality: Some Theoretical Considerations," in *Responses to Oliver Stone's "Alexander": Film, History, and Cultural Studies*, ed. Paul Cartledge and Fiona Rose Greenland (Madison: University of Wisconsin Press, 2010).

22. Plato, *Republic* 411e, trans. Griffith; Socrates' analysis of the soul appears primarily at *Republic* 4.439a—441e. Angela Hobbs, *Plato and the Hero: Courage, Manliness, and the Impersonal Good* (Cambridge: Cambridge University Press, 2000), 245–49, discusses the gender politics of Plato's conception of *thumos*, which does not exclude women from possessing it. Johnson's participation in the Finland conference was reported by FOIA Research, "Awakening Conference," 2019, https://www.foiaresearch.net/event/awakening-conference, accessed November 29, 2024. Johnson quotes Buckley's 1860 translation of the *Iliad.*

23. Francis Fukuyama, *The End of the History and the Last Man* (New York: Free Press, 1992), 162–66 on Plato, 182–91 on *thumos* in the contemporary world, and 333–39 on the threat *thumos* poses to political stability. A critique of Fukuyama's sanitized view of history is Peter Fritzsche, "Review of Francis Fukuyama, *The End of History and the Last Man*," *American Historical Review* 97, no. 3 (1992): 817–19; Tarik Kochi, "A Dangerous Text: Francis Fukuyama's Mischaracterisation of Identity, Recognition

and Right-Wing Nationalism," *Borderlands Journal* 20, no. 2 (October 1, 2021): 155–82, details the availability of his work to far right interpretation. Fukuyama's acceptance (xvi–xvii) of Hegel's idea that human freedom originates in the duels that he believed warrior-aristocrats practiced in prehistory places violence, if only implicitly, at the center of his analysis.

24. Homer, *Iliad* 5.253.
25. Homer, *Iliad* 1.149–71; and *Odyssey* 11.119–37.
26. Michael L. Silk, Ingo Gildenhard, and Rosemary J. Barrow, *The Classical Tradition: Art, Literature, Thought* (Hoboken, NJ: John Wiley & Sons, 2014), 265. On the varied reception of Achilles, see Joachim Latacz, "Achilles," in *The Classical Tradition*, ed. Glenn W. Most, Salvatore Settis, and Anthony Grafton, trans. Deborah Lucas Schneider (Cambridge, MA: Harvard University Press, 2010).
27. H. R. McMaster, "Preserving the Warrior Ethos," *National Review*, October 28, 2021, https://www.nationalreview.com/magazine/2021/11/15/preserving-the-warrior-ethos/. On the gods in *Troy*, see Charles C. Chiasson, "Redefining Homeric Heroism in Wolfgang Petersen's *Troy*," in *Reading Homer: Film and Text*, ed. Kostas Myrsiades (Cranbury, NJ: Associated University Presses, 2009), 186–207. On Homer in the poetry of the First World War, see Elizabeth Vandiver, *Stand in the Trench, Achilles: Classical Receptions in British Poetry of the Great War* (Oxford: Oxford University Press, 2010), especially 228–29. My treatment of Weil is based on that of Lisa Maurizio, *Classical Mythology in Context*, 2nd ed. (New York: Oxford University Press, 2023), 483–86.
28. Emily Wilson, trans., *Homer: The Odyssey* (New York: Norton, 2018), 105.
29. Edith Hall, *The Return of Ulysses: A Cultural History of Homer's Odyssey* (London: I. B. Tauris, 2012), 109, with 79 and 91 on the Cyclops episode. There is evidence that colonizers conceived of themselves as Odysseus and of the indigenous peoples they met as Cyclopes. On Christopher Columbus, see Michael Palencia-Roth, "Mapping the Caribbean: Cartography and the Cannibalization of Culture," in *History of Literature in the Caribbean*, vol. 3: *Cross-Cultural Studies*, ed. A. James Arnold (Amsterdam: John Benjamins, 1997). On John Smith, see Peter Hulme, *Colonial Encounters: Europe and the Native Caribbean, 1492–1797* (London: Methuen, 1986), 152–56.
30. Hall, *The Return of Ulysses*, 112–13. On *The Natural* as a "daring and exact reconfiguration of the *Iliad* and *The Odyssey* into American idiom," see Kevin Thomas Curtin, "*The Natural:* Our *Iliad* and *Odyssey*," *Antioch Review* 43, no. 2 (1985): 225–41.
31. Quoted by Martin M. Winkler, "Wolfgang Petersen on Homer and 'Troy,' " in *Return to Troy: New Essays on the Hollywood Epic*, ed. Martin M. Winkler (Leiden: Brill, 2015), 16–26. On the *Odyssey* in British public schools, the elite institutions that produced most of the officials that administered the British Empire, see Richard Jenkyns, *The Victorians and*

Ancient Greece (Cambridge, MA: Harvard University Press, 1980), 207–21; on imperial ideology in the schools more generally, J. A. Mangan, "Images of Empire in the Late Victorian Public School," *Journal of Educational Administration and History* 12, no. 1 (1980): 31–39. The function of Homer in American curricula and the imposition of American "individualism" onto its heroes is documented in Seth L. Schein, "An American Homer for the Twentieth Century," in *Homer in the Twentieth Century: Between World Literature and the Western Canon*, ed. Emily Greenwood and Barbara Graziosi (Oxford: Oxford University Press, 2007), especially 280–83. Levene, "Xerxes Goes to Hollywood," 395–400, argues that American accounts of Thermopylae, too, are shaped by the preoccupations of film westerns.

32. Walter Shrewring, trans., *Homer: The Odyssey* (Oxford: Oxford University Press, 1980), xix; Bernard Knox, introduction to *Homer: The Iliad*, trans. Robert Fagles (New York: Penguin, 1990), 24, 37. James M. Redfield, *Nature and Culture in the Iliad: The Tragedy of Hector* (Chicago: University of Chicago Press, 1975), ix, 123, expresses admiration for Hector, arguing that "the conflict between personal loyalty and collective loyalty is an element of the generic situation of the warrior." On Odysseus's "New Heroism": Hermann Fränkel, *Early Greek Poetry and Philosophy: A History of Greek Epic, Lyric, and Prose to the Middle of the Fifth Century*, trans. Moses Hadas and James Willis (New York: Harcourt Brace Jovanovich, 1973), 85–93. On the London Forum, see James Poulter, "The Neo-Nazi Home of the UK Alt-Right," *Vice*, March 12, 2018, https://www.vice.com/en/article/the-neo-nazi-home-of-the-uk-alt-right/.

33. These experiences are summarized by Benjamin F. Jones, "Looking for Bernard Knox: Warrior, Ancient and Modern," *War, Literature, and Arts* 15, nos. 1–2 (2003): 323–33.

34. Quoted by Meyer Reinhold, *Classica Americana: The Greek and Roman Heritage in the United States* (Detroit: Wayne State University Press, 1984), 98.

35. Plutarch, *Life of Cato the Elder* 8.2, trans. Perrin. Cato's "incitement to genocide" (Plutarch, *Cato* 27.1) is discussed in Ben Kiernan, "The First Genocide: Carthage, 146 BC," *Diogenes* 51, no. 3 (2004): 27. Elizabeth Manwell, "Real Roman Men and the Greeks Who Hate Them: Disciplina, Cato the Elder and Plutarch," in *Toxic Masculinity in the Ancient World*, ed. Melanie Racette-Campbell and Aven McMaster (Edinburgh: Edinburgh University Press, 2024), finds criticism of Cato's toxic masculinity in Plutarch's account of his life.

36. Elon Musk (@elonmusk), X.com, August 24, 2024, https://twitter.com/elonmusk/status/1820221050904359331.

37. The battle of the Horatii and Curiatii is described by Livy 1.25; Publius Decius Mus's *devotio:* Livy 10.28–29; Horatius at the bridge: Livy 2.10.

38. Livy, preface 9–10, trans. Foster. Polybius, too, described the Roman veneration of these figures in terms strikingly similar to those found in

white nationalist thought. "Enthusiasm and emulation for noble deeds . . . are engendered among the Romans by their customs," wrote Polybius, giving Horatius Cocles as his main example of veneration for these heroes (Polybius 6.55, trans. Shuckburgh).

39. Michael Anton, "The Flight 93 Election," *Claremont Review of Books*, 2016, https://claremontreviewofbooks.com/digital/the-flight-93-election/. On Anton's pseudonym, see Michael Warren, " 'Decius' Comes in from the Cold," *Weekly Standard*, February 13, 2017, 11–14; and on his politics, see Daniel W. Drezner, "Michael Anton and the Terrible, Horrible, No Good, Very Racist Argument on Birthright Citizenship," *Washington Post*, July 23, 2018, https://www.washingtonpost.com/news/posteverything/wp/2018/07/23/michael-antons-bad-no-good-very-racist-argument-on-birthright-citizenship/; and Paul Blest, "There Is Nothing More Highbrow Than White Supremacy," *Splinter*, 2018, https://splinternews.com/there-is-nothing-more-highbrow-than-white-supremacy-1825522090.

40. Malkin discusses her biography in an interview with Brian Lamb, Booknotes, December 8, 2002, https://booknotes.c-span.org/Watch/173558–1/Michelle-Malkin. On Malkin's identity and her appearance at the *American Renaissance* conference, see Hannah Gais, "Former Newsmax Host Speaks at White Nationalist Conference," Southern Poverty Law Center, December 17, 2021, https://www.splcenter.org/hatewatch/2021/12/17/former-newsmax-host-speaks-white-nationalist-conference. On her politics, see Bridge Initiative Team, "Factsheet: Michelle Malkin," Bridge, November 7, 2019, https://bridge.georgetown.edu/research/factsheet-michelle-malkin/; Leidig, *The Women of the Far Right*, 31; and David Neiwert, *The Age of Insurrection: The Radical Right's Assault on American Democracy* (New York: Penguin, 2023), 222–23. On Malkin's contributions to VDARE, see Alex Koppelman, "Michelle Malkin's White Supremacist Ties," *HuffPost*, May 12, 2006, https://www.huffpost.com/entry/michelle-malkins-white-su_b_20873.

41. Robert E. Sullivan, *Macaulay: The Tragedy of Power* (Cambridge, MA: Harvard University Press, 2010), 258; Joseph W. Elder, "The Decolonization of Educational Culture: The Case of India," *Comparative Education Review* 15, no. 3 (1971): 288–95. On Macaulay's classicism and imperialism, see Javed Majeed, "Comparativism and References to Rome in British Imperial Attitudes to India," in *Roman Presences: Receptions of Rome in European Culture*, ed. Catharine Edwards (Cambridge: Cambridge University Press, 1999), 88–109; and Phiroze Vasunia, *The Classics and Colonial India* (Oxford: Oxford University Press, 2013), 201–6. On the *Lays of Ancient Rome*, see Catharine Edwards, "Translating Empire? Macaulay's Rome," in *Roman Presences*, 70–87.

42. Ellen Moynihan, "White Supremacist James Jackson Reveals Deranged Desire to Kill Black Men to Save White Women in Jailhouse Interview,"

New York Daily News, March 26, 2017, https://www.nydailynews.com/news/national/james-jackson-twisted-regrets-killing-timothy-caughman-article-1.3009736. Michael E. Miller, "Hunting Black Men to Start a 'Race War,'" *Washington Post*, December 27, 2019. Reviews of Brand's book include Rose Mary Sheldon, "*Killing for the Republic: Citizen Soldiers and the Roman Way of War* by Steele Brand (Review)," *Classical Journal* 116, no. 1 (2020): 117–19; and Lee L. Brice, "Polemic as Flawed History," *Classical Review* 71, no. 1 (April 2021): 162–64. On violence and Grand Strategy video games featuring Rome, see Emily Joy Bembeneck, "Phantasms of Rome: Video Games and Cultural Identity," in *Playing with the Past: Digital Games and the Simulation of History*, ed. Matthew Wilhelm Kapell and Andrew B. R. Elliott (New York: Bloomsbury, 2013), 77–90; David Serrano Lozano, "Ludus (Not) Over: Video Games and the Popular Perception of Ancient Past Reshaping," in *Classical Antiquity in Video Games: Playing with the Ancient World*, ed. Christian Rollinger (London: Bloomsbury, 2020), 56–58; and Ross Clare, *Ancient Greece and Rome in Videogames: Representation, Play, Transmedia* (London: Bloomsbury, 2021), 83, 86. On stereotyped portrayals of "barbarians," see Dominic Machado, "Battle Narratives from Ancient Historiography to Total War: Rome II," in Rollinger, *Classical Antiquity in Video Games*, 97–100. On racism, misogyny, and video game culture, including the "Gamergate" harassment campaign that served as a precursor and feeder to the emergence of the so-called "Alt-Right," see Angela Nagle, *Kill All Normies: Online Culture Wars from 4Chan and Tumblr to Trump and the Alt-Right* (Winchester: Zero Books, 2017), 19–27; Kristin M. S. Bezio, "Ctrl-Alt-Del: GamerGate as a Precursor to the Rise of the Alt-Right," *Leadership* 14, no. 5 (2018): 556–66; and Hermansson, Lawrence, Mulhall, and Murdoch, *The International Alt-Right*, 114–16.

43. Kurt Raaflaub, "Caesar and Genocide: Confronting the Dark Side of Caesar's Gallic Wars," *New England Classical Journal* 48, no. 1 (May 14, 2021): 64. Interviews with January 6 rioters in Mark Danner, "'Be Ready to Fight,'" *New York Review of Books*, February 11, 2021, https://www.nybooks.com/articles/2021/02/11/stupid-coup-be-ready-to-fight-capitol-riot/.

Chapter Three. Predicting the New Dark Ages

1. The gender politics of the Roman Empire TikTok phenomenon are discussed by Sarah E. Bond and Stephanie Wong, "What Men Are Thinking about When They Think about the Roman Empire," MSNBC.com, September 19, 2023, https://www.msnbc.com/opinion/msnbc-opinion/men-roman-empire-tiktok-trend-rcna105780. On the popularity of modern stoicism and the inspiration that male supremacy groups take from it, see Donna Zuckerberg, *Not All Dead White Men: Classics and Misogyny in the Digital Age* (Cambridge, MA: Harvard University Press,

2018), 45–88. On masculinity in ancient Rome, see Craig A. Williams, *Roman Homosexuality* (Oxford: Oxford University Press, 2010).

2. Quoted by Brittany Wong, "Why Your Boyfriend or Husband Is Obsessed with the Roman Empire," *HuffPost*, September 19, 2023, https://www.huffpost.com/entry/men-thinking-about-roman-empire_l_65088b22e4b0584d7c6bcef7?fx.

3. On *OpenPsych*, see Aaron Panofsky, Kushan Dasgupta, and Nicole Iturriaga, "How White Nationalists Mobilize Genetics: From Genetic Ancestry and Human Biodiversity to Counterscience and Metapolitics," *American Journal of Physical Anthropology* 175, no. 2 (2021): 393–95.

4. Mike Duncan, *The Storm before the Storm: The Beginning of the End of the Roman Republic* (New York: Public Affairs, 2017), xx. Apocalyptic language taken from Cullen Murphy, "Rome's Slow Motion Catastrophe—And Ours," *Atlantic*, March 11, 2021, https://web.archive.org/web/20210311131206/https://www.theatlantic.com/magazine/archive/2021/04/no-really-are-we-rome/618075/; Sean Illing, "What America Can Learn from the Fall of the Roman Republic," *Vox*, January 1, 2019, https://www.vox.com/2019/1/1/18139787/rome-decline-america-edward-watts-mortal-republic; Tim Elliott, "America Is Eerily Retracing Rome's Steps to a Fall. Will It Turn around Before It's Too Late?" *Politico*, November 3, 2020, https://www.politico.com/news/magazine/2020/11/03/donald-trump-julius-caesar-433956. Other recent books that emphasize decline include Edward J. Watts, *Mortal Republic: How Rome Fell into Tyranny* (New York: Basic Books, 2018); and John Rapley and Peter Heather, *Why Empires Fall: Rome, America, and the Future of the West* (New Haven, CT: Yale University Press, 2023). Thomas E. Strunk, *On the Fall of the Roman Republic: Lessons for the American People* (London: Anthem, 2022) is notable for its use of Roman history to expose the violence that patriotic American self-identity often minimizes or ignores.

5. Vance is quoted by James Pogue, "Inside the New Right, Where Peter Thiel Is Placing His Biggest Bets," *Vanity Fair*, April 20, 2022, https://www.vanityfair.com/news/2022/04/inside-the-new-right-where-peter-thiel-is-placing-his-biggest-bets. On Hillsdale, see Erik Eckholm, "In Hillsdale College, a 'Shining City on a Hill' for Conservatives," *New York Times*, February 1, 2017. The advertisement for Hillsdale's course on the Roman Republic is archived at https://web.archive.org/web/20220215001003/https:/lp.hillsdale.edu/roman-republic-preregister/, accessed July 29, 2024.

6. Niall Ferguson, *Colossus: The Rise and Fall of the American Empire* (New York: Penguin, 2005), 14. This book was originally published in 2004 with a less apocalyptic subtitle, "The Price of America's Empire." Further examples of comparisons between America and Rome from this period are collected by Neville Morley, *Roman Empire: Roots of Imperialism* (London: Pluto, 2010), 6–8; and Paul Burton, "Pax Romana/Pax Americana:

Perceptions of Rome in American Political Culture, 2000–2010," *International Journal of the Classical Tradition* 18, no. 1 (2011): 66–104.

7. The quotation marks around "fall of Rome" are intended to signal to the reader that despite the familiarity of this and similar phrases such as "the fall of the Roman Empire," almost every aspect of this period of history is contested by professional historians, including whether one should speak of a "fall" at all.
8. The work most associated with this approach is Peter Brown, *The World of Late Antiquity: AD 150–750* (New York: Harcourt Brace Jovanovich, 1971). Averil Cameron, *The Mediterranean World in Late Antiquity, AD 395–600* (Abingdon: Routledge, 1993), resists and complicates narratives of decline throughout. See, too, her response to the attempt to separate "value-free" narratives of decline from "polemic" in J.H.W.G. Liebeschuetz, "The Uses and Abuses of the Concept of 'Decline' in Later Roman History; or, Was Gibbon Politically Incorrect?" in *Recent Research in Late-Antique Urbanism*, ed. Luke Lavan (Portsmouth, RI: Journal of Roman Archaeology, 2001), 238–39. On the arbitrariness of ignoring the political longevity of Constantinople, see Jonathan Theodore, *The Modern Cultural Myth of the Decline and Fall of the Roman Empire* (London: Palgrave Macmillan, 2016), 37.
9. Accessible reassessments of the so-called "Dark Ages" include Seb Falk, *The Light Ages: The Surprising Story of Medieval Science* (New York: Norton, 2020); and Matthew Gabriele and David Perry, *The Bright Ages: A New History of Medieval Europe* (New York: Harper Collins, 2022).
10. Neville Morley, "Review of *Why America Is Not a New Rome*, by Vaclav Smil," *Economic History Review* 64, no. 1 (2011): 339–40, calls for greater attention to the appeal of narratives of decline. On Rome as a model for the British Empire, see Javed Majeed, "Comparativism and References to Rome in British Imperial Attitudes to India," in *Roman Presences: Receptions of Rome in European Culture, 1789–1945*, ed. Catharine Edwards (Cambridge: Cambridge University Press, 1999), 109; and Phiroze Vasunia, "Greater Rome and Greater Britain," in *Classics and Colonialism*, ed. Barbara Goff (London: Bloomsbury, 2005), 38.
11. Theodore, *The Modern Myth of Decline and Fall*, 34–50.
12. On the fascist "myth of national decadence," see Roger Griffin, *The Nature of Fascism* (London: Routledge, 1993), 201. On decline and fascism, see further Roger Griffin, *Fascism: An Introduction to Comparative Fascist Studies* (Cambridge: Polity, 2018), 133; Robert O. Paxton, *The Anatomy of Fascism* (New York: Knopf, 2004), 186, 218; Jason Stanley, *How Fascism Works: The Politics of Us and Them* (New York: Random House, 2018), 3. Fear of decline is a recurring theme in the survey of American attitudes toward Rome in Margaret Malamud, *Ancient Rome and Modern America*, Classical Receptions (Malden, MA: Wiley-Blackwell, 2009).

13. On *Breitbart*, which straddles the boundary between mainstream conservatism and open white nationalism, see David Neiwert, *Alt-America: The Rise of the Radical Right in the Age of Trump* (New York: Verso Books, 2017), 243–48; Thomas J. Main, *The Rise of the Alt-Right* (Washington, DC: Brookings Institution Press, 2018), 210–30; and Barry J. Balleck, *Modern American Extremism and Domestic Terrorism: An Encyclopedia of Extremists and Extremist Groups* (Santa Barbara, CA: ABC-CLIO, 2018), 50–52.
14. On immigrants in the military, see Katherine Schaeffer, "The Changing Face of America's Veteran Population," Pew Research Center, November 8, 2023, https://www.pewresearch.org/short-reads/2023/11/08/the-changing-face-of-americas-veteran-population/. Musk's tweet: Elon Musk (@elonmusk), X.com, September 27, 2024, https://twitter.com/elonmusk/status/1839813945559003286, criticizing appointments that were reported by Matt Sepic, "New Recruits for Minneapolis Police Department Include First Somali-American Woman, First Non-U.S. Citizen," *MPR News*, September 27, 2024, https://www.mprnews.org/story/2024/09/27/minneapolis-police-department-first-somali-american-woman-first-non-us-citizen.
15. On Faye, see Jean-Yves Camus, "Guillaume Faye, from New Right Intellectual to Prophet of the Racial Civil War," in *Contemporary Far-Right Thinkers and the Future of Liberal Democracy*, ed. James McAdams and Alejandro Castrillon (London: Routledge, 2021), 66–81; and Ico Maly, "Guillaume Faye's Legacy: The Alt-Right and Generation Identity," *Journal of Political Ideologies* 28, no. 1 (2023): 35–61. MacDonald's argument about Rome appears in his self-published book that cites, for example, the genetic theories of the Nazi Party member and eugenicist Fritz Lenz to "present a biologically informed view of Western culture and civilization." The comparison between white and nonwhite immigration ignores the long history of American discrimination against all immigrants, including those who eventually came to be identified as white, and makes a concept that has no basis in genetics or biology—race—an explanatory cause for decline.
16. Main, *Rise of the Alt Right*, 27–29; Nick Confessore, Ben Decker, Jacob Silver, and Julie Tate, "Inside the Apocalyptic Worldview of *Tucker Carlson Tonight*," *New York Times*, April 30, 2022, https://www.nytimes.com/interactive/2022/04/30/us/tucker-carlson-tonight.html; Cassie Miller, "SPLC Poll Finds Substantial Support for 'Great Replacement' Theory and Other Hard-Right Ideas," Southern Poverty Law Center, June 1, 2022, https://www.splcenter.org/news/2022/06/01/poll-finds-support-great-replacement-hard-right-ideas.
17. On Cole's "pessimistic commentary on America's present and future" see Alan Wallach, "Thomas Cole: Landscape and the Course of American Empire," in *Thomas Cole: Landscape into History*, ed. William H. Truettner and Alan Wallach (New Haven, CT: Yale University Press, 1994), 94. Dan

Rather warned of a "downward spiral" for America in an October 9, 2016, post on Facebook (https://www.facebook.com/theDanRather/posts/10157537557070716).

18. Quotes from Peter Brimelow, *Alien Nation: Common Sense about America's Immigration Disaster* (New York: Harper Perennial, 1995), 131–33; and Peter Brimelow, "Conservatism and Immigration," *Commentary* 100, no. 5 (November 1995): 34–35. Positive reviews of *Alien Nation* include those of David C. Hendrickson in *Foreign Affairs* 74, no. 4 (July 1995): 140; and Miles Jack in *Atlantic Monthly* 275, no. 4 (1995): 130. Four essays on Brimelow's book were published in Samuel T. Francis et al., "Does Immigration Threaten to Undermine American Nationhood, as Peter Brimelow Contends in *Alien Nation*?" *National Review* 47, no. 8 (May 1, 1995): 76–80, including one by Samuel T. Francis, whose openly white nationalist work is discussed elsewhere in this book. The senator who sponsored the Alien Exclusion Act wrote in the *New York Times* that it passed because "thoughtful men began to apprehend that the United States was going the way that Rome went" (David A. Reed, "America of the Melting Pot Comes to an End," *New York Times*, April 27, 1924). I thank Joshua Nudell for the reference. On Peter Brimelow, see Kristina Shull, "Peter Brimelow (1947–)," in *Anti-Immigration in America: A Historical Encyclopedia*, ed. Kathleen R. Arnold (Santa Barbara, CA: ABC-Clio, 2012), 88–89; George Hawley, *Making Sense of the Alt-Right* (New York: Columbia University Press, 2017), 38–40; and Jane Coaston, "Peter Brimelow and VDare, the White Nationalist Website with Close Ties to the Right, Explained," *Vox*, August 22, 2018, https://www.vox.com/2018/8/22/17768296/peter-brimelow-vdare-kudlow-white-house-racism.

19. Cassius Dio, *Roman History* 60.17.6. Dio presents this claim as political propaganda against Claudius, not as an actual practice. On Malkin's appearance at AFPAC, see Will Sommer, "Michelle Malkin Endorses Racist CPAC Rival," *Daily Beast*, February 11, 2020, https://www.thedailybeast.com/right-richter-michelle-malkin-endorses-racist-cpac-rival-america-first-political-action-conference/.

20. Patrick J. Buchanan, *State of Emergency: The Third World Invasion and Conquest of America* (New York: Macmillan, 2006), 2. On Buchanan and white nationalism, see Chip Berlet and Matthew N. Lyons, *Right-Wing Populism in America: Too Close for Comfort* (New York: Guilford, 2000), 279–81; Leonard Zeskind, *Blood and Politics: The History of the White Nationalist Movement from the Margins to the Mainstream* (New York: Farrar, Straus & Giroux, 2009), 279–93; George Hawley, *Right-Wing Critics of American Conservatism* (Lawrence: University Press of Kansas, 2016), 186–90; Edward Ashbee, "Patrick J. Buchanan and the Death of the West," in *Key Thinkers of the Radical Right*, ed. Mark J. Sedgwick (Oxford: Oxford University Press, 2019), 121–36. Other references to Rome in Buchanan's books can be found in *A Republic, Not an Empire* (reprinted in 2002 as a

critique of President George W. Bush's attempts at immigration reform), and *The Death of the West* (2002). This latter book was a major influence on Matthew Heimbach, whom courts found liable for civil conspiracy for his involvement in the 2017 Unite the Right rally in Charlottesville, Virginia (Vegas Tenold, *Everything You Love Will Burn: Inside the Rebirth of White Nationalism in America* [New York: Nation Books, 2018], 56–58).

21. Buchanan on women: Patrick J. Buchanan, *The Death of the West: How Dying Populations and Immigrant Invasions Imperil Our Country and Civilization* (New York: Macmillan, 2002), 47–49. Schlafly is quoted by Edward J. Watts, *The Eternal Decline and Fall of Rome: The History of a Dangerous Idea* (New York: Oxford University Press, 2021), 236. In 2014, at age ninety, she appeared on the radio show of conspiracy theorist Alex Jones, where they agreed that America was "going the way of Rome" (Watts, *Eternal Decline,* 237). On Trump as continuator of Buchanan's strategy, see Ben Greenfield, "Donald Trump Is Pat Buchanan with Better Timing," *Politico,* 2016, https://www.politico.com/magazine/story/2016/09/donald-trump-pat-buchanan-republican-america-first-nativist-214221.

22. Mike Johnson on Rome: Erin Burnett, "Hear House Speaker's Past Comments Blaming the Fall of the Roman Empire on Homosexuality," CNN Politics, November 1, 2023, https://www.cnn.com/videos/politics/2023/11/01/kfile-house-speaker-homosexuality-ebof-vpx.cnn. Ben Carson: Andrew Kaczynski, "Ben Carson Blamed Same-Sex Marriage for 'Dramatic Fall of the Roman Empire,' " *BuzzFeed News,* September 29, 2015, https://www.buzzfeednews.com/article/andrewkaczynski/not-exactly-edward-gibbon. Richard Nixon: Curtis Dozier, "Nixon Claims Homosexuality Destroyed Greece, Rome . . . and America?" *Pharos: Doing Justice to the Classics,* April 19, 2019, https://pharos.vassarspaces.net/2019/04/19/nixon-claims-homosexuality-destroyed-greece-rome-and-america/. Ronald Reagan: "Remarks by Governor Ronald Reagan," Ronald Reagan Presidential Library, October 14, 1969, https://www.reaganlibrary.gov/public/digitallibrary/gubernatorial/pressunit/p18/40–840–7408624-p18–004–2017.pdf, quoted by Watts, *Eternal Decline,* 234.

23. Samuel P. Huntington, *Who Are We? The Challenges to America's National Identity* (New York: Simon & Schuster, 2004), 11–12, a book described as "Patrick Buchanan with footnotes" by Alan Wolfe, "Native Son: Samuel Huntington Defends the Homeland," *Foreign Affairs* 83, no. 3 (2004): 121. Similar arguments appear in a book by a classical scholar (Victor Davis Hanson, *Mexifornia: A State of Becoming* [San Francisco: Encounter Books, 2003]) that Peter Brimelow described in a review at VDARE as a "wonderful little book."

24. Niall Ferguson, "Empire Falls," *Vanity Fair,* October 17, 2006, https://www.vanityfair.com/news/2006/10/empire200610, modifying Juvenal, *Satires* 10.81. John Pincince, "Jerry Bentley, World History, and the Decline of the 'West,' " *Journal of World History* 25, no. 4 (2015): 637–38, points out how

predictions of decline are integral to Ferguson's celebration of "the West." On the similarities between Ferguson's analysis of Western civilization and those of overt white nationalists, see R. Charles Weller, " 'Western' and 'White Civilization': White Nationalism and Eurocentrism at the Crossroads," in *21st-Century Narratives of World History: Global and Multidisciplinary Perspectives*, ed. R. Charles Weller (London: Cham, 2017), 52–54, 59; and Andrew Gillett, "The Fall of Rome and the Retreat of European Multiculturalism: A Historical Trope as a Discourse of Authority in Public Debate," *Cogent Arts & Humanities* 4, no. 1 (January 1, 2017): 1–13, especially 10 on the similarity between Ferguson's "deploy[ment]" of the "classicizing appeal" of narratives concerning Rome's "decline" and that of "contemporary proponents of anti-immigration and anti-migration policies."

25. Cullen Murphy, *Are We Rome? The Fall of an Empire and the Fate of America* (Boston: Houghton Mifflin Harcourt, 2007), 83–90, 173, 178, 180–81. Murphy's description of the borders comes in a discussion of "cultural" rather than "political" borders, but the language of "invasive influences" suggests that the distinction is blurry. The description of Murphy's politics is that of Jed Esty, *The Future of Decline: Anglo-American Culture at Its Limits* (Redwood City, CA: Stanford University Press, 2022), 14.

26. Burr: Carl J. Richard, *The Founders and the Classics: Greece, Rome, and the American Enlightenment* (Cambridge, MA: Harvard University Press, 1995), 36. Jefferson: Richard, *Founders and the Classics*, 97. Webster: Carl J. Richard, *The Golden Age of the Classics in America: Greece, Rome, and the Antebellum United States* (Cambridge, MA: Harvard University Press, 2009), 179, noting the irony that Gibbon, in part, blamed Christianity for the fall of Rome. Gibbon himself only rarely drew comparisons with the present (see J.G.A. Pocock, *Barbarism and Religion*, vol. 3: *The First Decline and Fall* [Cambridge: Cambridge University Press, 2003], 8 for a decline-focused example). A study of the historiography of the fall of Rome before and after Gibbon is Ian Wood, *The Modern Origins of the Early Middle Ages* (Oxford: Oxford University Press, 2013).

27. On the debate over how preoccupied Gibbon was with each of these revolutions, see the following essays in Glen W. Bowersock, John Clive, and Stephen R. Graubard, eds., *Edward Gibbon and the Decline and Fall of the Roman Empire* (Cambridge, MA: Harvard University Press, 1977): Glen W. Bowersock, "Gibbon on Civil War and Rebellion in the Decline of the Roman Empire," 33–34; J.G.A. Pocock, "Between Machiavelli and Hume: Gibbon as Civic Humanist and Philosophical Historian," 115–16; Stephen R. Graunbard, "Edward Gibbon: Contraria Sunt Complementa," 133; Frank E. Manuel, "Edward Gibbon: Historien-Philosophe," 175–76. A critique of Gibbon's methods can be found in T. S. Brown, "Gibbon, Hodgkin, and the Invaders of Italy," in *Edward Gibbon and Empire*, ed. Roland Quinault and Rosamond McKitterick (Cambridge: Cambridge University Press, 1996), especially 139, 143, 159.

28. Watts, *Eternal Decline*, 233. On *The Darkening Age*, see the review of Tim Whitmarsh (*Guardian*, December 28, 2017, https://www.theguardian.com/books/2017/dec/28/the-darkening-age-the-christian-destruction-of-the-classical-world-by-catherine-nixey), who writes that Gibbon's "spirit permeates Catherine Nixey's book." The review of Averil Cameron (*Tablet*, September 23, 2017, https://www.thetablet.co.uk/books/10/11298/blame-the-christians) is more critical: "We imagined that we had made some progress in finally overturning the Gibbonian model … but, no." Bannon's admiration for Gibbon, as well as Thucydides and Plutarch's *Lives*, is documented by Keith Koffler, *Bannon: Always the Rebel* (Washington, DC: Regnery, 2017), 2. Bannon, who argues that Rome declined because "the empire became overrun by immigrants," refers to America as "the new Rome" (Koffler, *Bannon*, 100, 112). Bannon says he is a "populist," not a white nationalist, but in 2018 he exhorted members of France's National Rally party to regard the labels "racist" and "xenophobe" as a "badge of honor" (Morgan Winsor, "Steve Bannon: 'Let Them Call You Racist … Wear It as a Badge of Honor,'" *ABC News*, March 10, 2018, https://abcnews.go.com/Politics/steve-bannon-call-racist-wear-badge-honor/story?id=53656814). On Bannon's fascination with Greco-Roman antiquity, see Curtis Dozier, "The Biggest Name in White Nationalist Classics," *Pharos: Doing Justice to the Classics*, December 19, 2022, https://pharos.vassarspaces.net/2022/12/19/steve-bannon-classics-gibbon/. Iggy Pop, "Caesar Lives," appeared in *Classical Ireland* 2 (1995): 94–96 and was reprinted in *Arion* 23 no. 1 (2015): 187–88.
29. Quoted in Nathan O'Hagan, "Reaganite Rockers to Brexit Punks: 'The Kids Are Alt-Right,'" *Byline Times*, February 22, 2021, https://bylinetimes.com/2021/02/22/reaganite-rockers-to-brexit-punks-the-kids-are-alt-right/. Pop's comparison between America and Rome is Pop, "Caesar Lives," 94.
30. On Sailer, see Park MacDougald and Jason Willick, "The Man Who Invented Identity Politics for the New Right," *Intelligencer*, April 30, 2017, https://nymag.com/intelligencer/2017/04/steve-sailer-invented-identity-politics-for-the-alt-right.html; Angela Saini, *Superior: The Return of Race Science* (Boston: Beacon, 2019), 97–92; and Panofsky, Dasgupta, and Iturriaga, "How White Nationalists Mobilize Genetics," 391. On Buchanan and Gibbon, see Buchanan, *State of Emergency*, 5. For Gibbon's influence on Pierce, see William Luther Pierce, "Crisis in Rhodesia: White Survival Is at Stake," *Attack!* 45 (1976).
31. Since the many editions of Gibbon all have different pagination, I cite his chapter structure, which is consistent across editions. Gibbon describes Jewish people in part 1 of chapter 16; his remarks on homosexuality appear in part 8 of chapter 44. Pocock, "Between Machiavelli and Hume," 299, notes Gibbon's "abhorrence of the Jews." Gibbon describes Ethiopia in part 6 of chapter 47.
32. Quoted by Kirstofer Allerfeldt, "Rome, Race, and the Republic: Progressive America and the Fall of the Roman Empire, 1890–1920," *Journal of*

the Gilded Age and Progressive Era 7, no. 3 (2008): 314–15, who also collects examples of citations of Gibbon in the writings of Brooks Adams, Henry Adams, Henry Hay, and the political opponents of William McKinley. On Roosevelt and "race suicide" more generally, see Thomas G. Dyer, *Theodore Roosevelt and the Idea of Race* (Baton Rouge: Louisiana State University Press, 1980), 143–67; and Theodore Roosevelt, *Theodore Roosevelt on Race, Riots, Reds, Crime* (New York: Probe, 1968), an admiring collection of the president's proclamations edited by his son Archibald. Madison Grant, *The Passing of the Great Race; or, The Racial Basis of European History* (New York: Charles Scribner's Sons, 1916), 19, reproduces Gibbon's argument that Christianity harmed Rome; Lothrop Stoddard, *The Rising Tide of Color against White World-Supremacy* (New York: Charles Scribner's Sons, 1922), 116, describes the "mongrel chaos of the declining Roman Empire." On de Gobineau, see Wood, *Modern Origins*, 106–12. Gibbon may have laid the foundations for the racialist understanding of Roman population decline in, for example, his chapter 31, part 3, describing how "the vile and wretched populace of Rome" would have "been extinguished" if not for "the manumission of slaves and the influx of strangers" who brought with them the "vices of the universe." Pocock's study of the intellectual context of Gibbon's thought encompasses the six volumes of *Barbarism and Religion*, published from 1999 to 2015 (Cambridge: Cambridge University Press). Enlightenment texts relevant to the creation of the modern category of race are collected by Emmanuel Chukwudi Eze, *Race and the Enlightenment: A Reader* (Oxford: Blackwell, 1997).

33. Will Durant and Ariel Durant, *The Lessons of History* (New York: Simon & Schuster, 1968), 20. Their analysis of "biological factors" for the fall of Rome is in Will Durant, *The Story of Civilization*, vol. 3: *Caesar and Christ* (New York: Simon & Schuster, 1944), 665–66, quoted in Buchanan, *Death of the West*, 47. On the Durants' work as "the apotheosis of the Grand Narrative" of "the West," see David Gress, *From Plato to NATO: The Idea of the West and Its Opponents* (New York: Simon & Schuster, 1998), 35–36.

34. A. D. Nock, "Paganism in the Roman Empire," in *The Cambridge Ancient History*, vol. 12: *The Imperial Crisis and Recovery, A.D. 193–324*, ed. F. E. Adcock et al. (Cambridge: Cambridge University Press, 1939), 448. Martin P. Nilsson, "The Race Problem of the Roman Empire," appeared in a scientific journal devoted to genetics, *Hereditas* 2, no. 3 (1921): 370–90; on Nilsson's later retraction of this essay, see Anssi Saura, "A Tale of Two Papers," *Hereditas* 151, no. 6 (2014): 119–22. Tenney Frank, "Race Mixture in the Roman Empire," *American Historical Review* 21, no. 4 (1916): 689–708, was reprinted in the "Classics Corner" of the 2005 issue of the *Occidental Quarterly* with an appreciation by classical scholar E. Christian Kopff. Like Gibbon's *Decline and Fall*, Mommsen's *History of Rome* has ap-

peared in many editions with varied pagination. His account of "parasitic immigrants" appears in a section entitled "Depopulation of Italy" in chapter 11 of book 5.

35. Erin Burnett, "Hear House Speaker's Past Comments Blaming the Fall of the Roman Empire on Homosexuality," CNN Politics, November 1, 2023, https://www.cnn.com/videos/politics/2023/11/01/kfile-house-speaker-homosexuality-ebof-vpx.cnn. Contrary to the white nationalist defense of contemporary "censorship" of Frank, some aspects of his methods and findings were questioned soon after the publication of his article by Mary L. Gordon, "The Nationality of Slaves under the Early Roman Empire," *Journal of Roman Studies* 14 (1924): 93–111. But as Niall McKeown, *The Invention of Ancient Slavery?* (London: Duckworth, 2007), 12–24, notes in his critique of this "morally repugnant" understanding of history, Frank's arguments were "ignored rather than rebutted" because "the nature of the evidence . . . makes it oddly difficult to disprove them."

36. Peter Heather, *The Fall of the Roman Empire: A New History of Rome and the Barbarians* (Oxford: Oxford University Press, 2006), 459, reviewed by Michael Kulikowski, *Classical Outlook* 82, no. 1 (2006): 162–64. On the appeal of Heather's and other historians' work to "contemporary proponents of anti-immigration and anti-immigration policies," see Gillett, "The Fall of Rome," 7–10. Heather rejects Buchanan's work in Peter Heather, "Migration and the End of Empire," *Yale University Press Blog*, October 5, 2023, https://yalebooks.yale.edu/2023/10/05/migration-and-the-end-of-empire/.

37. Engels's interview was translated into English on a now-defunct pro-Orban blog, *Hungary Journal*, November 13, 2017, https://web.archive.org/web/20210716160009/https://thehungaryjournal.com/2017/11/13/belgian-historian-today-hungary-looks-a-lot-more-western-than-belgium/. Engels embraces the "Eurabia" conspiracy theory in David Engels, *Le déclin: La crise de l'Union européenne et la chute de la République romaine—Analogies historiques* (Paris: Editions Toucan, 2012), 78. On this theory, including its influence on the mass murderer Anders Behring Breivik, see Sindre Bangstad, "Bat Ye'or and Eurabia," in Sedgwick, *Key Thinkers of the Radical Right*, 170–86. The reviews of Engels cited here are those of Alex McAuley, *Bryn Mawr Classical Review* (2014), https://bmcr.brynmawr.edu/2014/2014.01.13/; and Manuel Tröster, "Ancient Rome as a Paradigm for the EU?" *Classical Review* 64, no. 2 (2014): 622–24. *American Renaissance* reprinted Peter Jones, "It Was Tribalism That Finished Rome, and It Will Finish Brussels Too," *Spectator*, January 1, 2005.

38. Watts, *Eternal Decline*, is one survey of Roman reflections on their own (supposed) decline. Those quoted by white nationalists include Livy, preface 9, trans. Foster; Sallust, *Conspiracy of Catiline* 10, trans. Rolfe; Tacitus, *Dialogue on Orators* 28, trans. Peterson; Ammianus Marcellinus, *Res Gestae* 14.6.4, 14.6.18, trans. Rolfe; Salvian, *De Gubernatore Dei* 7.6, trans.

Sanford. Cato's invectives against luxury are found in Plutarch's *Life of Cato the Elder* 4–9.

39. Seneca, *On Anger* 3.17, trans. Basore; Jerome, Letter 60.16 (Latin *beluae*); Libanius, *Orations* 19.13 (Greek *thêria*); Ammianus Marcellinus, *Res Gestae* 31.4.5, trans. Rolfe. On Roman prejudice against "barbarians," see Ralph W. Mathisen, "Violent Behavior and the Construction of Barbarian Identity in Late Antiquity," in *Violence in Late Antiquity*, ed. H. A. Drake (London: Routledge, 2006), 27–35. On *Gates of Vienna*, a site frequented by mass murderer Anders Behring Breivik, see Gabriella Lazaridis, Marilou Polymeropoulou, and Vasiliki Tsagkroni, "Networks and Alliances against the Islamisation of Europe: The Case of the Counter-Jihad Movement," in *Understanding the Populist Shift: Othering in a Europe in Crisis*, ed. Gabriella Lazaridis and Giovanna Campani (Abingdon: Routledge, 2017), 70–103; and Bridge Initiative Team, "Factsheet: Gates of Vienna," Bridge, September 18, 2020, https://bridge.georgetown.edu/research/factsheet-gates-of-vienna/.

40. Juvenal, *Satires* 3.60–65, linked to contemporary politics by Heather Vincent, "Xenophobia, Racism, and Hate Speech: Re-Reading Juvenal in the Era of Donald Trump" (paper delivered at the Classical Association of the Midwest and South annual meeting, April 7, 2021), abstract: https://camws.org/sites/default/files/101.EPluribusUnum.03.pdf; Propertius 3.13.1–24, quoted by Engels, *Le déclin*, 313n185; Suetonius, *Life of Nero* 28. On "incels" and Greco-Roman antiquity, see Zuckerberg, *Not All Dead White Men*, 178–79.

41. Polybius, *Histories* 37.9, trans. Shuckburgh; Ovid, *Nux* 24; Tacitus, *Annales* 3.25; Pliny the Younger, *Epistles* 4.15.3; Petronius, *Satyricon* 116 (a patently satirical passage); Codex Theodosianus 11.28.2; Hierocles quoted at Stobaeus 4.24.14; Augustus on foreigners: Cassius Dio, *Roman History* 56.7, trans. Foster; Suetonius, *Life of Augustus* 40, trans. Rolfe, with Lloyd A. Thompson, "The Concept of Purity of Blood in Suetonius' Life of Augustus," *Museum Africum* 7 (1981): 35–46, on the racial logic of the passage.

42. Mustafa Sagir and Stephen T. Mockabee, "Public Attitudes toward Immigration: Was There a Trump Effect?" *American Politics Research* 51, no. 3 (May 1, 2023): 381–96, analyze American xenophobia; for American anxieties about immigration and culture, see Jens Hainmueller and Daniel J. Hopkins, "Public Attitudes toward Immigration," *Annual Review of Political Science* 17, no. 1 (2014): 225–49. Deborah J. Schildkraut, "Does Becoming American Create a Better American? How Identity Attachments and Perceptions of Discrimination Affect Trust and Obligation," in *Fear, Anxiety, and National Identity: Immigration and Belonging in North America and Western Europe*, ed. Nancy Foner and Patrick Simon (New York: Russell Sage Foundation, 2015), 83–114, finds that discrimination determines the extent to which immigrants feel "trust in American political institutions" and "obligations to the national community."

43. Moral decline: Adam M. Mastroianni and Daniel T. Gilbert, "The Illusion of Moral Decline," *Nature* 618, no. 7966 (June 7, 2023): 782–89, with a summary of findings and implications in Mariana Lenharo, "Morality Is Declining, Right? Scientists Say That Idea Is an Illusion," *Nature* 618, no. 7965 (June 7, 2023): 441–42. On white anxiety, see Hui Bai and Christopher M. Federico, "Collective Existential Threat Mediates White Population Decline's Effect on Defensive Reactions," *Group Processes & Intergroup Relations* 23, no. 3 (April 1, 2020): 361–77; and Maria Abascal, "Contraction as a Response to Group Threat: Demographic Decline and Whites' Classification of People Who Are Ambiguously White," *American Sociological Review* 85, no. 2 (2020): 298–322. On "minority majority" as an artifact of census-taking, see Richard Alba, *The Great Demographic Illusion: Majority, Minority, and the Expanding American Mainstream* (Princeton, NJ: Princeton University Press, 2020).
44. On the conservatism of narratives of decline, see Theodore, *The Modern Myth of Decline and Fall*, 198. On white supremacy and decline, see Esty, *Future of Decline*, 30–31. Bowersock's lecture is Glen W. Bowersock, "The Vanishing Paradigm of the Fall of Rome," *Bulletin of the American Academy of Arts and Sciences* 49, no. 8 (1996): 43.
45. A recent argument that environmental factors caused the fall of Rome is Kyle Harper, *The Fate of Rome: Climate, Disease, and the End of an Empire* (Princeton, NJ: Princeton University Press, 2017), with the critique of Paul Erdkamp, "War, Food, Climate Change, and the Decline of the Roman Empire," *Journal of Late Antiquity* 12, no. 2 (2019): 422–65. On the fall of Rome as beneficial to Europe, see Walter Scheidel, *Escape from Rome: The Failure of Empire and the Road to Prosperity* (Princeton, NJ: Princeton University Press, 2019), with the critiques of Peter Thonemann, "But What If . . .: A Counterfactual Examination of the History of Europe," *Times Literary Supplement*, January 31, 2020; and Salman Sayyid and AbdoolKarim Vakil, "Critical Muslim Studies and the Remaking of the (Ancient) World," in *Critical Ancient World Studies: The Case for Forgetting Classics*, ed. Mathura Umachandran and Marchella Ward (Abingdon: Routledge, 2023), 35–50.

Chapter Four. The Descendants of Achilles

1. On Spencer, see George Hawley, *Making Sense of the Alt-Right* (New York: Columbia University Press, 2017), 51–66; Tamir Bar-On, "Richard B. Spencer and the Alt Right," in *Key Thinkers of the Radical Right*, ed. Mark J. Sedgwick (Oxford: Oxford University Press, 2019).
2. On William Regnery II, see Aram Anderson and Joel Roston, "The Moneyman behind the Alt-Right," *BuzzFeed News*, July 23, 2017, https://www.buzzfeednews.com/article/aramroston/hes-spent-almost-20-years-funding-the-racist-right-it.

3. Identity Evropa's flyers are collected by Ben Davis, "White Nationalism's New Love of Art History, Decoded," Artnet News, March 7, 2017, https://news.artnet.com/art-world/identity-evropa-posters-art-symbolism-881747. The Antidefamation League's list of Identity Evropa's campaigns in 2017 is available at https://www.adl.org/sites/default/files/Campus-Report-Table-2017.pdf, accessed March 13, 2025.
4. The bibliography demonstrating that race has no genetic basis is vast. Accessible summaries include Dorothy Roberts, *Fatal Invention: How Science, Politics, and Big Business Re-Create Race in the Twenty-First Century* (New York: New Press, 2011), especially 49–54, who also documents the persistence of race-thinking among medical doctors and other scientists; and Angela Saini, *Superior: The Return of Race Science* (Boston: Beacon, 2019), especially 55–57. On the toleration and even "embrace" of race science by academic geneticists, see too Aaron Panofsky, *Misbehaving Science: Controversy and the Development of Behavior Genetics* (Chicago: University of Chicago Press, 2014).
5. Claims of an "imaginary kinship" between modern Europeans and ancient Greeks are critiqued by Mathura Umachandran and Marchella Ward, "Towards a Manifesto for Critical Ancient World Studies," in *Critical Ancient World Studies: The Case for Forgetting Classics*, ed. Mathura Umachandran and Marchella Ward (Abingdon: Routledge, 2023), 14–19. Research on prehistoric DNA has shown that in fact nearly all populations throughout human history have continually intermingled with other populations: Saini, *Superior*, 116–18.
6. Race-thinking is defined by Paul C. Taylor, *Race: A Philosophical Introduction*, 2nd ed. (Cambridge: Polity, 2013), 49–67. The fundamental study of biological determinism is Richard C. Lewontin, "The Apportionment of Human Diversity," in *Evolutionary Biology*, ed. Theodosius Dobzhansky, Max K. Hecht, and William C. Steere (New York: Appleton-Century-Crofts, 1972), 381–98. Stephen Jay Gould, *The Mismeasure of Man* (New York: Norton, 1981), introduced the concept to the broader public.
7. Karen E. Fields and Barbara J. Fields, *Racecraft: The Soul of Inequality in American Life* (London: Verso, 2016), 23–74, offers a survey of many examples.
8. Meleager is described at *Iliad* 2.642, Agamede at *Iliad* 11.740. Penelope's cheeks: *Odyssey* 19.205. Theban women: Heraclides fr. 1.19.1. Descriptions of Romans: Plutarch, *Life of Cato the Elder* 1; *Life of Sulla* 2, 6; Suetonius, *Augustus* 79 (hair); Pliny, *Natural History* 11.143 (Augustus's eyes); Suetonius, *Nero* 51; John Malalas 11.13.
9. On the "Dorian invasion," see Jonathan M. Hall, *Ethnic Identity in Greek Antiquity* (Cambridge: Cambridge University Press, 1997), 64–65, also 122–28 on how archaeological evidence was originally interpreted in ways that sought to confirm the literary evidence. On Jaeger, see Hall, *Ethnic Identity*, 12–13. Jaeger's relationship to Nazism is discussed by

William M. Calder, "Werner Jaeger and Richard Harder: An Erklärung," *Quaderni di storia* 17 (1983): 99–121.

10. Vernon Ford, "Sarich, Vincent and Miele, Frank. *Race: The Reality of Human Differences*," *Booklist* 100, no. 12 (2004): 1031. On Coon, see John P. Jackson, *Science for Segregation: Race, Law, and the Case against Brown v. Board of Education*, Critical America (New York: New York University Press, 2005), 99–103, 159–72. On Jensen, see William H. Tucker, *The Science and Politics of Racial Research* (Urbana: University of Illinois Press, 1994), 195–239; and Robert W. Sussman, *The Myth of Race: The Troubling Persistence of an Unscientific Idea* (Cambridge, MA: Harvard University Press, 2014), 235–41. On Rushton, see William H. Tucker, *The Funding of Scientific Racism: Wickliffe Draper and the Pioneer Fund* (Urbana: University of Illinois Press, 2002), 197–203; and Sussman, *The Myth of Race*, 259–68. Sarich and Miele's book is dedicated to the University of Georgia psychology professor R. Travis Osborne who, at the time of the book's publication, was the director of the Pioneer Fund. Notable among many critical reviews of Sarich and Miele's book are Mark Nathan Cohen, "A Review Too Kind to Sarich and Miele: *Race: The Reality of Human Differences*," *American Anthropologist* 107, no. 3 (2005): 551; and Audrey Smedley, "*Race: The Reality of Human Differences:* Vincent Sarich and Frank Miele's Use of History," *Transforming Anthropology* 14, no. 1 (April 2006): 53–59.
11. Harriet Sherwood, "Cleopatra Was Light-Skinned, Egypt Tells Netflix in Row over Drama," *Guardian*, April 28, 2023, https://www.theguardian.com/tv-and-radio/2023/apr/28/cleopatra-was-light-skinned-egypt-tells-netflix-in-row-over-drama; Jabeen Waheed, "Adele James Discusses 'Blackwashing' Backlash to *Queen Cleopatra*," *Glamour UK*, May 4, 2023, https://www.glamourmagazine.co.uk/article/adele-james-queen-cleopatra-interview; Thomas Ling, "No, the BBC Is Not 'Blackwashing' *Troy: Fall of a City*," *RadioTimes*, February 12, 2019, https://www.radiotimes.com/tv/drama/troy-fall-of-a-city-blackwashing-casting-black-actors-greek-myth/.
12. Shelley Haley, "Black Feminist Thought and Classics: Re-Membering, Re-Claiming, Re-Empowering," in *Feminist Theory and the Classics*, ed. Nancy Sorkin Rabinowitz and Amy Richlin (New York: Routledge, 1993), 29. A recent example of scholarly conflation of Cleopatra's race and ancestry is Duane W. Roller, "Cleopatra's True Racial Background (and Does It Really Matter?)," *OUPBlog*, December 6, 2010, https://blog.oup.com/2010/12/cleopatra-2/. On *Troy: Fall of a City*, see Jackie Murray, "Race and Sexuality," in *A Cultural History of Race in Antiquity*, ed. Denise Eileen McCoskey (London: Bloomsbury, 2021), 137–56; and Rebecca Futo Kennedy, "Racist Reactions to Black Achilles," in *Screening Love and War in* Troy: Fall of a City, ed. Monica S. Cyrino and Antony Augustakis (London: Bloomsbury, 2022), 79–96. Critiques of reactions to Netflix's

Queen Cleopatra are Katherine Blouin and Rebecca Futo Kennedy, "Cleopatra VII: The Gift That Keeps on Giving," *Isis Naucratis*, 2023, https://isisnaucratis.medium.com/cleopatra-vii-the-gift-that-keeps-on-giving-f749b66c552c; and Sara Khorshid, "Why Netflix's *Queen Cleopatra* Has Egypt Up in Arms," *Foreign Policy*, January 12, 2024, https://foreignpolicy.com/2023/05/14/egypt-netflix-queen-cleopatra-race-history-heritage-imperialism-afrocentrism/.

13. Denise Eileen McCoskey, "What Would James Baldwin Do?" *Eidolon*, 2017, https://eidolon.pub/what-would-james-baldwin-do-a778947c04d5; Heidi Morse, "Classics and the Alt-Right: Historicizing Visual Rhetorics of White Supremacy," *Learn, Speak, Act*, February 15, 2018, https://sites.lsa.umich.edu/learn-speak-act/2018/02/15/classics-and-the-alt-right/. On the nineteenth-century material: Debbie Challis, " 'The Ablest Race': The Ancient Greeks in Victorian Racial Theory," in *Classics and Imperialism in the British Empire*, ed. Mark Bradley (Oxford: Oxford University Press, 2010), 96–111. The fullest treatment of the "polychromy" of ancient statuary is the collection of essays in Vinzenz Brinkmann, Oliver Primavesi, and Max Hollein, eds., *Circumlitio: The Polychromy of Antique and Mediaeval Sculpture* (Munich: Hirmer Verlag, 2010).

14. On Odysseus's black skin, see James H. Dee, "Black Odysseus, White Caesar: When Did 'White People' Become 'White'?" *Classical Journal* 99, no. 2 (2003–4): 161. Snowden's earliest discussion of the absence of racism (as he defined it) in Greco-Roman antiquity was Frank M. Snowden, "The Negro in Classical Italy," *American Journal of Philology* 68, no. 3 (1947): 288; but see Lloyd A. Thompson, *Romans and Blacks* (Norman: University of Oklahoma Press, 1989). On anti-Blackness in scholarly treatments of Africans, see Sarah F. Derbew, *Untangling Blackness in Greek Antiquity* (Cambridge: Cambridge University Press, 2022), 23–24, on Snowden and Thompson; I have followed Derbew in capitalizing "Blackness" only when it refers to the application of modern racial logics.

15. Denise Eileen McCoskey, "Naming the Fault in Question: Theorizing Racism among the Greeks and Romans," *International Journal of the Classical Tradition* 13, no. 2 (2006): 251. On the reception of Snowden, see Denise Eileen McCoskey, "By Any Other Name? Ethnicity and the Study of Ancient Identity," *Classical Bulletin* 79, no. 1 (2003): 93, 97–109; Bernard Knox, *The Oldest Dead White European Males and Other Reflections on the Classics* (New York: Norton, 1993), 12, discussed by Rebecca Futo Kennedy, " 'Western Civilization,' White Supremacism, and the Myth of a Greco-Roman Past," in *Polarized Pasts: Heritage and Belonging in Times of Political Polarization*, ed. Elisabeth Niklasson (New York: Berghahn Books, 2023), 101–3; Peter Jones, *Vote for Caesar: How the Ancient Greeks and Romans Solved the Problems of Today* (London: Orion, 2008), 4–5.

16. Xenophanes D13 (B16). Frank M. Snowden, *Blacks in Antiquity: Ethiopians in the Greco-Roman Experience* (Cambridge, MA: Harvard University Press, 1970), collects extensive evidence of Africans in the Greco-Roman world, evidence that is routinely ignored in later surveys, according to Patrice D. Rankine, "Black Apollo? Martin Bernal's *Black Athena: The Afroasiatic Roots of Classical Civilization*, Volume III, and Why Race Still Matters," in *African Athena: New Agendas*, ed. Daniel Orrells, Gurminder K. Bhambra, and Tessa Roynon (Oxford: Oxford University Press, 2011), 53. Snowden himself, however, maintained that the Greeks and Romans themselves were white. See Christopher Stedman Parmenter, " 'A Happy Coincidence': Race, the Cold War, and Frank M. Snowden, Jr's Blacks in Antiquity," *Classical Receptions Journal* 13, no. 4 (October 1, 2021): 486.
17. Taki Theodoracopulos, "Black Belts and Golden Dawn," *Taki's Magazine*, July 19, 2013, https://www.takimag.com/article/black_belts_and_golden_dawn_taki/2/. On Sailer, see Park MacDougald and Jason Willick, "The Man Who Invented Identity Politics for the New Right," *Intelligencer*, April 30, 2017, https://nymag.com/intelligencer/2017/04/steve-sailer-invented-identity-politics-for-the-alt-right.html; Saini, *Superior*, 87–92; Aaron Panofsky, Kushan Dasgupta, and Nicole Iturriaga, "How White Nationalists Mobilize Genetics: From Genetic Ancestry and Human Biodiversity to Counterscience and Metapolitics," *American Journal of Physical Anthropology* 175, no. 2 (2021): 391.
18. Denise Eileen McCoskey, "On Black Athena, Hippocratic Medicine, and Roman Imperial Edicts: Egyptians and the Problem of Race in Classical Antiquity," in *Race and Ethnicity: Across Time, Space and Discipline*, ed. Rodney D. Coates (Leiden: Brill, 2004), 313–21; Benjamin H. Isaac, *The Invention of Racism in Classical Antiquity* (Princeton, NJ: Princeton University Press, 2004), 56–101; David Kaufman, "Race and Science," in *A Cultural History of Race in Antiquity*, ed. Denise Eileen McCoskey (London: Bloomsbury, 2021), 68.
19. Isaac, *The Invention of Racism*, 149–62; Kaufman, "Race and Science," 77. Deduction of character from appearance can be found in a wide array of ancient authors; see Elizabeth C. Evans, *Physiognomics in the Ancient World* (Philadelphia: American Philosophical Society, 1969), 6–7, who also notes (9n28) that, except in the case of Africans, the *Physiognomy* assigns characteristics only to individuals; Egyptians and Ethiopians, by contrast, are assumed to share (primarily undesirable) characteristics. That is, the treatise racializes Africans while treating other people as individuals. Hannah Čulík-Baird and Mathias Hanses, "Africa Ipsa Parens: Racializing Representations of Sardinians in Cicero's Pro Scauro (54 B.C.E.)," *TAPA* 154, no. 1 (2024): 105–8, discuss the intricacies of colorism in Rome, as illustrated by Cicero's dehumanizing rhetoric against Sardinians.
20. Isaac, *The Invention of Racism*, 8–13, 102–8; McCoskey, "On Black Athena," 321–23. On the Middle Ages, see Cord J. Whitaker, *Black*

Metaphors: How Modern Racism Emerged from Medieval Race-Thinking (Philadelphia: University of Pennsylvania Press, 2019), 79–88; and Joseph Ziegler, "Text and Context: On the Rise of Physiognomic Thought in the Later Middle Ages," in *De Sion Exibit Lex et Verbum Domini de Hierusalem: Essays on Medieval Law, Liturgy, and Literature in Honour of Amnon Linder*, ed. Yitzhak Hen (Turnhout: Brepols, 2001), especially 182. Cuvier was also the dissector of the body of Sarah Baartman, the African woman who was displayed throughout Europe as a curiosity and known as the "Hottentot Venus".

21. Strabo 2.5.26, 3.3.8, 4.1.12. On *Mankind Quarterly*, see Tucker, *The Funding of Scientific Racism*, 90–97. On Lynn and Francis, see Sussman, *The Myth of Race*, 268–72, 276–77. Francis's career is covered in detail by Leonard Zeskind, *Blood and Politics: The History of the White Nationalist Movement from the Margins to the Mainstream* (New York: Farrar, Straus & Giroux, 2009), especially 288–93, 424–28, with Michael Brendan Dougherty, "How an Obscure Adviser to Pat Buchanan Predicted the Wild Trump Campaign in 1996," *Week*, November 12, 2016, https://theweek.com/articles/599577/how-obscure-adviser-pat-buchanan-predicted-wild-trump-campaign-1996, on how Francis anticipated Trump's campaign strategy.
22. Tacitus, *Agricola* 11; Homer, *Odyssey* 4.611, trans. Murray.
23. Theognis 183–92; Plato, *Republic* 459a–460b; Plutarch, *Life of Lycurgus* 15.8, trans. Clough.
24. Herodotus 8.144, trans. Waterfield.
25. Samuel P. Huntington, *The Clash of Civilizations and the Remaking of World Order* (New York: Simon & Schuster, 1996), 42, with the criticism of Amartya Kumar Sen, "Democracy as a Universal Value," *Journal of Democracy* 10, no. 3 (1999): 3–17. Rebecca Futo Kennedy, "How Obama Became American: Herodotus and the Rhetoric of Ethnos in the 2008 Election," *Classics at the Intersections*, February 24, 2009, https://rfkclassics.blogspot.com/2009/02/how-obama-became-american-rhetoric-of.html, quotes both John Adams and the *Federalist*, no. 2 (John Jay). On Herodotus's definition of Greekness, see Hall, *Ethnic Identity*, 44–47; and David Konstan, "To Hellenikon Ethnos: Ethnicity and the Construction of Ancient Greek Identity," in *Ancient Perceptions of Greek Ethnicity*, ed. Irad Malkin (Washington, DC: Center for Hellenic Studies, 2001), 33–36.
26. Plato, *Republic* 470c–d, trans. Waterfield; *Laws* 693a, trans. Saunders.
27. These are the *Brill Dictionary of Ancient Greek* (ed. Montanari, English edition 2015), and the *Cambridge Greek Lexicon* (2021). The translations cited by the *Occidental Observer* are Robin Waterfield, trans., *Plato: Republic* (Oxford: Oxford University Press, 1993); Robin Waterfield, trans., *Herodotus: The Histories* (Oxford: Oxford University Press, 1998); Trevor J. Saunders, trans., *Plato: The Laws* (London: Penguin, 1970).

28. Iosif Lazaridis, Alissa Mittnik, Nick Patterson, Swapan Mallick, Nadin Rohland, Saskia Pfrengle, Anja Furtwängler, et al., "Genetic Origins of the Minoans and Mycenaeans," *Nature* 548, no. 7666 (August 2017): 214–18.
29. As reported by Yannis Hamilakis, "Who Are You Calling Mycenaean?" *London Review of Books* blog, August 10, 2017, https://www.lrb.co.uk/blog/2017/august/who-are-you-calling-mycenaean. The *Greek Reporter*'s report is in Tasos Kokkinidis, "Greeks Are Descendants of the Mycenaeans, DNA Study Confirms," GreekReporter.com, November 22, 2023, https://greekreporter.com/2023/11/22/new-evidence-supports-modern-greeks-having-dna-of-ancient-mycenaeans/. See also the discussion of Raphael Greenberg and Yannis Hamilakis, *Archaeology, Nation, and Race: Confronting the Past, Decolonizing the Future in Greece and Israel* (Cambridge: Cambridge University Press, 2022), 145–48. The nineteenth-century theory of Greek racial identity is quoted by Thomas Leeb, *Jakob Philipp Fallmerayer: Publizist und Politiker zwischen Revolution und Reaktion (1835–1861)* (Munich: Beck, 1996), 55. See also Johanna Hanink, *The Classical Debt: Greek Antiquity in an Era of Austerity* (Cambridge, MA: Harvard University Press, 2017), 167–70; and Greenberg and Hamilakis, *Archaeology, Nation, and Race*, 134–36.
30. Hamilakis, "Who Are You Calling Mycenaean?" with the more technical discussions of Joseph Maran, "Archaeological Cultures, Fabricated Ethnicities and DNA Research: 'Minoans' and 'Mycenaeans' as Case Examples," in *Material, Method, and Meaning: Papers in Eastern Mediterranean Archaeology in Honor of Ilan Sharon*, ed. Uri Davidovich, Naama Yahalom-Mack, and Sveta Matskevich (Münster: Zaphon, 2022), 13–18; and Christopher Stedman Parmenter, "The Twilight of the Gods? Genomic History and the Return of Race in the Study of the Ancient Mediterranean," *History and Theory* 63, no. 1 (2024): 52–66. Nadia Abu El-Haj, *The Genealogical Science: The Search for Jewish Origins and the Politics of Epistemology* (Chicago: University of Chicago Press, 2012), 219–47, attempts to differentiate "genetic history" from race science.
31. Katharine Tyler, "Genetic Ancestry Testing, Whiteness and the Limits of Anti-Racism," *New Genetics and Society* 40, no. 2 (April 3, 2021): 216–35. See too Henry T. Greely, "Genetic Genealogy: Genetics Meets the Marketplace," in *Revisiting Race in a Genomic Age*, ed. Barbara A. Koenig, Sandra Soo-Jin Lee, and Sarah S. Richardson (New Brunswick, NJ: Rutgers University Press, 2008), 215–34; Roberts, *Fatal Invention*, 327–28; Catherine Nash, *Genetic Geographies: The Trouble with Ancestry* (Minneapolis: University of Minnesota Press, 2015), 51–53; Mark A. Jobling, Rita Rasteiro, and Jon H. Wetton, "In the Blood: The Myth and Reality of Genetic Markers of Identity," *Ethnic and Racial Studies* 39, no. 2 (January 26, 2016): 142–61. Discussions of DNA tests in white nationalist Web forums are summarized in Panofsky, Dasgupta, and Iturriaga, "How White

Nationalists Mobilize Genetics," 389–91, with Susanne E. Hakenbeck, "Genetics, Archaeology, and the Far Right: An Unholy Trinity," *World Archaeology* 51, no. 4 (2019): 517–27; and Catherine J. Freeman and Daniela Hofmann, "Present Pasts in the Archaeology of Genetics, Identity, and Migration in Europe: A Critical Essay," *World Archaeology* 51, no. 4 (2019): 528–45, on their interest in DNA-based studies of prehistoric populations and their movements. On race pseudoscience and genetic ancestry testing more generally, see Antonio Regalado, "More Than 26 Million People Have Taken an At-Home Ancestry Test," *MIT Technology Review*, February 11, 2019, https://www.technologyreview.com/2019/02/11/103446/more-than-26-million-people-have-taken-an-at-home-ancestry-test/; Roberts, *Fatal Invention*, 202–25; and Troy Duster, "Ancestry Testing and DNA: Uses, Limits, and Caveat Emptor," in *Race and the Genetic Revolution: Science, Myth, and Culture*, ed. Sheldon Krimsky and Kathleen Sloan (New York: Columbia University Press, 2011), 99–115.

32. White House Council of Economic Advisors, "Racial Discrimination in Contemporary America," the White House, July 3, 2024, https://www.whitehouse.gov/cea/written-materials/2024/07/03/racial-discrimination-in-contemporary-america/.

Chapter Five. The Prometheans

1. These are executive orders 13769, 13767, 13768, 13950, and 13958, respectively. Criticism of the 1776 Commission by historians was reported by Gillian Brockell, " 'A Hack Job,' 'Outright Lies': Trump Commission's '1776 Report' Outrages Historians," *Washington Post*, January 22, 2021, https://www.washingtonpost.com/history/2021/01/19/1776-report-historians-trump/. Executive order 13967, "Promoting Beautiful Federal Civic Architecture," is available at the Federal Register: https://www.federalregister.gov/documents/2020/12/23/2020–28605/promoting-beautiful-federal-civic-architecture.
2. The American Institute of Architects webpage no longer carries their press release, which can be found in Ned Cramer, "An Executive Order on Federal Architecture Is Serious Business," *Architect*, February 6, 2020, https://www.architectmagazine.com/design/editorial/an-executive-order-on-federal-architecture-is-serious-business_o. The archaeologists' statement is "Archaeological Institute of America Weighs In about Ancient Architecture as a Responsive Tradition," Archaeological Institute of America, February 7, 2020, https://www.archaeological.org/archaeological-institute-of-america-weighs-in-about-ancient-architecture-as-a-responsive-tradition/. On fascist architecture and the executive order, see Morgan Baskin, " 'Classical' Architecture Is Just One Way Tyrants Build in Their Own Image," *Slate*, February 14, 2020, https://slate.com/

business/2020/02/trump-classical-architecture-executive-order.html; Juan Sebastián Pinto, "The Dark Side of Trump's Architectural Fantasy," *Forbes*, February 7, 2020, https://www.forbes.com/sites/juansebastianpinto/2020/02/07/the-dark-side-of-trumps-architectural-fantasy/; Steve Rose, "Will Trump Make Architecture Great Again? The Dark History of Dictator Chic," *Guardian*, February 5, 2020, https://www.theguardian.com/artanddesign/shortcuts/2020/feb/05/trump-wants-more-neoclassical-buildings-but-dictating-to-architects-has-a-dark-history. Trump's remarks to CPAC were reported by Tim Hains, "Trump Wants to 'Build New Cities,' 'Get Rid of Ugly Buildings,' Encourage 'New Baby Boom,' " Real Clear Politics, March 5, 2023, https://www.realclearpolitics.com/video/2023/03/05/trump_wants_to_build_new_cities_get_rid_of_ugly_buildings_support_new_baby_boom.html.

3. Glenn Brown, *History of the United States Capitol* (Washington, DC: U.S. Government Printing Office, 1900), xv.
4. UNESCO, "UNESCO Logo Toolkit," 2011, 2, https://unesdoc.unesco.org/ark:/48223/pf0000191825. UNESCO, "Convention concerning the Protection of the World Cultural and Natural Heritage," UNESCO World Heritage Centre, 1972, https://whc.unesco.org/en/conventiontext/.
5. Lyra Monteiro, "How a Trump Executive Order Aims to Set White Supremacy in Stone," *Hyperallergic*, 2021, http://hyperallergic.com/614175/how-a-trump-executive-order-aims-to-set-white-supremacy-in-stone/. Curtis Dozier, "Not Just Hitler and Mussolini: Neo-Nazis Love Neoclassical Architecture, Too," *Pharos: Doing Justice to the Classics*, February 20, 2020, https://pharos.vassarspaces.net/2020/02/20/not-just-hitler-and-mussolini-neo-nazis-love-neoclassical-architecture-too/, documents their embrace of Trump's executive order. On Stormfront and its founder Don Black, see Carol M. Swain and Russ Nieli, *Contemporary Voices of White Nationalism in America* (Cambridge: Cambridge University Press, 2003), 153–65; Jessie Daniels, *Cyber Racism: White Supremacy Online and the New Attack on Civil Rights* (Lanham, MD: Rowman & Littlefield, 2009), 61–90; Barry J. Balleck, *Modern American Extremism and Domestic Terrorism: An Encyclopedia of Extremists and Extremist Groups* (Santa Barbara, CA: ABC-CLIO, 2018), 33–34, 347–48; and Eli Saslow, *Rising out of Hatred: The Awakening of a Former White Nationalist* (New York: Doubleday, 2018).
6. On the Eurocentric politics of UNESCO, see Lylaah L. Bhalerao, "Away from 'Civilisational' Heritage in the Eastern Mediterranean: Embracing Classical and Islamic Cultural Co-Presences and Simultaneous Histories at the Parthenon and Ayasofia," in *Critical Ancient World Studies: The Case for Forgetting Classics*, ed. Mathura Umachandran and Marchella Ward (Abingdon: Routledge, 2023), 162–69. Data from "World Heritage List Statistics," UNESCO, https://whc.unesco.org/en/list/?action=stat&, with analysis by Chloé Maurel, "Whose World Heritage? The Problem with

UNESCO's Famous List," *Equal Times*, July 20, 2017, https://www.equaltimes.org/whose-world-heritage-the-problem. Ford's declaration of February as Black History Month is quoted from https://www.blackhistorymonth.gov/About.html.

7. This description of the Parthenon is taken from Wikipedia, s.v. "Parthenon," as it appeared in February 2024. Thousands of tourists in Athens learned to view the Parthenon in this way from the Acropolis Sound and Light Show that celebrated the "Golden Age of Athens" from 1959 until well into the twenty-first century, as described by Johanna Hanink, *The Classical Debt: Greek Antiquity in an Era of Austerity* (Cambridge, MA: Harvard University Press, 2017), 180–82; and Elisabeth Marlowe, "Cold War Illuminations of the Classical Past: 'The Sound and Light Show' on the Athenian Acropolis," *Art History* 24, no. 4 (2001): 578–97. Hanink, *The Classical Debt*, 32–69, traces the origin of idealizing perceptions of the Parthenon to the propaganda of classical Athens itself.
8. Elizabeth W. Thill, "Classical Architecture and the Attack on the Capitol," Society for Classical Studies, January 15, 2021, https://classicalstudies.org/scs-blog/elizabeth-w-thill/blog-classical-architecture-and-attack-capitol.
9. Yannis Hamilakis, *The Nation and Its Ruins: Antiquity, Archaeology, and National Imagination in Greece* (Oxford: Oxford University Press, 2007), 78–98; Bhalerao, "Away from 'Civilisational' Heritage," 158–62.
10. UNESCO's citation of "Acropolis, Athens" (https://whc.unesco.org/en/list/404) mentions only the "significant historical phases" of the site without specifying them, focusing instead on the Acropolis as a "universal" symbol of the "classical spirit." On African American commentary on the Capitol, see John Levi Barnard, *Empire of Ruin: Black Classicism and American Imperial Culture* (Oxford: Oxford University Press, 2018), 77–79, quoting also Thomas Jefferson's imperial understanding of the Capitol as a building that would embellish "with Athenian taste the course of a nation looking far beyond the range of Athenian destinies."
11. Socrates is quoted at Diogenes Laertius, *Lives and Opinions of Eminent Philosophers* 1.33, trans. Hicks. Aristotle's declaration of Greek superiority is found at *Politics* 1327b, trans. Kennedy, discussed by David Kaufman, "Race and Science," in *A Cultural History of Race in Antiquity*, ed. Denise Eileen McCoskey (London: Bloomsbury, 2021), 71–73. A survey of Greek attitudes toward barbarians is John E. Coleman, "Ancient Greek Ethnocentrism," in *Greeks and Barbarians: Essays on the Interactions between Greeks and Non-Greeks in Antiquity and the Consequences for Eurocentrism*, ed. John E. Coleman and Clark A. Walz (Bethesda, MD: CDL, 1997).
12. Hannah Gais, "The Alt-Right Doesn't Know What to Do with White Women," *New Republic*, 2017, https://newrepublic.com/article/145325/alt-right-doesnt-know-white-women; and Alexandra Minna Stern, *Proud*

Boys and the White Ethnostate: How the Alt-Right Is Warping the American Imagination (Boston: Beacon, 2019), 83. Hannah Gais, Megan Squire, and Rachael Fugardi, "White Nationalist and Male Supremacist Identified," identified Moore by comparing passages between Moore's dissertation and a book he published pseudonymously: Southern Poverty Law Center, August 28, 2024, https://www.splcenter.org/hatewatch/2024/08/29/white-nationalist-male-supremacist-author-identified.

13. Herodotus 5.78, 7.135, trans. Purvis.
14. Erich S. Gruen, *Rethinking the Other in Antiquity* (Princeton, NJ: Princeton University Press, 2011), 21–39, is the most prominent recent argument that Herodotus rejects Greek superiority; Thomas Harrison, "Reinventing the Barbarian," *Classical Philology* 115, no. 2 (2020): 139–63, reasserts the case for the xenophobia of the ancient category. Bury is quoted by Benjamin H. Isaac, *The Invention of Racism in Classical Antiquity* (Princeton, NJ: Princeton University Press, 2004), 257, along with other similar interpretations from nineteenth-century scholars. The others quoted here are from Thomas Harrison and Joseph Skinner, introduction to *Herodotus in the Long Nineteenth Century*, ed. Thomas Harrison and Joseph Skinner (Cambridge: Cambridge University Press, 2020), 5–6. The prominence of Herodotus in Oxford's curriculum is described in Joseph Skinner, "Imagining Empire through Herodotus," in Harrison and Skinner, *Herodotus in the Long Nineteenth Century*, 126. Oxford students' trajectories to the Indian Civil Service are described by Phiroze Vasunia, "Greek, Latin, and the Indian Civil Service," *Cambridge Classical Journal* 51 (2005): 35–71. The examples given here focus on the influence of Herodotus in particular, but many aspects of Greek thought about the Persians have been enlisted in support of what Edward Said termed "Orientalism": see Phiroze Vasunia, "Hellenism and Empire: Reading Edward Said," *Parallax* 9, no. 4 (2003): 88–97; and Edith Hall, *The Theatrical Cast of Athens: Interactions between Ancient Greek Drama and Society* (Oxford: Oxford University Press, 2006), 220–26. The example of the French traveler Comte de Marcellus is analyzed in Gonda Van Steen, *Liberating Hellenism from the Ottoman Empire: Comte de Marcellus and the Last of the Classics* (New York: Palgrave Macmillan, 2010), especially 148–68.
15. Barry Strauss, "Herodotus's Wheel," *New Criterion* 27, no. 3 (2008): 16–20; Victor Davis Hanson, *Carnage and Culture: Landmark Battles in the Rise of Western Power* (New York: Anchor, 2001), 47; Anthony Pagden, *Worlds at War: The 2,500-Year Struggle between East and West* (New York: Random House, 2008), 7–8, quoting Herodotus 5.78 at 28; Donald Kagan, "The Athenian Empire," YouTube, 2008, https://youtu.be/EuvkY7l8w-Y?t=1094. In a lecture in the same series entitled "Athenian Democracy," Kagan ranks the Athenian "commitment to political freedom" as the quality that makes their culture "closer to the dominant ideas

and values of our own era than any other." On Kagan's politics, see John Bloxham, *Ancient Greece and American Conservatism: Classical Influence on the Modern Right* (London: Bloomsbury, 2018), 174–203; and, less sympathetically, Paige DuBois, *Trojan Horses: Saving the Classics from Conservatives* (New York: New York University Press): 30–34; Rebecca Futo Kennedy, "Classics and Western Civilization: The Troubling History of an Authoritative Narrative," in *Authority and History: Ancient Models, Modern Questions*, ed. Marques J. Bastos and Federico Santangelo (London: Bloomsbury, 2022), 103–4; and Rebecca Futo Kennedy, " 'Western Civilization,' White Supremacism, and the Myth of a Greco-Roman Past," in *Polarized Pasts: Heritage and Belonging in Times of Political Polarization*, ed. Elisabeth Niklasson (New York: Berghahn Books, 2023), 96–97. On Hanson, see Eric Adler, *Classics, the Culture Wars, and Beyond* (Ann Arbor: University of Michigan Press, 2016), 173–212; and Bloxham, *Ancient Greece and American Conservatism*, 198–203; less sympathetically, DuBois, *Trojan Horses*, 34–41; and Francisco Javier González García and Pedro López Barja de Quiroga, "Neocon Greece: V. D. Hanson's War on History," *International Journal of the Classical Tradition* 19, no. 3 (2012): 129–51. Despite the similarity between some of Kagan's and Hanson's views of Greco-Roman antiquity with those of white nationalists, neither Kagan (probably because he is Jewish) nor Hanson (because he advocates U.S. military intervention abroad and is supportive of Israel) is cited with approval by them. As for Pagden, many reviews in both academic and mainstream publications highlighted the Eurocentrism and knee-jerk hostility to Islam in Pagden's book, noting its "reification as historically inevitable" of ancient Greek rhetoric about the Persians: see Prasenjit Duara, "*Worlds at War: The 2,500 Year Struggle between East and West* (Review)," *Common Knowledge* 15, no. 3 (2009): 511. Fakhreddin Azimi, "Book Review: Anthony Pagden, *Worlds at War: The 2,500-Year Struggle between East and West*," *European History Quarterly* 41, no. 1 (January 1, 2011): 153–55, describes the book's perspective as that of "an unreconstructed Orientalist." Pagden's "perpetual enmity" seems to be taken from De Selincourt's 1954 translation of Herodotus 1.4.4: "From [the Trojan War] sprang [the Persians'] belief in the perpetual enmity of the Grecian world toward them." This translation was retained in the 1996 revision. A more accurate translation would be "The Persians always believed that the Trojan War was the source of Greek hatred toward them"; Herodotus only says the belief, not the hatred itself, was perpetual.

16. Orlando Patterson, *Freedom in the Making of Western Culture* (New York: Basic Books, 1991). Kurt A. Raaflaub, *The Discovery of Freedom in Ancient Greece* (Chicago: University of Chicago Press, 2004).
17. Hanson, *Carnage and Culture*, 4, 56.
18. R. Charles Weller, " 'Western' and 'White Civilization': White Nationalism and Eurocentrism at the Crossroads," in *21st-Century Narratives of*

World History: Global and Multidisciplinary Perspectives, ed. R. Charles Weller (London: Cham, 2017), 59, links mainstream and white nationalist treatments of Western civilization. See, too, Kennedy, " 'Western Civilization' "; and Rebecca Futo Kennedy, "Race and the Athenian Metic Revisioned," in *Identities in Antiquity*, ed. V. Manalopoulou, J. Skinner, and C. Tsouparopolou (New York: Routledge, forthcoming), on racialized concepts of Western civilization in classics. King's remarks were reported by Trip Gabriel, "Before Trump, Steve King Set the Agenda for the Wall and Anti-Immigrant Politics," *New York Times*, January 10, 2019, https://www.nytimes.com/2019/01/10/us/politics/steve-king-trump-immigration-wall.html. King went on to ask, "Why did I sit in classes teaching me about the merits of our history and our civilization?" a probable reference to the study of classical Greece. Thornton's essay is Bruce Thornton, "Free Citizens Do Not Kneel," *Front Page Magazine*, June 12, 2020, https://www.frontpagemag.com/free-citizens-do-not-kneel-bruce-thornton/; on the David Horowitz Freedom Center, see Southern Poverty Law Center, "David Horowitz," Southern Poverty Law Center, https://www.splcenter.org/fighting-hate/extremist-files/individual/david-horowitz, accessed February 8, 2024. Thornton quotes Herodotus 7.136.

19. Bruce S. Thornton, *Greek Ways: How the Greeks Created Western Civilization* (San Francisco: Encounter Books, 2002), 2. Erlich won the Nobel Prize for his work on antibiotics; Hata was nominated three times but never won. Titles of books by classical scholars that trade on the celebration of Western civilization include Michael Grant's *Founders of the Western World* (1991); Hanson's *The Other Greeks: The Family Farm and the Agrarian Roots of Western Civilization* (1995); Strauss's *Battle of Salamis: The Naval Encounter That Saved Greece—and Western Civilization* (2004); Billows's *Marathon: How One Battle Changed Western Civilization* (2010); Garland's *Everyday Life in the Birthplace of Western Civilization* (2013); McKeown's *Cabinet of Greek Curiosities: Strange Tales and Surprising Facts from the Cradle of Western Civilization* (2013); Klavan's *How to Save the West: Ancient Wisdom for Five Modern Crises* (2023).

20. Ian Almond, "Five Ways of Deconstructing Europe," *Journal of European Studies* 44, no. 1 (2014): 50–58, delineates five ways that historians have destabilized the idea of "Europe"; each is applicable to the idea of Western civilization as well. An example of a scholar who emphasizes the synthesis of diverse cultures is Jack A. Goldstone, *Why Europe? The Rise of the West in World History, 1500–1850* (Boston: McGraw-Hill, 2009). One who emphasizes the violence underlying European accomplishments is Robert B. Marks, *The Origins of the Modern World: A Global and Ecological Narrative from the Fifteenth to the Twenty-First Century* (Lanham, MD: Rowman & Littlefield, 2002). The best-known discussion of luck, particularly of environmental and geographic factors, in Europe's rise is Jared M. Diamond, *Guns, Germs, and Steel: The Fates of Human Societies*

(New York: Norton, 1997), but see also Kenneth Pomeranz, *The Great Divergence: China, Europe, and the Making of the Modern World Economy* (Princeton, NJ: Princeton University Press, 2000). The historical range of the data these scholars employ to answer their questions is expanded by Ian Morris, *Why the West Rules—for Now: The Patterns of History, and What They Reveal about the Future* (New York: Farrar, Straus & Giroux, 2010). See too, however, the critique of Salman Sayyid and AbdoolKarim Vakil, "Critical Muslim Studies and the Remaking of the (Ancient) World," in Umachandran and Ward, *Critical Ancient World Studies*, 37–39. Classical scholars have begun to interrogate the grand narrative of "the West": Naoíse Mac Sweeney, *The West: A New History in Fourteen Lives* (New York: Dutton, 2023); and Josephine Quinn, *How the World Made the West: A 4,000-Year History* (London: Bloomsbury, 2024).

21. Ricardo Duchesne, *The Uniqueness of Western Civilization* (Leiden: Brill, 2011). The quoted promotion was taken from Brill's webpage in February 2024 (https://web.archive.org/web/20231202123145/https://brill.com/display/title/18312). On Duchesne, see Weller, " 'Western' and 'White Civilization,' " 46–48; and Ron Dart, "The Canadian Red Tory Tradition: Janus," in *The Right and Radical Right in the Americas: Ideological Currents from Interwar Canada to Contemporary Chile*, ed. Tamir Bar-On and Bàrbara Molas (Lanham, MD: Lexington Books, 2021), 117–18. On the University of New Brunswick faculty's open letter, see Bailey Martens, "Over 100 University of New Brunswick Faculty 'Condemn' Ricardo Duchesne's Extremist Views," *HuffPost*, 2019, https://www.huffpost.com/archive/ca/entry/ricardo-duchesne-unb-faculty-condemn_ca_5ceda269e4b0793c2346ca52. Before the publication of *Uniqueness*, Duchesne contributed to the *Occidental Observer* under the classical pseudonym Domitius Corbulo: an essay criticizing scholarship on the influence of the Near East on Greek culture published under that name is identical to a section of Duchesne's later book *Faustian Man in a Multicultural Age*, published by Arktos. On Jonathan Bowden, see George Hawley, Richard T. Marcy, and José Pedro Zúquete, "Examining the Performance and Political Influence of Far Right Vanguard Leaders: The Case of Jonathan Bowden," *Journal of Political Ideologies* (2023): 1–19.

22. Krishnan J. Ram-Prasad, "Comparative Philology and Critical Ancient World Studies," in Umachandran and Ward, *Critical Ancient World Studies*, 93–94, describes the reconstruction of this language.

23. Léon Poliakov, *The Aryan Myth: A History of Racist and Nationalist Ideas in Europe*, trans. Edmund Howard (New York: Basic Books, 1974), traces the history of European racialization of prehistory, with Ram-Prasad, "Comparative Philology," 94–98, on the ongoing legacy of this understanding of historical linguistics in classical studies. For Pearson, see Chip Berlet

and Matthew N. Lyons, *Right-Wing Populism in America: Too Close for Comfort*, Critical Perspectives (New York: Guilford, 2000), 187; William H. Tucker, *The Funding of Scientific Racism: Wickliffe Draper and the Pioneer Fund* (Urbana: University of Illinois Press, 2002), 159–79; William H. Tucker, *The Cattell Controversy: Race, Science, and Ideology* (Urbana: University of Illinois Press, 2009), 120–26; Robert W. Sussman, *The Myth of Race: The Troubling Persistence of an Unscientific Idea* (Cambridge, MA: Harvard University Press, 2014), 242–48. The fiftieth anniversary issue of the *Journal of Indo-European Studies* discussed Pearson's role in founding the journal and made no reference to his racist activism. On Carto and the Institute for Historical Review, see Leonard Zeskind, *Blood and Politics: The History of the White Nationalist Movement from the Margins to the Mainstream* (New York: Farrar, Straus & Giroux, 2009), 3–16, 52–59.

24. Duchesne, *Uniqueness*, 370, celebrates the capacity to inflict violence as one of the distinguishing traits of Western civilization, citing Hanson, *Carnage and Culture*, for "Westerners" being "the most deadly soldiers in the history of civilization."

25. Duchesne, *Uniqueness*, 370, 440–41. He bases his analysis on the theories of Nietzsche, a favorite philosopher of far-right thinkers according to Ronald Beiner, *Dangerous Minds: Nietzsche, Heidegger, and the Return of the Far Right* (Philadelphia: University of Pennsylvania Press, 2018). On Renan, see Poliakov, *The Aryan Myth*, especially 206–9; Martin Bernal, *Black Athena: The Afroasiatic Roots of Classical Civilization*, vol. 1: *The Fabrication of Classical Greece, 1785–1985* (New Brunswick, NJ: Rutgers University Press, 1987), 341–50; and Shmuel Almog, "The Racial Motif in Renan's Attitude to Jews and Judaism," in *Antisemitism through the Ages*, ed. Shmuel Almog (Oxford: Pergamon, 1988). Critiques of the idealizing politics of "Greek Miracle" rhetoric include Hanink, *The Classical Debt;* and Rebecca Futo Kennedy, "We Condone It by Our Silence," *Eidolon*, May 11, 2017, https://eidolon.pub/we-condone-it-by-our-silence-bea76fb59b21. Historians of science have begun to try to define what is distinctive about ancient Greek intellectual thought without falling into claims of superiority: Reviel Netz, "The Problematic Greek Miracle," *Syllecta Classica* 31, no. 31 (2020): 1–37; and G.E.R. Lloyd, *Expanding Horizons in the History of Science: The Comparative Approach* (Cambridge: Cambridge University Press, 2021), 32–43.

26. Jaeger is quoted by Duchesne, *Uniqueness*, 451; Duchesne's main treatments of Snell are at 435–36 and 447. On Snell, see Brooke Holmes, "Bruno Snell, *The Discovery of the Mind*," *Public Culture* 32, no. 2 (91) (May 1, 2020): 365.

27. Wynter is quoted in David Scott, "The Re-Enchantment of Humanism: An Interview with Sylvia Wynter," *Small Axe* 8 (2000): 192–93. See too Paul Gilroy, *The Black Atlantic: Modernity and Double Consciousness* (Cambridge, MA: Harvard University Press, 1993), 74, on "the obvious complicity which

both plantation slavery and colonial regimes revealed between [Western] rationality and the practice of racial terror." Other examples of appropriation of Prometheus in far-right literature include John Bruce Leonard's *The New Prometheans*, and Jason Reza Jorjani's books *Prometheus and Atlas* and *Prometheism* (all published by Arktos). On James Edwards, see David Neiwert, *Alt-America: The Rise of the Radical Right in the Age of Trump* (London: Verso, 2017), 252; and "Extremist Files: James Edwards," Southern Poverty Law Center, https://www.splcenter.org/fighting-hate/extremist-files/individual/james-edwards, accessed November 23, 2024.

28. John Knox Jessup, ed., *The Ideas of Henry Luce* (New York: Atheneum, 1969), 210. Michael Augspurger, "Henry Luce, Fortune, and the Attraction of Italian Fascism," *American Studies* 41, no. 1 (2000): 115–39, describes how Luce's publications promoted fascism. David Landes's *Unbound Prometheus* (1969) is an influential work of economic history that celebrates European ingenuity.
29. Katherine Blouin, "History Is Not a Plant: Some Thoughts on High School and Undergraduate (Ancient) History Curricula," *Everyday Orientalism*, 2017, https://everydayorientalism.wordpress.com/2017/08/29/history-is-not-a-plant-some-thoughts-on-high-school-and-undergraduate-ancient-history-curricula/; and Katherine Blouin, "Ralph W. Mathisen, Ancient Mediterranean Civilizations: Sources in Ancient Mediterranean Civilizations (Review)," Bryn Mawr Classical Review, 2017, https://bmcr.brynmawr.edu/2017/2017.11.03.
30. Amy Zhao Yu, Shahar Ronen, Kevin Hu, Tiffany Lu, and César A. Hidalgo, "Pantheon 1.0, a Manually Verified Dataset of Globally Famous Biographies," *Scientific Data* 3, no. 150075 (2016).
31. Zeskind, *Blood and Politics*, 417–23, 464–69; Rebecca Hersher, "What Happened When Dylann Roof Asked Google for Information about Race?" NPR.org, 2017, https://www.npr.org/sections/thetwo-way/2017/01/10/508363607/what-happened-when-dylann-roof-asked-google-for-information-about-race. The poster announcing the CCC's 2018 "National Solutions" conference featured an image of the classical sculpture known as the Discobolus, which Hitler particularly admired; see Sarah E. Bond, "The Political Uses of a Figure of Male Beauty from Antiquity," *Hyperallergic*, June 27, 2018, http://hyperallergic.com/447769/the-political-uses-of-a-figure-of-male-beauty-from-antiquity.
32. Wikipedia itself maintains an extensive description of its biases and omissions (https://en.wikipedia.org/wiki/Criticism_of_Wikipedia). At the time of writing, seven of the top ten and forty of the top fifty in Pantheon's rankings are European (counting Lenin and Stalin as Europeans). There are only four women, one of whom is Mary, the mother of Jesus. Che Guevara is the only figure born in the Western Hemisphere. Cleopatra and Moses, if he was a historical figure at all, are the only Afri-

cans. Pantheon has stopped claiming to measure how "memorable" historical figures are and now claims to measure their popularity.

33. Yu, Ronen, Hu, Lu, and Hidalgo, "Pantheon 1.0," 9, 15, describe their use of Murray's book in "validating" Pantheon's rankings. On the legacy of *The Bell Curve*, see William H. Tucker, *"The Bell Curve" in Perspective: Race, Meritocracy, Inequality and Politics* (Cham, Switzerland: Palgrave Macmillan, 2024), with 7–8 on *Human Accomplishment* and its methodological flaws. Murray's interview was with Steve Sailer, "Q&A: Charles Murray's *Human Accomplishment*," *UPI Odd Newsletter*, October 16, 2003, https://www.upi.com/Odd_News/2003/10/16/QA-Charles-Murrays-Human-Accomplishment/63221066339488/. *Human Accomplishment* inspired a contributor to the forums at Stormfront to create a list of the "scientific, technical, and technological accomplishments of the white race," beginning with fifteen ancient Greek thinkers, including Thales, Pythagoras, Anaximander, and Ptolemy.

34. Francis Galton, *Hereditary Genius: An Inquiry into Its Laws and Consequences* (London: Macmillan, 1869), 340, 342. On Galton, see Debbie Challis, *The Archaeology of Race: The Eugenic Ideas of Francis Galton and Flinders Petrie* (London: Bloomsbury, 2013), 45–59; and Adam Rutherford, *Control: The Dark History and Troubling Present of Eugenics* (London: Hachette, 2022), 37–51, with 130–31 on the removal of Galton's name from buildings and institutions at University College London (UCL) in 2020. In 2018, Ben Van Der Merwe, "Exposed: London's Eugenics Conference and Its Neo-Nazi Links," called attention to an annual gathering of eugenicists at UCL; one of the attendees has attempted to use historical DNA to demonstrate the cognitive superiority of the ancient Athenians: *London Student*, January 10, 2018, https://web.archive.org/web/20180110131144/http://londonstudent.coop/news/2018/01/10/exposed-london-eugenics-conferences-neo-nazi-links/.

35. Galton, *Hereditary Genius*, 339, 342. Charles A. Murray, *Human Accomplishment: The Pursuit of Excellence in the Arts and Sciences, 800 B.C. to 1950* (New York: HarperCollins, 2003), 73, cites Galton as his predecessor and declares that the Greek "contribution to philosophy during the seminal period" is "one of the enduring mysteries of human accomplishment" (223). On the historical context in which Galton wrote, see Challis, *The Archaeology of Race*, 48–49. The year 1868 witnessed the Opelousas, Camilla, and St. Bernard's Parish massacres in the United States.

36. Jaclyn Schildkraut, *Mass Shootings in America: Understanding the Debates, Causes, and Responses* (Santa Barbara, CA: ABC-Clio, 2018), xxv, reports that white people commit about half of mass shootings in the United States; her analysis of gender (47–53) finds that the vast majority of shooters are men.

37. This figure is quoted by Alan Cameron from a pseudoscientific book; see "Crantor and Posidonius on Atlantis," *Classical Quarterly* 33, no. 1 (January

1983): 81–91. Critiques of Hancock's methods include Garrett G. Fagan, "Diagnosing Pseudoarchaeology," in *Archaeological Fantasies: How Pseudoarchaeology Misrepresents the Past and Misleads the Public*, ed. Garrett G. Fagan (London: Routledge, 2006), 30–42; and Christopher Hale, "The Atlantean Box," in Fagan, *Archaeological Fantasies*, 242–56.

38. On Donnelly, see Jason Colavito blog, "Ignatius Donnelly and the Politics of Atlantis," Jason Colavito, July 27, 2018, http://www.jasoncolavito.com/1/post/2018/07/ignatius-donnelly-and-the-politics-of-atlantis.html. On Nazi occultism, see Eric Kurlander, " 'One Foot in Atlantis, One in Tibet': The Roots and Legacies of Nazi Theories on Atlantis, 1890–1945," *Leidschrift: Historische Tijdschrif* 32, no. 1 (2017): 82. From Graham Hancock, *Fingerprints of the Gods* (New York: Three Rivers, 1995), Dibble collected the following racializing passages in a thread on X.com (https://twitter.com/FlintDibble/status/1591867883088662529, accessed November 24, 2024), 59, 73, 107, 108, to which may be added 53, 56–57, 105–6, 262. Hancock calls the prehistoric white civilizer a "universal figure." See also Flint Dibble, "With Netflix's *Ancient Apocalypse*, Graham Hancock has Declared War on Archaeologists," *Conversation*, November 18, 2022, https://theconversation.com/with-netflixs-ancient-apocalypse-graham-hancock-has-declared-war-on-archaeologists-194881; and Stephanie Halmhoffer, "Manufacturing History: Atlantis, Aryans, and the Use of Pseudoarchaeology by the Far-Right," in *Conspiracy Theories and Extremism in New Times*, ed. Christopher T. Conner, Matthew N. Hannah, and Nicholas J. MacMurray (Lanham, MD: Lexington Books, 2024).

39. Hancock condemns white supremacy in Max Channon, "Netflix *Ancient Apocalypse:* Graham Hancock Slams Neo-Nazis Using Work to Spread Hate," *Express*, October 18, 2024, https://www.express.co.uk/news/world/1963394/netflix-ancient-apocalypse-graham-hancock. On indigenous protests of filming in the Grand Canyon, see Annette McGivney and Oliver Milman, "Netflix's *Ancient Apocalypse* Scraps US Filming Plans after Outcry from Native American Groups," *Guardian*, July 1, 2024, https://www.theguardian.com/us-news/article/2024/jul/01/netflix-ancient-apocalypse-canceled. The Society for American Archaeology statement on the show may be found at https://documents.saa.org/container/docs/default-source/doc-governmentaffairs/saa-letter-ancient-apocalypse.pdf, accessed November 24, 2024.

40. On the racial politics of *Ancient Aliens*, see Joan Braune, "*Ancient Aliens* Down to Earth: Conspiracy Theories, Antisemitism, and 'Anonymous Authority,' " in *Critical Theory and the Critique of Antisemitism*, ed. Marcel Stoetzler (London: Bloomsbury, 2023), 155–74. For the popularity of such theories on Stormfront and other white nationalist websites, see Stephanie Halmhofer, "Did Aliens Build the Pyramids? And Other Racist Theories," *Discover Magazine*, October 14, 2021, https://www.discovermagazine.com/planet-earth/did-aliens-build-the-pyramids-and-other-racist-theories.

Chapter Six. The (Un)Natural Order

1. On the *fasces* at Charlottesville, see Sarah E. Bond, "Fasces, Fascism, and How the Alt-Right Continues to Appropriate Ancient Symbols," *Hyperallergic*, September 13, 2018, https://hyperallergic.com/459504/fasces-fascism-and-how-the-alt-right-continues-to-appropriate-ancient-roman-symbols/. On the Charlottesville rally more generally, see Shane Burley, *Fascism Today: What It Is and How to End It* (Chico, CA: AK, 2017), 223–27; Nicole Hemmer, "The Alt-Right in Charlottesville: How an Online Movement Became a Real-World Presence," in *A Field Guide to White Supremacy*, ed. Kathleen Belew and Ramon A. Gutiérrez (Berkeley: University of California Press, 2021), 287–303; and the first-person account of Vegas Tenold, *Everything You Love Will Burn: Inside the Rebirth of White Nationalism in America* (New York: Nation Books, 2018), 286–93.
2. Michelle Renee Salzman, "Aurelian and the Cult of the Unconquered Sun: The Institutionalization of Christmas, Solar Worship, and Imperial Cult," in *Expressions of Cult in the Southern Levant in the Greco-Roman Period: Manifestations in Text and Material Culture*, ed. Oren Tal and Zeev Weiss (Turnhout: Brepols, 2017), 46, on Augustus's interest in solar worship.
3. On the symbolic history of the *fasces*, see T. Corey Brennan, *The Fasces: A History of Ancient Rome's Most Dangerous Political Symbol* (Oxford: Oxford University Press, 2022), especially 119–35. The Anti-Defamation League's "Hate Symbol: Fasces" documents examples of the symbolism in white nationalist logos (https://www.adl.org/resources/hate-symbol/fasces).
4. A recent definition of fascism that emphasizes the centrality of hierarchy to that ideology is that of Burley, *Fascism Today*, 50: "inequality through mythologized and essentialized identity." On Spencer's comparison, see Curtis Dozier, "A New Roman Empire for White People," *Pharos: Doing Justice to the Classics*, July 26, 2019, https://pharos.vassarspaces.net/2019/07/26/a-new-roman-empire-for-white-people/. On Italian fascism and Greco-Roman antiquity, see Marla Stone, "A Flexible Rome: Fascism and the Cult of Romanitá," in *Roman Presences: Receptions of Rome in European Culture, 1789–1945*, ed. Catharine Edwards (Cambridge: Cambridge University Press, 1999); and the essays collected in Helen Roche and Kyriakos Demetriou, *Brill's Companion to the Classics, Fascist Italy and Nazi Germany* (Leiden: Brill, 2018). The classical historian Ramsay MacMullen, *Roman Social Relations, 50 B.C. to A.D. 284* (New Haven, CT: Yale University Press, 1974), 38, summarized the history of the Roman Empire with the phrase "less have more."
5. Nicole Maurantonio, *Confederate Exceptionalism: Civil War Myth and Memory in the Twenty-First Century*, Culture America (Lawrence: University Press of Kansas, 2019), presents a history of the myriad ways that nostalgia for the Confederacy has sanitized white supremacy, from southern folk music of the 1870s to "Heritage, not hate" slogans in the internet era.

6. Lyra Monteiro, "Power Structures: White Columns, White Marble, White Supremacy," Medium, 2020, https://intersectionist.medium.com/american-power-structures-white-columns-white-marble-white-supremacy-d43aa091b5f9. The murderer's photographs at Boone Hall, Magnolia Plantation and Gardens, and Macleod Plantation are collected by Neely Tucker and Peter Holley, "Dylann Roof's Eerie Tour of American Slavery at Its Beginning, Middle and End," *Washington Post*, July 1, 2015, https://www.washingtonpost.com/news/post-nation/wp/2015/07/01/dylann-roofs-eerie-tour-of-american-slavery-at-its-beginning-middle-and-end/.
7. On states' rights and Greco-Roman antiquity, see Carl J. Richard, *The Golden Age of the Classics in America: Greece, Rome, and the Antebellum United States* (Cambridge, MA: Harvard University Press, 2009), 49–50. On Gildersleeve, see David Lupher and Elizabeth Vandiver, "Yankee She-Men and Octoroon Electra: Basil Lanneau Gildersleeve on Race, Slavery, and Abolition," in *Ancient Slavery and Abolition: From Hobbes to Hollywood*, ed. Edith Hall, Richard Alston, and Justine McConnell (Oxford: Oxford University Press, 2011). See also Page DuBois, *Slaves and Other Objects* (Chicago: University of Chicago Press, 2003), 15–17, on the incoherence of Gildersleeve's analogy: he saw the Confederacy in the slaveholding, agrarian society of Sparta but linked the Confederate defeat to that of Athens at the hands of Sparta. The wider context of Gildersleeve's nostalgia is examined by Denise Eileen McCoskey, "Basil Gildersleeve and John Scott: Race and the Rise of American Classical Philology," *American Journal of Philology* 143, no. 2 (2022): 247–77.
8. On the dedication of Silent Sam, see Kelly McArdle, "Removing 'Silent Sam': Confederate Statues and the Misuse of Classics at UNC-Chapel Hill," Society for Classical Studies, May 20, 2018, https://classicalstudies.org/scs-blog/kmcardle/blog-removing-silent-sam-confederate-statues-and-misuse-classics-unc-chapel-hill; and Andrew Tobolowsky, "A Historian Annotates the Horrific Speech Given at the Dedication of 'Silent Sam,'" *Eidolon*, October 1, 2018, https://eidolon.pub/a-historian-annotates-the-horrific-speech-given-at-the-dedication-of-silent-sam-96acf5cea5af. On the Arlington Confederate Memorial, see Margaret Malamud, *African Americans and the Classics: Antiquity, Abolition and Activism* (London: I. B. Tauris, 2016), 142–46. On the Nashville Parthenon, see Savannah Marquardt, "The Nashville Parthenon Glorifies Ancient Greece—and the Confederacy," *Eidolon*, 2018, https://eidolon.pub/the-heirs-of-athens-of-the-south-a8b730b84de3.
9. On Fleming, Hill, and the "League of the South," see Euan Hague, Heidi Beirich, and Edward H. Sebesta, *Neo-Confederacy: A Critical Introduction* (Austin: University of Texas Press, 2008), 1–7, 116–18, quoting Thomas Fleming, "Grow Old along with Me," *Chronicles* 23, no. 9 (1999): 10–12; and Thomas Fleming, "Burn This Book," *Chronicles* 24, no. 9 (2000): 10–12.

10. On the Helots as slaves, see Paul Cartledge, "The Helots: A Contemporary Review," in *The Cambridge World History of Slavery*, vol. 1: *The Ancient Mediterranean World*, ed. Keith Bradley and Paul Cartledge (Cambridge: Cambridge University Press, 2011), 78–82. White nationalists regard the Helots as an ancient parallel to (and therefore justification for) racial slavery, since Spartan ideology held that the Helots were indigenous inhabitants of Laconia whom the invading Spartans had conquered and enslaved. Historians have begun to question the long-held assumption that ancient slavery was not based on race: see Christopher S. Parmenter, " 'But They Were a Race of Whites': Race and the Making of Ancient Slavery in the Anglophone World, 1785–1980," *TAPA* 154, no. 1 (2024): 295–330.
11. On Aristotle's justification of "natural slavery" (*Politics* 1255a, trans. Rackham), see Rachana Kamtekar, "Studying Ancient Political Thought through Ancient Philosophers: The Case of Aristotle and Natural Slavery," *Polis* 33, no. 1 (2016): 151–57; Emily Greenwood, "Reconstructing Classical Philology: Reading Aristotle *Politics* 1.4 after Toni Morrison," *American Journal of Philology* 143, no. 2 (2022): 337–40; and Parmenter, " 'But They Were a Race of Whites,' " 302–3. Peter Hunt, *Ancient Greek and Roman Slavery* (Hoboken, NJ: Wiley-Blackwell, 2017), 207–8, discusses the lack of abolitionist activism in antiquity. On the fine-grained hierarchies of Athenian civic life, see Deborah Kamen, *Status in Classical Athens*, Course Book (Princeton, NJ: Princeton University Press, 2013), with Rebecca Futo Kennedy, "Race and the Athenian Metic Revisioned," in *Identity in Antiquity*, ed. V. Manapopulou, J. Skinner, and C. Tsouparopolou (New York: Routledge, forthcoming), on "Metic" as a racialized category.
12. One source white nationalists cite for this understanding of slavery is Elmer Pendell, *Why Civilizations Self Destruct* (Cape Canaveral, FL: H. Allen, 1977). Pendell was a professor of economics who taught at Cornell University, Pennsylvania State University, and the University of Arkansas. His argument about slavery was summarized in *American Renaissance*: "The modern analogue of slavery is immigration."
13. Aristotle, *Politics* 1254b12, 1259a37, trans. Barker, with the analysis of Marguerite Deslauriers, "Political Unity and Inequality," in *The Cambridge Companion to Aristotle's "Politics,"* ed. Maguerite Deslauriers and Pierre Destrée (Cambridge: Cambridge University Press, 2013).
14. Eric Havelock, "Plato's *Politics* and the American Constitution," *Harvard Studies in Classical Philology* 93 (1990): 3–6, contrasts Popper and Bloom, quoting Allan Bloom, *The Closing of the American Mind: How Higher Education Has Failed Democracy and Impoverished the Souls of Today's Students* (New York: Simon & Schuster, 1987), 266. On Popper, see Michael L. Silk, Ingo Gildenhard, and Rosemary J. Barrow, *The Classical Tradition: Art, Literature, Thought* (Hoboken, NJ: John Wiley & Sons, 2014), 403–5.

On Bloom, see Eric Adler, *Classics, the Culture Wars, and Beyond* (Ann Arbor: University of Michigan Press, 2016), 19–22, whose generally sympathetic presentation does not conceal the hierarchical dimension of Bloom's book: "According to Bloom, the university must encourage elitist philosophical contemplation anathema to the pragmatic leveling of American democracy."

15. Justifications for rule: Plato, *Laws* 690a–c, trans. Saunders, quoting Pindar fr. 169a Maehler. Definition of "true justice": *Laws* 757d, a section of the dialogue that also includes claims that "friendship between [masters and slaves] is impossible" (756e) and "indiscriminate equality for all amounts to inequality, and both fill a state with quarrels between its citizens" (757a). White nationalists also quote the recommendation of "proportional inequality" from *Laws* 744c. From the *Republic*, white nationalists quote 455c on "naturally competent" and "naturally incompetent" people; 495c and 545a on "inferior kinds of people"; and 518c on the view that education can no more change a foolish man than it can teach a blind man to see.
16. Plato, *Republic* 557a–563c, trans. Griffith.
17. For this interpretation of Socrates' execution, see Mogens Herman Hansen, *The Trial of Sokrates—from the Athenian Point of View* (Copenhagen: Kgl. Danske Videnskabernes Selskab, 1995). I. F. Stone, *The Trial of Socrates* (Boston: Little, Brown, 1988), is a popular explanation along these lines. The Athenian orator Aeschines, speaking fifty years after Socrates' death, was at least aware of this interpretation: "Did you put to death Socrates, fellow citizens, because he was shown to have been the teacher of Critias, one of the Thirty who put down the democracy?" (1.173). The geneticist who compared David Duke to Socrates was Glayde Whitney, on whom see William H. Tucker, *The Funding of Scientific Racism: Wickliffe Draper and the Pioneer Fund* (Urbana: University of Illinois Press, 2002), 181–82; and William H. Tucker, *The Cattell Controversy: Race, Science, and Ideology* (Urbana: University of Illinois Press, 2009), 151.
18. Gregory R. Johnson, "The First Founding Father: Aristotle on Freedom and Popular Government," in *Liberty and Democracy*, ed. Tibor R. Machan (Stanford, CA: Hoover Institution Press, 2002). Donald Morrison, "Aristotle's Definition of Citizenship: A Problem and Some Solutions," *History of Philosophy Quarterly* 16, no. 2 (1999): 144–45, discusses the "incoherence" of Aristotle's theory. On the relationship between libertarianism and white nationalism, see Melinda Cooper, "The Alt-Right: Neoliberalism, Libertarianism and the Fascist Temptation," *Theory, Culture & Society* 38, no. 6 (November 1, 2021): 29–50.
19. Aristotle, *Politics* 1280a13–14, trans. Barker.
20. For the citation of Aristotle and Greco-Roman antiquity to justify slavery, see Mavis Campbell, "Aristotle and Black Slavery: A Study in Race Preju-

dice," *Race* 15, no. 3 (1974): 283–301; J. Drew Harrington, "Classical Antiquity and the Proslavery Argument," *Slavery and Abolition* 10, no. 1 (1989): 60–72; Richard, *Golden Age of the Classics*, 181–93; and Sara Monoson, "Recollecting Aristotle: Pro-Slavery Thought in Antebellum Argument and the Argument of *Politics* Book I," in Hall, Alston, and McConnell, *Ancient Slavery and Abolition*, 247–78. The claim that slavery produced the "high civilization" of Greece is quoted by Malamud, *African Americans and the Classics*, 128. For the role of Platonic thought in justifying slavery, see Cedric Robinson, "Slavery and the Platonic Origins of Anti-Democracy," *National Political Science Review* 5 (1995): 18–35. For classical scholars sanitizing the influence of Greek and Roman slavery, see, for example, Victor Davis Hanson, *Carnage and Culture: Landmark Battles in the Rise of Western Power* (New York: Anchor, 2001), 50: "The sins of the Greeks—slavery, sexism, economic exploitation, ethnic chauvinism—are largely the sins of man common to *all* cultures at *all* times"; Bruce S. Thornton, *Greek Ways: How the Greeks Created Western Civilization* (San Francisco: Encounter Books, 2002), 11: "These sins are really the sins of humanity, discoverable in all times and places"; and Lefkowitz, quoted in Zbigniew Janowski, "A Conversation with Mary Lefkowitz," Postil Magazine, May 1, 2020, https://www.thepostil.com/a-conversation-with-mary-lefkowitz/, on those who "only [consider] the downside of Western Civ, which is pretty much the downside of human nature generally." In a lecture, "Classification of Slaves in Ancient Greece," for a course Daily Life in the Ancient World hosted by the streaming platform the Great Courses, Robert Garland claimed that "slavery was an ideal condition for some people in ancient Greece": see Robert Garland, "Classification of Slaves in Ancient Greece," Wondrium Daily, August 11, 2020, https://web.archive.org/web/20220524030220/https://www.wondriumdaily.com/classification-of-slaves-in-ancient-greece/. Cotton's remarks on slavery are reported by Bryan Armen Graham, "Tom Cotton Calls Slavery 'Necessary Evil' in Attack on *New York Times*' 1619 Project," *Guardian*, July 26, 2020, https://www.theguardian.com/world/2020/jul/26/tom-cotton-slavery-necessary-evil-1619-project-new-york-times.

21. Plato, *Republic* 459d–e, 460c, trans. Waterfield. Aristotle, *Politics* 1335b19, trans. Barker. Plutarch, *Life of Lycurgus* 16.1–2, trans. Perrin. Plato, *Laws* 735d–736a, trans. Saunders.

22. On infanticide in antiquity, see Debby Sneed, "Disability and Infanticide in Ancient Greece," *Hesperia* 90, no. 4 (2021): 747–72. Jefferson's letter of October 28, 1813, to Adams is quoted by M. Andrew Holowchak, "Jefferson's Platonic Republicanism," *Polis* 31 (2014): 378–79. In that letter, Jefferson goes on to reject the idea of eugenic programs because the populace would not accept the regulation of sexuality, "obliging us to continue acquiescence under the 'weakening of the stock of citizens' which Theognis (183–192) complains of," a hypocritical concession for a

man who fathered several children with Sally Hemings, a woman he enslaved. (Jefferson quotes Theognis's original Greek, which I have translated in this quotation.) Edwin Black, *War against the Weak: Eugenics and America's Campaign to Create a Master Race* (New York: Thunder's Mouth, 2004), is an accessible history of eugenics in the United States that sometimes errs on the side of the sensational. More sober is Daniel J. Kevles, *In the Name of Eugenics: Genetics and the Uses of Human Heredity*, Collection Sueurs Froides (New York: Knopf, 1985).

23. R. A. Fisher, *The Genetical Theory of Natural Selection* (Oxford: Clarendon, 1930), 202–4. Darwin's message can be found in Charles B. Davenport, Harry F. Perkins, Clarence G. Campbell, Madison Grant, Harrison R. Hunt, Frederick Osborn, Paul Popenoe, Laurence H. Snyder, and Harry H. Laughlin, eds., *A Decade of Progress in Eugenics: Scientific Papers of the Third International Congress of Eugenics* (Baltimore: Williams & Wilkins, 1934), 23–24. On Fisher, who is described as a "genius" by Anders Hald, *A History of Mathematical Statistics* (New York: Wiley, 1998), 738, see Adam Rutherford, *Control: The Dark History and Troubling Present of Eugenics* (London: Hachette, 2022), 95–99, 135.

24. Roper's praise for Plato and Aristotle is in Allen G. Roper, *Ancient Eugenics: The Arnold Prize Essay for 1913* (Oxford: Blackwell, 1913), 70. The PPIE's history is quoted by Mireille M. Lee, "Classical Nudity and Eugenics at the Panama-Pacific International Exposition," *International Journal of the Classical Tradition* 28, no. 1 (2021): 61, on the use of Greco-Roman statuary to promote eugenics at that exposition.

25. Kevin Bales, Zoe Trodd, and Alex Kent Williamson, *Modern Slavery: The Secret World of 27 Million People* (Oxford: Oneworld, 2009), is a survey of the issue. The organ trafficker is quoted by Siddharth Kara, *Modern Slavery: A Global Perspective* (New York: Columbia University Press, 2017), 120, who documents extensive examples of the experiences of the enslaved. On slavery and global capitalism, see Julia O'Connell Davidson, *Modern Slavery: The Margins of Freedom* (London: Palgrave Macmillan, 2015). Along similar lines, it is argued in Emily Kenway, *The Truth about Modern Slavery* (London: Pluto, 2021), that the terminology of "slavery" hampers efforts to end exploitation. On the representation of slavery in Latin textbooks, see Kelly Dugan, "The 'Happy Slave' Narrative and Classics Pedagogy: A Verbal and Visual Analysis of Beginning Greek and Latin Textbooks," *New England Classical Journal* 46, no. 1 (January 1, 2019): 62–87. On slave auctions, see Dani Bostick, "The Shame of Mock Slave Auctions in Secondary Classics," *Sententiae Antiquae*, October 29, 2019, https://sententiaeantiquae.com/2019/10/29/the-shame-of-mock-slave-auctions-in-secondary-classics/; and Dani Bostick, "Not for All: Nostalgic Distortions as a Weapon of Segregation in Secondary Classics," *American Journal of Philology* 141, no. 2 (2020): 291–92.

26. These examples of forced sterilizations are collected from Philip R. Reilly, "Eugenics and Involuntary Sterilization: 1907–2015," *Annual Review of Genomics and Human Genetics* 16 (2015): 351–68; and Alexandra Minna Stern, *Eugenic Nation: Faults and Frontiers of Better Breeding in Modern America*, 2nd ed. (Oakland: University of California Press, 2016). On the white supremacist fear of the fertility of women of color, see Leo R. Chavez, "Fear of White Replacement: Latina Fertility, White Demographic Decline, and Immigration Reform," in Belew and Gutiérrez, *A Field Guide to White Supremacy*, 177–202. For critiques of the eugenic principles of "Quality Adjusted Life Years," see Ron Amundson, "Disability, Ideology, and Quality of Life: A Bias in Biomedical Ethics," in *Quality of Life and Human Difference: Genetic Testing, Health Care, and Disability*, ed. David Wasserman, Jerome Bickenbach, and Robert Wachbroit (Cambridge: Cambridge University Press, 2005); and Pepper Stettler, "The Eugenic Roots of 'Quality Adjusted Life Years,' and Why They Matter," *Washington Post*, March 8, 2023, https://www.washingtonpost.com/made-by-history/2023/03/08/qlay-disabilities/. On the popularity of "transhumanism" among Silicon Valley billionaires, see Jennifer Huberman, *Transhumanism: From Ancestors to Avatars* (Cambridge: Cambridge University Press, 2021), 232–34. Philosopher Susan Levin details transhumanist citations of Plato and Aristotle, as well as the mythological figure of Prometheus, whom I discussed as a symbol of white superiority in my fifth chapter; see Susan B. Levin, "Antiquity's Missive to Transhumanism," *Journal of Medicine and Philosophy* 42, no. 3 (June 1, 2017): 279–83. On the parallels between transhumanist and eugenic thought, see Susan B. Levin, *Posthuman Bliss? The Failed Promise of Transhumanism* (New York: Oxford University Press, 2021), 172–90.
27. Alexander Jacob, *Nobilitas: A Study of European Aristocratic Philosophy from Ancient Greece to the Early Twentieth Century* (Lanham, MD: University Press of America, 2001), 2. Jacob's translations include the work of Houston Stewart Chamberlain, whose "Foundations of the Nineteenth Century" informed the Nazi Party's antisemitism; Jean-François Thiriart, a Belgian collaborator with the Nazis; and Otto Böckel, whose 1887 pamphlet "The Jews: Kings of Our Times" was an early deployment of antisemitism for political gain in Germany.
28. *Federalist*, no. 55 (James Madison).
29. Madison is quoted by Richard, *Golden Age of the Classics*, 75. Jefferson has a reputation for despising Plato but in fact his political philosophy was highly Platonic; see M. Andrew Holowchak, "Jefferson's Platonic Republicanism," *Polis* 31 (2014): 369–86. On Jefferson's "natural aristocracy" in American political thought, see Judith N. Shklar, *Redeeming American Political Thought* (Chicago: University of Chicago Press, 1998), 147–50, who sees the framers' debates about "aristocracy" as symptomatic of the

contradiction between the Declaration's language of equality and the "wholly inegalitarian" structure of their new nation. Sarah Teets, "Classical Slavery and Jeffersonian Racism," links Jefferson's educational philosophy, and the architecture of the University of Virginia's campus, to the Charlottesville rally: *Eidolon*, August 10, 2018, https://eidolon.pub/classical-slavery-and-jeffersonian-racism-28cbcdf53364.

30. On the *fasces* in American art and architecture before the Civil War, see Brennan, *The Fasces*, 140–74, with 167 on Jefferson Davis.
31. Brennan, *The Fasces*, 175–77, with 158 on the National Park Service's description of the *fasces* as the "theme of the [Lincoln] memorial."
32. On the similarities between contemporary and Jim Crow voter suppression, see Gilda R. Daniels, *Uncounted: The Crisis of Voter Suppression in America* (New York: New York University Press, 2020), with Charles S. Bullock, Ronald Keith Gaddie, and Justin J. Wert, *The Rise and Fall of the Voting Rights Act* (Norman: University of Oklahoma Press, 2016), 151–69, on the Supreme Court decision that ended federal oversight of these practices. See Jesse H. Rhodes, *Ballot Blocked: The Political Erosion of the Voting Rights Act* (Redwood City, CA: Stanford University Press, 2017), on the long campaign following the passage of the Voting Rights Act in 1965 that led to that decision. American authoritarianism: Burley, *Fascism Today*, 2. Polybius applies Greek political philosophy to Rome's constitution in his book 6.
33. Jeff Fuhrer, *The Myth That Made Us: How False Beliefs about Racism and Meritocracy Broke Our Economy (and How to Fix It)* (Cambridge, MA: MIT Press, 2023), 57–112, documents the inequalities that pervade American life. Williams is quoted by Jo Littler, *Against Meritocracy: Culture, Power and Myths of Mobility* (Abingdon: Routledge, 2018), 3, who also analyzes how meritocracy justifies and racializes hierarchy (151–55). Wilkerson's explanation of her analogy between American racism and hierarchical caste systems is found in Isabel Wilkerson, *Caste: The Origins of Our Discontents* (New York: Random House, 2020), 68–72. The term *meritocracy* was coined by Michael Young, *The Rise of the Meritocracy* (London: Thames & Hudson, 1958); in a new preface for the second edition, Young recalled that "a friend, a Classical scholar," advised him not to use the term because he would be "laughed to scorn" for combining Latin (*merito-*) and Greek (*-cracy*) roots in a new coinage.
34. Joel Christensen, "Fake Aristotle Fakely Rails against Fighting Inequality," *Sententiae Antiquae*, March 23, 2019, https://sententiaeantiquae.com/2019/03/23/fake-aristotle-fakely-rails-against-fighting-inequality/.

Chapter Seven. The Dream of a White Homeland

1. Powell's speech quoted *Aeneid* 6.87. Biographical details from Powell's life are cited from Robert Shepherd, *Enoch Powell* (London: Hutchinson, 1996), 35–36; and Simon Heffer, *Like the Roman: The Life of Enoch Powell* (London: Weidenfield & Nicholson, 1998), 35, 47–78, 252. On Powell's influence among British white nationalists, see Graham Macklin, *Failed Führers: A History of Britain's Extreme Right* (London: Routledge, 2020), 155–56, 227–28. For the influence of the American civil rights movement on Powell's thought and the influence of his speech in America, see Clive Webb, "Enoch Powell's America/America's Enoch Powell," in *Global White Nationalism: From Apartheid to Trump*, ed. Daniel Geary, Camilla Schofield, and Jennifer Sutton (Manchester: Manchester University Press, 2020).
2. Powell and then president Donald Trump are compared in Barry Eichengreen, "For a Better Parallel with Donald Trump, Try Enoch Powell," *Guardian*, January 12, 2017, https://www.theguardian.com/business/2017/jan/12/donald-trump-enoch-powell-rivers-of-blood. Austrian rally: Julia Müller, "Pop Culture against Modernity," in *Classical Controversies: Reception of Graeco-Roman Antiquity in the Twenty-First Century*, ed. Kim Beerden and Timo Epping (Leiden: Sidestone, 2022), 106–11.
3. On Vox Day, see George Hawley, *Making Sense of the Alt-Right* (New York: Columbia University Press, 2017), 97–99; and Tamir Bar-On, "The Metapolitics of the Alt-Right: A 'Cultural War' for the United States, European Identity, and the 'White Race,' " in *The Right and Radical Right in the Americas: Ideological Currents from Interwar Canada to Contemporary Chile*, ed. Tamir Bar-On and Bàrbara Molas (Lanham, MD: Lexington Books, 2021), 197–201.
4. Aristotle, *Politics* 1303a25. This passage provides yet another example of a popular translation employing language that asserts the biological reality of racial identity: the word Aristotle uses is *homophulon*, which refers only to shared ancestry. The line "Tolerance and apathy are the last virtues of a dying society" is often attributed to Aristotle but appears nowhere in his work, as discussed by Joel Christensen, "Racists Use This Fake Quote from Aristotle," *Sententiae Antiquae*, September 29, 2018, https://sententiaeantiquae.com/2018/09/29/racists-use-this-fake-quote-from-aristotle/. It appears without mention of Aristotle in the manifesto of the man who murdered ten Black people at a supermarket in Buffalo, New York, in 2022. Highbrow white nationalists do not cite this fake quotation because they can find enough support for their ideas in authentic works.
5. Aristotle's description of humankind is at *Politics* 1353a4. On the definition of the *polis* and its extent in the ancient Greek world, see John Ma, *Polis: A New History of the Ancient Greek City-State from the Early Iron Age*

to the End of Antiquity (Princeton, NJ: Princeton University Press, 2024), 13–19. On the white nationalist ethnostate, see Alexandra Minna Stern, *Proud Boys and the White Ethnostate: How the Alt-Right Is Warping the American Imagination* (Boston: Beacon, 2019), 51–70. The conference where Leonard spoke was reported on by FOIA Research, "Nova Europa Society," FOIA Research, March 12, 2020, https://www.foiaresearch.net/organization/nova-europa-society.

6. Azar Gat, with contributions by Alexander Yakobson, *Nations: The Long History and Deep Roots of Political Ethnicity and Nationalism* (Cambridge: Cambridge University Press, 2013), 68–69.
7. Ryszard Kulesza, "Citizenship and the Spartan Kosmos," in *Citizenship in Antiquity: Civic Communities in the Ancient Mediterranean*, ed. Jakub Filonik, Christine Plastow, and Rachel Zelnick-Abramovitz (London: Routledge, 2023), 209–25, provides an overview of citizenship in Sparta, including the enslaved soldiers who were freed for their military service and then known as *neodamodes* (219–20).
8. Xenophon, *Constitution of the Lacedaemonians* 14, trans. Talbert; Plutarch, *Life of Lycurgus* 27.3, trans. Perrin; Thucydides 1.144.2, 2.39.1; Aristophanes, *Birds* 1012–1014; Plato, *Protagoras* 342c.
9. Helen Roche, "Mussolini's 'Third Rome,' Hitler's Third Reich and the Allure of Antiquity: Classicizing Chronopolitics as a Remedy for Unstable National Identity?" *Fascism* 8, no. 2 (2019): 142, quotes Hitler on Sparta. Tampa exhibition: "Ancient Athens: Birthplace of Democracy," Tampa Museum of Art, October 25, 2024, https://web.archive.org/web/20241118000951/https://tampamuseum.org/ancient-athens-birthplace-of-democracy/, archived November 18, 2024. For the history of naive celebration of Pericles' claim of Athenian openness (Thucydides 2.39, trans. Smith), see Nicole Loraux, *The Invention of Athens: The Funeral Oration in the Classical City*, trans. Alan Sheridan (Cambridge, MA: Zone Books, 2006), 33, 429n40; and Johanna Hanink, *The Classical Debt: Greek Antiquity in an Era of Austerity* (Cambridge, MA: Harvard University Press, 2017), 275. London buses: Hanink, *The Classical Debt*, 54. European Union constitutional treaty: Wilfried Nippel, *Ancient and Modern Democracy: Two Concepts of Liberty?* (Cambridge: Cambridge University Press, 2015), 368–69; and Paul Cartledge, *Ancient Greece: A History in Eleven Cities* (Oxford: Oxford University Press, 2009), 105.
10. Dark side of the *polis:* Ma, *Polis*, 480–540. Racial citizenship in Athens: Susan Lape, *Race and Citizen Identity in the Classical Athenian Democracy* (Cambridge: Cambridge University Press, 2010). On the influence of ancient Athenian propaganda on modern perceptions of antiquity, see Hanink, *The Classical Debt*, 35.
11. On the Athenian ideology of autochthony, see David Konstan, "To Hellenikon Ethnos: Ethnicity and the Construction of Ancient Greek Identity," in *Ancient Perceptions of Greek Ethnicity*, ed. Irad Malkin (Washington, DC: Center for Hellenic Studies, 2001), 34–40.

12. On Pericles' law, see Plutarch, *Life of Solon* 22.1, with Edwin Carawan, "Pericles the Younger and the Citizenship Law," *Classical Journal* 103, no. 4 (2008): 383–406, on the later revision. On the number of *metics* in Athens, see Ben Akrigg, *Population and Economy in Classical Athens* (Cambridge: Cambridge University Press, 2019), 120–26. On *metics,* see Deborah Kamen, *Status in Classical Athens* (Princeton, NJ: Princeton University Press, 2013), 43–54. Somewhat puzzlingly, Robert Garland, *Wandering Greeks: The Ancient Greek Diaspora from the Age of Homer to the Death of Alexander the Great* (Princeton, NJ: Princeton University Press, 2014), suggests that Athens was "open to immigrants" (5) before detailing the systemic oppression of *metics* under Athenian law (155–65).
13. Appeal of Athens to white nationalists: Rebecca Futo Kennedy, "We Condone It by Our Silence," *Eidolon*, May 11, 2017, https://eidolon.pub/we-condone-it-by-our-silence-bea76fb59b21. Plutarch, *Life of Pericles* 37, is the fullest ancient source for Pericles' citizenship law, on which see Chris Carey, "The Citizen Body," in Filonik, Plastow, and Zelnick-Abramovitz, *Citizenship in Antiquity*, 288–91. It is true that Athens occasionally granted citizenship to individuals who had earned the gratitude of the city-state, but this must have affected only a tiny number of elites and in any case is best understood as an act not of generosity but of political expedience: when Athens granted citizenship to refugees from Plataea following the outbreak of the Peloponnesian War, for example, they did so to create an enticement to other, wavering, allies to remain loyal. Ancient comparisons between free and enslaved populations include Plato, *Laws* 777d, trans. Saunders, and Aristotle, *Politics* 1330a28. On the number of slaves in Athens, see Akrigg, *Population and Economy*, 89–96. Rebecca Futo Kennedy, "Classics and Western Civilization: The Troubling History of an Authoritative Narrative," in *Authority and History: Ancient Models, Modern Questions*, ed. Marques J. Bastos and Federico Santangelo (London: Bloomsbury, 2022), 97–99, notes an example of a prominent scholar asserting the homogeneity of Athens.
14. On the Pelasgians, see Lionel Scott, ed., *Historical Commentary on Herodotus Book 6* (Leiden: Brill, 2005), 444–46; and Jeremy McInerney, "Pelasgians and Leleges: Using the Past to Understand the Present," in *Valuing the Past in the Greco-Roman World*, ed. Christopher Pieper and James Ker (Leiden: Brill, 2014). On the "aboriginal Pelasgian hordes" in the work of Robert Knox, a nineteenth-century proponent of scientific racism, see Athena S. Leoussi, "Making Nations in the Image of Greece: Classical Greek Conceptions of the Body in the Construction of National Identity in Nineteenth-Century England, France, and Germany," in *Graeco-Roman Antiquity and the Idea of Nationalism in the 19th Century*, ed. Thorsten Fögen and Richard Warren (Berlin: De Gruyter, 2016), 54.
15. Herodotus 6.137–38, trans. Waterfield.

16. Dan-el Padilla Peralta, "Barbarians inside the Gate, Part 1," *Eidolon*, November 9, 2015, https://eidolon.pub/barbarians-inside-the-gate-part-i-c175057b340f. Nandini Pandey, "The Roman Roots of Racial Capitalism," *Berlin Journal* 34 (2021): 16–20, wrestles with the tension between Rome's apparent openness to and dependence on a diverse population and the imperial violence that produced the cosmopolitan empire. On the anachronisms of Herodotus's account of the conflict between Athens and Lemnos, see Scott, *Historical Commentary*, 448–51.
17. Johann Chapoutot, *Greeks, Romans, Germans: How the Nazis Usurped Europe's Classical Past*, trans. Richard R. Nybakken (Berkeley: University of California Press, 2016), 266.
18. For the reception of *Alexander: The Making of a God* in Greece, see Sian Cain, "Alexander the Great Netflix Show Labelled 'Extremely Poor-Quality Fiction' by Greek Minister," *Guardian*, February 20, 2024, https://www.theguardian.com/tv-and-radio/2024/feb/20/alexander-the-great-netflix-show-greece-minister-for-culture-lina-mendoni-gay-characters, with Jon Solomon, "The Popular Reception of *Alexander*," in *Responses to Oliver Stone's "Alexander": Film, History, and Cultural Studies*, ed. Paul Cartledge, Fiona Rose Greenland, and Oliver Stone (Madison: University of Wisconsin Press, 2010), on the broader homophobia that Oliver Stone's 2004 *Alexander* faced. On Turner, see "Right Now! A Forum for Eugenicists," *Searchlight*, July 1998, https://web.archive.org/web/20040508063548/http://www.searchlightmagazine.com/stories/genewar03.htm; and Matthew Collins, "What's Derek Turner Up to Right Now?" *Hope Not Hate: Insiders' Blog*, August 10, 2022, https://hopenothate.org.uk/2022/08/10/whats-derek-turner-up-to-right-now/.
19. Aristotle's advice: Plutarch, *On the Fortune of Alexander* 329b. Alexander's adoption of Persian customs: Arrian, *Anabasis of Alexander* 7.4.5–6; and Promotion of intermarriage: Plutarch, *Life of Alexander* 70.2, with the discussion of A. B. Bosworth, "Alexander and the Iranians," *Journal of Hellenic Studies* 100 (1980): 1–21.
20. Arrian 7.6.2–5, trans. Brunt, with Bosworth, "Alexander and the Iranians," 11. The idea that Alexander "dreamed" of a "brotherhood of man" seems to have originated with William W. Tarn, "Alexander the Great and the Unity of Mankind," *Proceedings of the British Academy* 19 (1933): 123–66, whose interpretations of ancient evidence are refuted by Ernst Badian, "Alexander the Great and the Unity of Mankind," *Historia* 7, no. 4 (1958): 425–44.
21. One survey of Hellenistic settlements is Katja Mueller, *Settlements of the Ptolemies: City Foundations and New Settlement in the Hellenistic World* (Leuven: Peeters, 2006). On more voluntary immigration, see Zosia H. Archibald, "Mobility and Innovation in Hellenistic Economies: The Causes and Consequences of Human Traffic," in *The Economies of Hellenistic Societies, Third to First Centuries BC*, ed. Zosia H. Archibald, John K. Davies, and Vincent Gabrielsen (Oxford: Oxford University Press, 2011).

22. For a treatment of ancient refugees displaced by war, see Angelos Chaniotis, "Mobility of Persons during the Hellenistic Wars: State Control and Personal Relations," in *La mobilité des personnes en Mediterranee, de l'antiquite a l'epoque moderne: Procedures de controle et documents d'identification*, ed. Claudia Moatti (Rome: Ecole française de Rome, 2004), 481–500. Polybius 34.14 = Strabo 17.12 describes Alexandria. A review of David Engels, *Le déclin: La crise de l'Union européenne et la chute de la République romaine—Analogies historiques* (Paris: Editions Toucan, 2012), in the *Occidental Observer* cites his discussion of these passages (pp. 67–68 in Engels). Phiroze Vasunia, "Alexander and Asia: Droysen and Grote," in *Memory and History: The Legacy of Alexander in Asia*, ed. Himanshu Prabha Ray and Daniel T. Potts (New Delhi: Aryan Books International, 2007), 98, finds the same interpretation of these passages in the work of George Grote.
23. Critique of Polybius: Ian S. Moyer, *Egypt and the Limits of Hellenism* (Cambridge: Cambridge University Press, 2011), 24n89. Unequal relations: Jean Bingen, "Greco-Roman Egypt and the Question of Cultural Interactions," in *Hellenistic Egypt: Monarchy, Society, Economy, Culture*, ed. Roger S. Bagnall and Jean Bingen (Edinburgh: Edinburgh University Press, 2007), 242. *Oracle of the Potter* in Greek: Thomas Landvatter, "Contact Points: Alexandria, a Hellenistic Capital in Egypt," in *Beyond the Nile: Egypt and the Classical World*, ed. T. Potts, J. Spier, and S. E. Cole (Los Angeles: J. Paul Getty Museum, 2018), 129. László Török, *Hellenizing Art in Ancient Nubia 300 B.C.–A.D. 250 and Its Egyptian Models: A Study in Acculturation* (Leiden: Brill, 2011), 41–50, is a critique of Bingen's "apartheid" model.
24. Volker Losemann, "The Nazi Concept of Rome," in *Roman Presences: Receptions of Rome in European Culture, 1789–1945*, ed. Catharine Edwards (Cambridge: Cambridge University Press, 1999), 221–35; and Marla Stone, "A Flexible Rome: Fascism and the Cult of Romanitá," 205–20, in the same volume.
25. Eugene N. Borza, *The Impact of Alexander the Great: Civilizer or Destroyer?* (Hinsdale, IL: Dryden, 1974), considers Alexander's legacy critically. On the violence of Alexander's campaigns, see Brooke Allen, "Alexander the Great: Or the Terrible?" *Hudson Review* 58, no. 2 (2005): 220–30; see also Yousuf Chughtai, "Revisiting the 'Hellenistic' Period," *Eidolon*, May 21, 2018, https://eidolon.pub/revisiting-the-hellenistic-period-5ff7e96b9fad. Discussions of Persian attitudes toward Alexander include F. M. Kotwal and P. G. Kreyenbroek, "Alexander the Great, ii: In Zoroastrian Tradition," in *Encyclopaedia Iranica, Online Edition*, 2006; Parivash Jamzadeh, *Alexander Histories and Iranian Reflections* (Leiden: Brill, 2012), 173–83; and Josef Wiesehöfer, "The 'Accursed' and the 'Adventurer': Alexander the Great in Iranian Tradition," in *A Companion to Alexander Literature in the Middle Ages*, ed. Z. David Zuwiyya (Leiden: Brill, 2011). On the view

of Alexander as a "civilizer," see Peter Green, *Alexander to Actium: The Historical Evolution of the Hellenistic Age* (Berkeley: University of California Press, 1993), xv. For this view of his influence in Egypt, see Moyer, *Egypt and the Limits of Hellenism*, 11–21; and in India, see Vasunia, "Alexander and Asia"; and Phiroze Vasunia, *The Classics and Colonial India* (Oxford: Oxford University Press, 2013), 99–103. On Droysen's predecessors, see Pierre Briant, "Alexander and the Persian Empire, between 'Decline' and 'Renovation': History and Historiography," in *Alexander the Great: A New History*, ed. Waldemar Heckel and Lawrence A. Tritle (Malden, MA: Wiley-Blackwell, 2009), 172–76. On exchange and hybridity in the Hellenistic world, see, for example, Fergus Millar, "The Problem of Hellenistic Syria," in *Hellenism in the East*, ed. A. Kuhrt and S. Sherwin-White (Berkeley: University of California Press, 1987), on Syria; on Central Asia, see Rachel Mairs, *The Hellenistic Far East: Archaeology, Language, and Identity in Greek Central Asia* (Berkeley: University of California Press, 2014); and on Iran, see Rolf Strootman, "Hellenism and Persianism in Iran: Culture and Empire after Alexander the Great," *Dabir* 7, no. 1 (November 30, 2020): 201–27. The idea of "Romanization" is critiqued in D. J. Mattingly, *Imperialism, Power, and Identity: Experiencing the Roman Empire* (Princeton, NJ: Princeton University Press, 2011).

26. For the traditional prejudice against the Hellenistic period, see Glenn R. Bugh, introduction to *The Cambridge Companion to the Hellenistic World*, ed. Glenn R. Bugh (Cambridge: Cambridge University Press, 2006), 1. On Schachermeyr: Grant Parker, "Race and Politics," in *A Cultural History of Race in Antiquity*, ed. Denise Eileen McCoskey (London: Bloomsbury, 2021), 97, with Chapoutot, *Greeks, Romans, Germans*, 347–51, on Nazi ambivalence toward Alexander. Diller: Denise Eileen McCoskey, introduction to McCoskey, *Cultural History of Race*, 1–3. Grote: Vasunia, "Alexander and Asia," 93–96; and Vasunia, *The Classics and Colonial India*, 46. A review of Diller by the Oxford University archaeologist John Linton Myers (*The Classical Review* 52, no. 1 [1938]: 32) began by declaring, "Race-problems always occur when different peoples come into prolonged contact." On ambivalence toward Alexander in imperial Britain, see Vasunia, *The Classics and Colonial India*, 50, 89, 145.

27. Green, *Alexander to Actium*, 85, 453, 587, with further examples of twentieth-century scholarship asserting "hybridization and decline" collected by Moyer, *Egypt and the Limits of Hellenism*, 21–24. "Fusion of the Races": William Woodthorpe Tarn, "Alexander: The Conquest of the Far East," in *The Cambridge Ancient History*, vol. 6: *Macedon, 401–301 BC*, ed. J. B. Bury, S. A. Cook, and F. E. Adcock (Cambridge: Cambridge University Press, 1933), 431; and Will Durant, *The Story of Civilization 2: The Life of Greece* (New York: Simon & Schuster, 1939), 577–78. On Tarn see also Grant Parker, "Hellenism in an Afghan Context," in Prabha Ray and

Potts, *Memory and History*, 177–78; and Vasunia, *The Classics and Colonial India*, 99–103, with Daniel Ogden, "Alexander's Sex Life," in Heckel and Tritle, *Alexander the Great*, 204–5, on Tarn's bowdlerization of Alexander's sexuality. The racialist language employed by Diller belied that his findings anticipated those of later scholars who challenged the application of such language to antiquity. See Christopher S. Parmenter, " 'But They Were a Race of Whites': Race and the Making of Ancient Slavery in the Anglophone World, 1785–1980," *TAPA* 154, no. 1 (2024): 317–19.

28. One example is Ernst Curtius, on whom see Nippel, *Ancient and Modern Democracy*, 228, 336n128. On Schachermeyr's assessment of Pericles, see Parker, "Race and Politics," 96, building on Martina Pesditschek, "Die Karriere des Althistorikers Fritz Schachermeyr im Dritten Reich und in der Zweiten Republik," *Mensch, Wissenschaft, Magie Mitteilungen* 25 (2005): 41–71.

29. On the Greek *polis* in Enlightenment thought, see Anthony D. Smith, "Classical Ideals and the Formation of Modern Nations in Europe," in Fögen and Warren, *Graeco-Roman Antiquity and the Idea of Nationalism*, 25; and Ma, *Polis*, 547–50. Hans Kohn and Craig Calhoun, *The Idea of Nationalism: A Study in Its Origins and Background* (Abingdon: Transaction, 2004), 576, makes Athens one of the "fundamental inspirations" of "civic" nationalism; see ix–l for a critical orientation to Kohn's theories. On the artificiality of the distinction between "civic" and "ethnic" nationalism, see Taras Kuzio, "The Myth of the Civic State: A Critical Survey of Hans Kohn's Framework for Understanding Nationalism," *Ethnic and Racial Studies* 25, no. 1 (January 2002): 20–39; Rogers Brubaker, "The Manichean Myth: Rethinking the Distinction between 'Civic' and 'Ethnic' Nationalism," in *Nation and National Identity: The European Experience in Perspective*, ed. Hanspeter Kriesi, Klaus Armingeon, Hannes Siegrist, and Andreas Wimmer (West Lafayette, IN: Purdue University Press, 2004); and Yael Tamir, "Not So Civic: Is There a Difference between Ethnic and Civic Nationalism?" *Annual Review of Political Science* 22 (May 11, 2019): 419–34.

30. David Theo Goldberg, *The Racial State* (Malden, MA: Blackwell, 2002), treats race in the founding of European nations. Daniele Conversi, "Can Nationalism Studies and Ethnic/Racial Studies Be Brought Together?" *Journal of Ethnic & Migration Studies* 30, no. 4 (2004): 815–29, argues for the linking of the study of nationalism and race. On the history of the word *nation*, see Aira Kemiläinen, *Nationalism: Problems concerning the Word, the Concept, and Classification* (Jyväskylä: Jyväskylän Kasvatusopillinen Korkeakoulu, 1964), 13–59. On the much more varied meanings of *natio* in antiquity, see Kelly Nguyen, "Pham Duy Khiem, Classical Reception, and Colonial Subversion in Early 20th Century Vietnam and France," *Classical Receptions Journal* 12, no. 3 (2020): 340–56. On the persistence of the equation of "race" and "nation," see Steve Fenton, "Race

and the Nation," in *The SAGE Handbook of Nations and Nationalism*, ed. Gerard Delanty and Krishan Kumar (London: SAGE, 2006), 198–201. See, too, Alastair Bonnett, *Multiracism: Rethinking Racism in Global Context* (Cambridge: Polity, 2022), 25–27, noting Niall Ferguson's promotion of "primordialist" understandings of fixed racial identities. Leoussi, "Making Nations," 47–66, implicates the model of Athens in the nineteenth-century shift from conceptions of citizenship based on ideals to those based on race, developing an analysis of Anthony D. Smith, *The Ethnic Origins of Nations* (Oxford: Blackwell, 1986), 136, 216. On the language of "ethnicity" as an evasion of race, see Denise Eileen McCoskey, "By Any Other Name? Ethnicity and the Study of Ancient Identity," *Classical Bulletin* 79, no. 1 (2003).

31. Gregory T. Carter, "Race and Citizenship," in *The Oxford Handbook of American Immigration and Ethnicity*, ed. Ronald H. Bayor (Oxford: Oxford University Press, 2016). White women received citizenship but could not vote.

32. Melting pot: Heike Paul, *The Myths That Made America: An Introduction to American Studies* (Bielefeld: Transcript, 2014), 257–98. On the conflicting ideologies within the American Colonization Society, see Eric Burin, *Slavery and the Peculiar Solution: A History of the American Colonization Society* (Gainesville: University Press of Florida, 2005), with Thomas Jefferson's arguments in favor of "colonization" of African Americans, *Notes on the State of Virginia* (1785), ed. Robert Pierce Forbes (New Haven, CT: Yale University Press, 2022), 223. On Lincoln, see Ibram X. Kendi, *Stamped from the Beginning: The Definitive History of Racist Ideas in America* (New York: Bold Type Books, 2016), 214–28.

33. For King's remarks, see Andrew Kaczynski and Christopher Massie, "Steve King: Defend White People from Attacks or Face the Dark Ages," *BuzzFeed News*, July 21, 2016, https://www.buzzfeednews.com/article/andrewkaczynski/say-what; and Sarah E. Bond, "What Rep. Steve King Gets Wrong about the Dark Ages—and Western Civilization," *Forbes*, July 25, 2016, https://www.forbes.com/sites/drsarahbond/2016/07/23/stevekingandthedarkages/. For Poe's, see Frank Argote-Freyre and Christopher M. Bellitto, "The Fall of Ancient Rome and Modern U.S. Immigration: Historical Model or Political Football?" *Historian* 74, no. 4 (2012): 789–90. Jefferson's comparison of Roman and American slavery is in Jefferson, *Notes on the State of Virginia*, 218–21, discussed by Eric Ashley Hairston, *The Ebony Column: Classics, Civilization, and the African American Reclamation of the West* (Knoxville: University of Tennessee Press, 2013), 36–37; and Parmenter, " 'But They Were a Race of Whites,' " 298–302. On the abolitionist response, see Margaret Malamud, *African Americans and the Classics: Antiquity, Abolition and Activism* (London: I. B. Tauris, 2016), 106–19.

34. Trump's 2024 comments on immigrants: Ellie Quinlan Houghtaling, "Trump's Rally Just Went Full Nazi with Bloodthirsty Immigration

Threat," *New Republic*, October 11, 2024, https://newrepublic.com/post/187115/donald-trump-rally-nazi-bloodthirsty-immigration-threat. During the 2024 presidential campaign Trump continued to say immigration brings "carnage and chaos and killing from all over the world"; see Joey Cappelletti, Jill Colvin, and Adriana Gomez, "Trump Accuses Biden of Causing a Border 'Bloodbath' as He Escalates His Immigration Rhetoric," AP News, April 2, 2024, https://apnews.com/article/trump-immigration-crime-battleground-election-aa4b09123 22dee09cf475ffad7c8cec7. Examples of "Diversity Is Not Our Strength" op-eds include Thomas Sowell, "Diversity Is Our Strength? There's No Evidence of That," *Columbian*, June 14, 2016, https://www.columbian.com/news/2016/jun/14/sowell-diversity-is-our-strength-theres-no-evidence-of-that/; Jonah Goldberg, "What If Diversity Isn't America's Strength?" *Los Angeles Times*, January 15, 2018, https://www.latimes.com/opinion/op-ed/la-oe-goldberg-diversity-strength-20180115-story.html; David French, "Is Diversity Really Our Strength?" *National Review*, September 10, 2018, https://www.nationalreview.com/2018/09/american-diversity-requires-common-creed/; and, for Steve King quoting Hungary's Victor Orbán to this effect, Luke Nozicka, "Dems Call on Reynolds to Disassociate from King After 'Diversity Is Not Our Strength' Tweet," *Des Moines Register*, December 8, 2017, https://www.desmoinesregister.com/story/news/politics/2017/12/08/dems-ask-reynolds-remove-king-staff-diversity-not-our-strength/936999001/. DeSantis's remarks are recorded in Florida Governor's Office, "Governor Ron DeSantis Signs Strongest Anti-Illegal Immigration Legislation in the Country to Combat Biden's Border Crisis," May 10, 2023, https://www.flgov.com/2023/05/10/governor-ron-desantis-signs-strongest-anti-illegal-immigration-legislation-in-the-country-to-combat-bidens-border-crisis/. The comments of New York State elected officials are in Asher Stockler, " 'Smells Like Jim Crow Law': Federal Judge Furious over Asylum Seeker Executive Orders," *Rockland/Westchester Journal News*, June 1, 2023, https://www.lohud.com/story/news/2023/06/01/nyc-asylum-seekers-federal-judge-furious-over-ny-executive-orders/70278231007/.

35. On 2019 levels of segregation, see Stephen Menedian, Samir Gambhir, and Arthur Gailes, "Twenty-First Century Racial Residential Segregation in the United States," Othering and Belonging Institute, June 21, 2021, https://belonging.berkeley.edu/roots-structural-racism. On school segregations and the impact of "secessions" on integration, see Jacqueline M. Nowicki, "K-12 Education: Student Population Has Significantly Diversified, but Many Schools Remain Divided along Racial, Ethnic, and Economic Lines," Government Accountability Office, 2022, https://www.gao.gov/assets/gao-22–104737.pdf. A critical study of the phenomenon is Heather Beth Johnson and Thomas M. Shapiro, "Good Neighborhoods, Good Schools: Race and the 'Good Choices' of White Families," in *White Out: The Continuing Significance of Racism*, ed. Ashley W. Doane

and Eduardo Bonilla-Silva (New York: Routledge, 2003), 173–88. On segregation in the twenty-first-century United States more generally, see John R. Logan, "The Persistence of Segregation in the 21st Century Metropolis," *City & Community* 12, no. 2 (2013): 160–68. On its history, see David Theo Goldberg, "The New Segregation," in *City Visions*, ed. David Bell and Azzedine Haddour (London: Routledge, 2000), 182–96.

36. Studies refuting any link between immigration and crime are collected by Ramiro Martinez Jr. and Kimberly Mehlman-Orozco, "Latino/Hispanic Immigration and Crime," in *The Oxford Handbook of Ethnicity, Crime, and Immigration*, ed. Sandra M. Bucerius and Michael Tonry (Oxford: Oxford University Press, 2014); Daniel E. Martínez and Rubén G. Rumbaut, *The Criminalization of Immigration in the United States* (Washington, DC: American Immigration Council, 2015); and Saundra Trujillo and María B. Vélez, "Ethnicity and Crime," in *The Handbook of Race, Ethnicity, Crime, and Justice*, ed. Ramiro Martinez Jr., Meghan E. Hollis, and Jacob I. Stowell (Hoboken, NJ: Wiley-Blackwell, 2018), 44–49. Belief in this link has been fostered by a century of xenophobic representations of immigrants as criminal. See Mae Ngai, *Impossible Subjects: Illegal Aliens and the Making of Modern America* (Princeton, NJ: Princeton University Press, 2004); Leo Chavez, *The Latino Threat: Constructing Immigrants, Citizens, and the Nation* (Redwood City, CA: Stanford University Press, 2008); and Philip M. Pendergast, Tim Wadsworth, and Joshua LePree, "Immigration, Crime, and Victimization in the US Context: An Overview," in Martinez, Hollis, and Stowell, *The Handbook of Race, Ethnicity, Crime, and Justice*, 66–68.

Conclusion

1. The Daily Stormer quotes Carl J. Richard, *The Golden Age of the Classics in America: Greece, Rome, and the Antebellum United States* (Cambridge, MA: Harvard University Press, 2009), x. On the "founders' " interest in Cincinnatus, Solon, and Polybius's concept of decay, see Carl J. Richard, *The Founders and the Classics: Greece, Rome, and the American Enlightenment* (Cambridge, MA: Harvard University Press, 1995), 55–56, 69–71, 132–33.
2. For instance, see Bret Devereaux, "This. Isn't. Sparta. Part I: Spartan School," *A Collection of Unmitigated Pedantry*, August 16, 2019, https://acoup.blog/2019/08/16/collections-this-isnt-sparta-part-i-spartan-school/; Owen Rees, "Did the Spartans Bring Their War Dead Back on Their Shields?" *Bad Ancient*, August 21, 2020, https://www.badancient.com/claims/spartans-war-dead/; Roel Konijnendijk, "Did 300 Spartans Try to Put a Halt to the Persian Advance at Thermopylae?" *Bad Ancient*, May 15, 2020, https://www.badancient.com/claims/did-300-spartans-halt-persian-advance-thermopylae/; Myke Cole, *The Bronze Lie: Shattering the Myth of Spartan Warrior Supremacy* (Oxford: Osprey, 2021).

3. Alexandra Desanctis, "Old School," *National Review*, August 10, 2023, https://www.nationalreview.com/magazine/2023/08/28/old-school-4/; Nick Anderson, "Florida Approved an SAT Alternative, but Experts Say the Test Is Unproven," *Washington Post*, October 11, 2023, https://www.washingtonpost.com/education/2023/10/06/clt-test-florida-sat-act-alternative/; Emma Green, "Have the Liberal Arts Gone Conservative?" *New Yorker*, March 11, 2024, https://web.archive.org/web/20240311152653/https://www.newyorker.com/magazine/2024/03/18/have-the-liberal-arts-gone-conservative. On homeschooling, see Peter Jamison, Laura Meckler, Prayag Gordy, Clara Ence Morse, and Chris Alcantara, "Home Schooling's Rise from Fringe to Fastest-Growing Form of Education," *Washington Post*, October 31, 2023, https://www.washingtonpost.com/education/interactive/2023/homeschooling-growth-data-by-district/.
4. On the contemporary politics of "classical education," see Joel Christensen, "Classical Deception: Reactionary Misappropriation of Greek Classics Fuel Culture Wars in Education," *Neos Kosmos*, April 30, 2023, https://neoskosmos.com/en/2023/04/30/dialogue/opinion/classical-deception-us-conservatives-misappropriate-greek-classics-to-fuel-the-culture-wars-in-education/; Annie Abrams and Roosevelt Montás, "The Defenders of Liberal Education Are Destroying It," *Atlantic*, March 15, 2023, https://www.theatlantic.com/ideas/archive/2023/03/liberal-education-desantis-humanities-western-canon/673395/; Emily Waller Singeisen, "Trojan Horse Universities: How Tech Billionaires and Alt-Right Figures Legitimise Intolerance in Classics," Working Classicists, https://www.workingclassicists.com/post/trojan-horse-universities-how-tech-billionaires-and-alt-right-figures-legitimise-intolerance-in-cla; Green, "Have the Liberal Arts Gone Conservative?" Florida's "Don't Say Gay" law is summarized in "What You Need to Know about Florida's 'Don't Say Gay' and 'Don't Say They' Laws, Book Bans, and Other Curricula Restrictions," National Education Association, June 2023, https://www.nea.org/sites/default/files/2023–06/30424-know-your-rights_web_v4.pdf. The Association of Classical Christian Schools, which boasts more than five hundred member schools, stipulates in its "Statement of Faith" (https://classicalchristian.org/statement-of-faith/, accessed November 29, 2024) that "God defined marriage as the life-long covenant between one man and one woman, and that all forms of sexual activity outside of marriage are sin." On Wilson and Fleming, see Mark Potok, "Doug Wilson's Religious Empire Expanding in the Northwest," Southern Poverty Law Center, April 20, 2004, https://www.splcenter.org/fighting-hate/intelligence-report/2004/doug-wilson%E2%80%99s-religious-empire-expanding-northwest; and Euan Hague, Heidi Beirich, and Edward H. Sebesta, *Neo-Confederacy: A Critical Introduction* (Austin: University of Texas Press, 2008), 47, 63–64, 207–11.

5. "CLT Author Bank," CLTexam.com, https://www.cltexam.com/tests/authors/, accessed November 29, 2024; and "The Classical Reader," https://www.classicalreader.com/, accessed November 29, 2024.
6. Zack Withers, "Why Your Child Needs a Classical Education," Great Hearts America, October 10, 2022, https://www.greatheartsamerica.org/why-your-child-needs-a-classical-education/; Lulu Garcia-Navarro, "Why Conservatives Can't Stop Talking about Aristotle," *New York Times*, May 4, 2023, https://www.nytimes.com/2023/05/04/opinion/classical-education-conservative-movement.html; Kevin Mahnken, "Classical Academies: What if Education's Next Big Thing Is 2,500 Years Old?" *The74*, March 22, 2023, https://www.the74million.org/article/amid-the-pandemic-a-classical-education-boom-what-if-the-next-big-school-trend-is-2500-years-old/.
7. Stephen Blackwood, "Colleges Are Failing in Their Fundamental Mission, but There's Still Hope," Foundation for Economic Education, January 21, 2021, https://fee.org/articles/colleges-are-failing-in-their-fundamental-mission-but-there-s-still-hope/; Garcia-Navarro, "Why Conservatives Can't Stop Talking about Aristotle."
8. Great Hearts America, "Our View of Learning," https://www.greatheartsamerica.org/great-hearts-life/great-hearts-philosophy/, accessed November 29, 2024. Green, "Have the Liberal Arts Gone Conservative?" On Michael Levin, who is both Jewish and a white nationalist, see Carol M. Swain and Russ Nieli, *Contemporary Voices of White Nationalism in America* (Cambridge: Cambridge University Press, 2003), 133–52; and "Extremist Files: Michael Levin," Southern Poverty Law Center, https://www.splcenter.org/fighting-hate/extremist-files/individual/michael-levin, accessed November 29, 2024.
9. Neville Morley, *Classics: Why It Matters* (Cambridge: Polity, 2018), 78. Canceling classics: Rod Dreher, "Cancel Cult Comes for Homer," *American Conservative*, December 28, 2020, https://www.theamericanconservative.com/cancel-cult-comes-for-homer/; Jeremy Tate, "Nobody Wants to Cancel the Classics—Except Academic Elites," *National Review*, May 6, 2021, https://www.nationalreview.com/2021/05/nobody-wants-to-cancel-the-classics-except-academic-elites/; Rich Lowry, "Are the Classics Racist?" *National Review*, February 9, 2021, https://www.nationalreview.com/2021/02/are-the-classics-racist/; Daisy Dunn, "Don't Cancel the Classics," *UnHerd*, February 25, 2021, https://unherd.com/2021/02/dont-cancel-the-classics/; Roger Kimball, "Canceling Classics," *New Criterion*, February 24, 2021, https://newcriterion.com/article/canceling-classics/. From a different perspective, Angel Adams Parham, "Don't Cancel the Classics, Broaden and Diversify Them," *Wall Street Journal*, May 20, 2022, https://www.wsj.com/articles/dont-cancel-the-classics-broaden-and-diversify-them-education-college-charter-school-choice-systemic-racism-diversity-and-inclusion-clt-crt-ancients-greece-rome-homer-

toni-morrison-11653079858. Counter-Currents' headline is "Homer Gets Cancelled"; VDARE's is "Classics under Attack from PC Mob."

10. Mathura Umachandran and Marchella Ward, "Towards a Manifesto for Critical Ancient World Studies," in *Critical Ancient World Studies: The Case for Forgetting Classics*, ed. Mathura Umachandran and Marchella Ward (Abingdon: Routledge, 2023), 3. Rachel D. Friedman, "A Reformed Classical Pedagogy," *Classical Receptions Journal* 5, no. 2 (2013): 226–37, links name change with curricular change. On the name *classics*, see Josephine Crawley Quinn, "Time to Move On," *Times Literary Supplement*, September 21, 2018, with James Tatum, "What Was a Classic?" *Classical World* 114, no. 1 (2020): 85–97, on the decision in 2013 of the professional association of classical scholars to change its name from the American Philological Association to the Society for Classical Studies: "The philologists a.k.a. classicists have thus shifted their association's name from an intellectual activity . . . to a word conferring status" (85).

11. Dan-el Padilla Peralta, "Some Thoughts on AIA-SCS 2019," Medium, 2019, https://medium.com/@danelpadillaperalta/some-thoughts-on-aia-scs-2019-d6a480a1812a, with Arum Park, "Race, Data, and Classics," *TAPA* 154, no. 1 (2024): 17–61, on the overwhelming whiteness of practitioners within the field. Proposals for disciplinary reform are usefully summarized by Rebecca Futo Kennedy and Max Goldman, "Changing 'Classics': What Do We Want? Not What Some People Keep Saying We Want," *Classics at the Intersections*, 2021, https://rfkclassics.blogspot.com/2021/02/changing-classics-what-do-we-want-not.html. Specific proposals include Shelley Haley, "Classics and Minorities," in *Classics: A Discipline and Profession in Crisis?* ed. Phyllis Culham and Lowell Edmunds (Lanham, MD: University Press of America, 1989); Patrice D. Rankine, "The Classics, Race, and Community-Engaged or Public Scholarship," *American Journal of Philology* 140, no. 2 (2019): 345–59; J. Mira Seo, "Classics for All: Future Antiquity from a Global Perspective," *American Journal of Philology* 140, no. 4 (2019): 699–715; Dani Bostick, "Not for All: Nostalgic Distortions as a Weapon of Segregation in Secondary Classics," *American Journal of Philology* 141, no. 2 (2020): 283–306; Mathura Umachandran, "Disciplinecraft: Towards an Anti-Racist Classics," *TAPA* 152, no. 1 (2022): 25–31; Sasha-Mae Eccleston and Dan-el Padilla Peralta, "Racing the Classics: Ethos and Praxis," *American Journal of Philology* 143, no. 2 (2022): 199–218; Patrice D. Rankine, "Racializing Antiquity, Post-Diversity," *TAPA* 154, no. 1 (2024): 1–15; Sasha-Mae Eccleston, "On Yearning, from the Spectacular to the Speculative," *TAPA* 154, no. 1 (2024): 331–47.

12. Eric Ashley Hairston, *The Ebony Column: Classics, Civilization, and the African American Reclamation of the West* (Knoxville: University of Tennessee Press, 2013), 63; Phiroze Vasunia, *The Classics and Colonial India* (Oxford:

Oxford University Press, 2013), 240–52; Kelly Nguyen, "Pham Duy Khiem, Classical Reception, and Colonial Subversion in Early 20th Century Vietnam and France," *Classical Receptions Journal* 12, no. 3 (2020): 340–56; Kenneth W. Goings and Eugene O'Connor, "Black Athena before Black Athena: The Teaching of Greek and Latin at Black Colleges and Universities during the Nineteenth Century," in *African Athena: New Agendas*, ed. Daniel Orrells, Gurminder K. Bhambra, and Tessa Roynon (Oxford: Oxford University Press, 2011); César Augusto Baldi, "Decolonizing Greek Theater: Black Experimental Theater," in *Receptions of the Classics in the African Diaspora of the Hispanophone and Lusophone Worlds: Atlantis Otherwise*, ed. Elisa Rizo and Madeleine Henry (Lanham, MD: Lexington Books, 2016), 43–60; Emily Greenwood, *Afro-Greeks: Dialogues between Anglophone Caribbean Literature and Classics in the Twentieth Century* (Oxford: Oxford University Press, 2009), 112–85.

13. Tessa Roynon, "A New 'Romen' Empire: Toni Morrison's 'Love' and the Classics," *Journal of American Studies* 41, no. 1 (2007): 31–47; and Tessa Roynon, "The Africanness of Classicism in the Work of Toni Morrison," in *African Athena: New Agendas*, ed. Daniel Orrells, Gurminder K. Bhambra, and Tessa Roynon (Oxford: Oxford University Press, 2011).

Index